DECISION TIME

DECISION TIME

Can a Teenager Make a Life Decision?

A Memoir of My Life

Shane McGuire

Copyright © 2006 by Shane McGuire.

Library of Congress Control Number: 2005908132
ISBN: Hardcover   1-59926-686-5
         Softcover   1-59926-685-7

All rights reserved. No part of this book may be reproduced or transmitted in any form or by any means, electronic or mechanical, including photocopying, recording, or by any information storage and retrieval system, without permission in writing from the copyright owner.

This book was printed in the United States of America.

To order additional copies of this book, contact:
Xlibris Corporation
1-888-795-4274
www.Xlibris.com
Orders@Xlibris.com

CONTENTS

An Invitation to You, the Reader vii

Preface ix

Introduction xi

Acknowledgements xxi

Chapter 1: How I Got Here 1

Chapter 2: Early Memories 7

Chapter 3: Stricken with Osteomyelitis 19

Chapter 4: The Dog and the Birds and More 28

Chapter 5: Parents Romance and Backgrounds 35

Chapter 6: Two Years Away From Home 42

Chapter 7: Coming Home After Two Years 69

Chapter 8: Life on the Farm 75

Chapter 9: Eighth Grade and the Bully 83

Chapter 10: Economic War, Depression and the Ninth Child 88

Chapter 11: Secondary Boarding School and War 91

Chapter 12: Deciding the Future 98

Chapter 13: Novitiate—A Spiritual Year 106

Chapter 14: Philosophy and Theology 116

Chapter 15: The Osteomyelitis Comes Back 128

Chapter 16: Before Ordination 135

Chapter 17: Ordination and Coming Home 141

Chapter 18: My Father Dies 149

Chapter 19: Ministry in Scotland 154

Chapter 20: Rome 164

Chapter 21: Coming to the United States 178

Chapter 22: Ministry, Parish, Hospital and University 185

Chapter 23: My Mother Dies 202

Chapter 24: Variety in Ministries 207

Chapter 25: Bayshore Parish 212

Chapter 26: Called to be a Pastor 228

Chapter 27: The Church In Transition 253

Chapter 28: The Church in Turmoil 260

Chapter 29: Semi-Retirement 273

Epilogue 277

Addendum: My Sisters and Brothers 283

DEDICATION

I dedicate this memoir to my parents Bernard and Mary Ellen McGuire, in gratitude for the way they loved, sacrificed and shared their lives and their faith with all of us, their children.

An Invitation to You, the Reader

My writing this memoir was quite exciting,
to share it with me, 'tis you I'm inviting.
I will make you laugh and make you cry,
with human feelings I can't deny.

My life unfolds as you turn these pages,
and I lead you along in gentle stages.
Through a happy boyhood turning to pain,
to achieve life's calling not looking for gain.

There are interesting stories and anecdotes,
poetic verses giving spice to the thoughts.
Turns on the road at life's gentle speed,
some narratives you'll find hard to believe.

Many interesting people who crossed my path,
some who really left their mark.
Can I take you gently by the hand,
to read on and you'll understand.

PREFACE

The title of this memoir is "Decision Time". This title ties in with my picture on the cover as a boy of sixteen. At that time and for several more years I was struggling to make a life decision. As a subtitle or handle I have, "Can a teenager make a life decision?"

As I relive my life in writing these treasured memories, I invite you, the reader, to come with me, sharing my experiences, from a very happy, active boyhood to great pain and suffering, beginning at age ten, caused by a then incurable bone disease, from near despair in a "home for cripples" to a fruitful life in ministry, going through very interesting stages along the way.

Please come with me through my life's journey. The intention in writing this memoir was primarily for family and friends. While enjoying the writing I felt I was also writing for myself. Now I present it for all to read and enjoy.

In a way I lived three lives but in a good sense, under the three names of Shane (to the family); Father David (while a monk in the passionist order) and Monsignor John (in the United States).

I was christened John Aloysius but my family called me by a Gaelic form of John, Shane. I was known as Shane where I grew up and all the way through school until I became a monk by entering the passionist order, where they gave me the name David, but the family and all who knew me as Shane continued to call me Shane and do so to this day.

During the time I ministered in Scotland and Rome I was Father David. It was a new world I had entered into with a new name. I got used to it easily enough because all the other members of the order called me David. When I transferred from the order to parish ministry in the United States, I became known as Father John, and later as Monsignor John, after receiving papal honors. When friends ask me how I adjusted to the different names, I think of the old saying "a rose by any other name . . ."

I thank my good friends who encouraged me to write this memoir. It has been a very good experience, giving me deeper insights on my life. From this perspective, as I look at how my life unfolded, many thoughts come to my mind on how different it could have been if I had made different decisions. I strive to be factual and true in writing about all that really happened and not to speculate about what could have been.

I feel I have a lot to offer young people, but a piece of advice I ask you all to remember: your decisions must be yours and don't drift along, at any stage in your life, doing what others expect of you, or even pressure you to do. It may sound strange but, writing the story of my life has made me appreciate life all the more.

I feel there are contrary drives within me, and probably in varying degrees within everyone who shares the one human nature.

> There is selfishness and there is love.
> There are temptations and there are decisions.
> I am not my temptations.
> I am my decisions.
>
> I have decided to love everyone in the whole world.
>
> Love is not love 'til it's given away.

INTRODUCTION

My memoir flashes back across my life like a bee buzzing from flower to flower. I was born into a large family on a farm, with grassland and crops and a flowing river. I had a happy childhood until stricken with a bone disease called osteomyelitis.

From running and vaulting in the meadows along the riverbank, I found myself lying in pain, or moving slowly around on crutches. The country doctor could do nothing, so gossip had it I was incurable and would have to go to a home for cripples. Mean children taunted my family at school, and how they suffered. I felt I was being dumped on the garbage heap of the useless, ignorant and suffering for life in the dregs of humanity to be avoided, a stigma on my family, a burden to others always, hopes that blossomed, now withering, the joy of running and vaulting just a memory, a bright mind eclipsed by pain's dark cloud.

> I needed friends and a high self esteem.
> The friends were sympathetic and never a mean word,
> The mean ones never ran out of mean words,
> getting pleasure from taunting, reflected in grinning faces.
>
> The school master made light of my pain,
> and came down heavy with his cane.
> His slapping hand benumbed my brain,
> putting me under unbearable strain.
> Coming home at a sickening trot,

trying to shake off what I'd got.
A swollen face and purple ear,
and throbbing brain beset by fear.
Harsh punishment most undeserved,
loss of faith in one who served,
To lead a child to his full potential
in respect and learning so essential,
To building up of the human race,
With no child slapped across the face.
On painful days resting in the field,
to black despair I refuse to yield.
Lying at my feet man's best friend,
Licking my sores my leg to mend.
The blackbird singing from the sycamore,
makes my leg feel much less sore.
I hold my leg in the flowing river,
Until the cold just makes me shiver.

We went to see an old bonesetter,
who failed to make my leg feel better.
Neighbors told us of a famous quack,
who cured and pain would not come back.

It took all day for us to go,
he touched the leg, but even so,
The pain did not go away,
we felt it had come to stay.

To look for help we had no choice,
we followed the neighbors' best advice.
Drawing from ancestral ways to cure,
streams and nettles and cow manure.

The doctor was baffled by my leg,
lancing would cure me he said.
I bore the pain of a cutting knife,
I cried alone by day and night.

One week I was getting better,
the next week was worse than ever.
The family tried to give me hope,
and did their best to help me cope.

Go to the infirmary and wear a cast,
to protect the bone while time passed.
Long months went by and nothing was done,
one incurable boy with incurable men.

No schooling and no future hopes,
wasting time studying form and betting on horses.
The excitement of the grand national race,
it was my first bet and my last penny . . .
Golden Miller went down at a jump,
with him we all fell into a slump.
The men in horror at the fall
called the horse names, I won't recall.

When she could, mother would come,
bringing comfort to her lonely son.
Assuring me of the family love,
and daily prayers to God above.
For eight long months I saw none other,
the only one my loving mother.
Lonely, frustrated and sexually abused,
I demand to go home and won't be refused.

While thinking I was going to my own home, I was taken instead to another hospital, having the name of being a home for cripples. It was Coole Sanitarium for boys with bone disease.

In the middle of a long row of beds,
I could see through the open space ahead.
Boys lying there who could not walk,
making up for that with plenty of talk.
All the boys had the bone disease,

with pain and suffering in varying degrees.
The open air relieved the stench
of rotting bones and running sores.
Some boys in iron frames lay,
looking straight up all the day.
When outside they could see the sky,
and watch the clouds go floating by.
All of us tried so hard to cope,
out on the veranda we felt new hope.
We longed for weekends and all the sports,
radios and newspapers were our source.
We were on the fields running and scoring,
enjoying success we joined in the roaring.
Sister Maryann gave me special attention,
the boy's teasing not to mention.
She came with chocolate for me alone,
which I shared when she was gone.
This went on for a while
then she suddenly changed her style.
Now she gave me the blackthorn stick,
on the backs of the hands until I felt sick.
I tried to sleep with knuckles aching,
and grim anticipation on awaking!
She went from chocolates to a blackthorn stick,
from a winning smile to a grin that was sick.
I'm trying to put it all together,
her mood, changing like the weather.
A victim in shock by a nun abused,
dismayed, dejected and confused.
Sister Gabriel x-rayed my leg,
I see some hope for you she said.
A surgeon chiseled out the rotting bone,
When it all healed up they sent me home.

I thought now the disease was dead,
again it would raise it's ugly head.
When I was sure it had gone away,
it said, no, I came to stay.

DECISION TIME

In the eighth grade we have a real bully,
who makes life miserable for so many.
He sneers and torments and instills fear,
but eases off when ever I am near.
My younger siblings suffered greatly,
when I was away he taunted them saying,
Your brother Shane has a rotten bone,
and will spend his life in a cripple's home.
The girl to whom I was attracted most,
had told me of his empty boast.
That he had beaten better boys than me,
and told them to just wait and see.
We crossed a wall to the fighting hollow,
all the others were happy to follow.
And assemble in the bottom of the bowl,
the students were shouting and cheering us on.
There were those who were bullied and scared,
there were those he hurt by his vile mouth.
Excitement mounted as we faced each other,
all roared and shouted, "Start the fight."
The bully attacked with fists flying,
I fended him off, but he kept trying.
An opening came and I got him on the nose,
as the punching continued his blood flowed.
It caked on his lips as the weather was cold,
the blood soon covered his mouth and froze.
The spectators all joined in the shout,
bully your liver is coming out of your mouth.
As cheering mounted and excitement grew,
he drew back with faltering steps a few.
He took a fistful of liver off his mouth,
and looked at it while hearing the shout.
He flicked his liver to the ground,
and slunk away without a sound.

I am coming to the end of the high school years, and planning for the future ahead. There are three strong callings arising within me just about every day:

The calling to marriage and family life.
The calling to have money and possessions.
The calling to sacred ministry.

Firstly, the calling to marriage and family life:
Girls occupy much of my thoughts and feelings, both during the day and in my dreams at night. In the daytime I am attending classes, studying hard under pressure and trying to push all distractions out of my mind at night. I dream a lot, often waking up embracing a girl, then feeling all alone and coming to grips with reality, the feelings lingering often into the daytime. These feelings and thoughts come to me even when I pray.

> I feel within me a real strife,
> calling me to settle for an easier life.
> I am so committed to succeed,
> I dismiss these thoughts and proceed.

Secondly, I feel the calling to have money and possessions. Deep in my heart I have a great longing to own a big house and farm of my own. When we drove through the countryside in the horse drawn trap with my father and mother, they always commented on the farms we passed on the way, the bigger the house meant the bigger the farm. My unspoken dream is a big farm, a big house, with horses, cows sheep and cattle, a loving wife and devoted children. I love to look at beautiful cars, Daimlers, Bentleys and Jaguars. Possessing appears to be the be all and the end all of life. I become what I possess, the greater my possessions, the greater am I. So people become their possessions? Those with most are they the greatest? They seem to be self sufficient and depending on no one. They are always looking for more of what this world has to offer. More gives them more problems. More places them above their neighbors. Does more make me a better person? What can make me a better person? Do I have to learn and have to endure? Do I have to grow and have to mature? When I give my heart to possessions I sense the pain of a vacuum within my being. The potential within me is quasi infinite. When I grow mentally there is still room for more. No matter how much I grow spiritually, there is never an end. Possessions do not make me great. Growing to full potential is true greatness. Possessions can be taken away. What I become is here to stay.

Possessions don't fully satisfy all my longings. Growth in the spirit is most fulfilling. The true spiritual life is union with God, and service of neighbor. This greatness lasts forever.

Thirdly, there is the calling to the priesthood. Sometimes I have an awareness that God may be calling me to ministry. The sacrifices would be very great, no wife, no children and no possessions. One day I think I may be getting a call. The next day I want to forget it all. The cost is so great, I am unable to take this seriously. I swing from one side to the other. Deep down I want it to go away. I am vacillating from day to day. This is going on for several years. During the last year at high school I am thinking more seriously about the possible call to ministry. At the same time the pressure is telling me I can't do this. The next day my mind is full of it again. I am torn apart inside and I pray hard, telling God I cannot do this: I am not able.

The balance of the scales is the thought of helping people, ministering, counseling, sympathizing, sharing and empathizing. People are waiting, looking, expecting a minister. They should not be disappointed, deprived or neglected. It is a privilege to serve people in need. Then this day when the thoughts of the call and the sacrifices come into my mind, I feel different. A change has come over me. The call is so strong, I feel new courage and I am saying in my heart: Yes I can do it. I am speaking to God in silence. I am saying to him in my inmost being, I accept the call and I can make the sacrifices. I have a new strength and feel surprised and happy. I have taken a step up higher and feel I have started to climb the mountain.

The study of philosophy made me think and ask many questions, especially about the great religions of the world; Hinduism, Buddhism, Judaism, Christianity and Islam. Hinduism, dates back about six thousand years. Buddhism came from Hinduism, Judaism started about four thousand years ago, Christianity two thousand years, Islam 600 years after Christ in the seventh century.

People came first in time, religion second. People are more important than religion. Religion is for people not people for religion. We speak of the living faith. There can be no faith except in the faithful. Jesus said, "Man was not made for the Sabbath, the Sabbath was made for man." There can be people without religion. There cannot be religion without people. For religion binds people to God. We can say God does everything in his own good time. There is a fullness of time for everything including you and I getting life.

The two great works of God are creation and revelation. By creation, God made the universe. Through revelation, God spoke to humans, revealing himself. We see creation all around us. Revelation calls for faith which is a gift.

In my ministry in different countries, some homosexuals approached me. I respected them but was not attracted to them. You may find it hard to believe what a homosexual in Edinburgh said. He and some friends believed strange things about Christ and his disciples. I always took time to listen and heard a lot. Sometimes I was shocked.

I was always strongly heterosexual and found it very difficult at times being sorely tempted to say this is too much and seek a dispensation to leave and get married as so many priest friends, including my brother Mike, had done. The call I received in my early life continued and prevailed. The people I served were my strength.

The four years in Rome as an international guestmaster at a monastery opened up a larger world to me, giving me more varied experiences. I learned to look into life or get a glimpse of it as others see it. From seeing it through two eyes, I now see it through thousands of eyes. From around the world I hear the many languages of men and women and see the faces and smiles of people who traveled so many miles to see the eternal city, learn from its past and experience what it has to offer today.

They leave here with their lives enriched and enlarged leaving behind what cannot be described, but I feel something changed within me. I am better and a more mature person because we met and we shared our lives together. We talked, we listened and we learned from one another. I made lasting friendships, among them the friendships with the Woods and the Sulzbergers who had a key role in my coming to the United States.

Then we had the church in transition. I was in Rome when Pope John XXIII was elected Pope and stood in St. Peter's Square when he gave his first blessing to the world as Pope. I can still see him there and hear him speak, as we all clapped and chanted, "Viva il Papa." It was a universal voice of people from around the world.

He called all the bishops of the world to come to Rome from the Second Vatican Ecumenical Council. The council was to renew the church, especially in liturgical worship and reach out to all churches inviting them to renew their efforts for unity. Indeed he reached out to all people on this earth to work together to build one human family of justice and peace.

What was most evident in the parishes after the council was parish councils, greater involvement of the laity in ministry, a change from Latin to English in liturgical worship and the altar turned around leaving the priest facing the people.

It became easier for the religious to get dispensed from their vows and return to the lay state. Many sisters and brothers were leaving and the number joining declined dramatically. In some orders no one was joining. Many priests were seeking dispensations, leaving the priesthood and most of them getting married. The church was in transition.

I experienced this close up. My first two priest associates in the new parish left and got married as did my own brother, Mike. Many new members signed up in the parish and told me they were ex-brothers or ex-sisters or ex-priests. They use their experience and talent in the service of the parish. They are very helpful in building up the community. Most of them are happily married and have their own families.

Now we have the church in turmoil. Each morning, after mass and morning prayer, my associate and I would sit down for a simple breakfast, open the morning papers and, discuss what is going on in the world. This morning the headlines are about priests accused of molesting children. We are shocked and saddened. We express our feelings over what is being reported. We feel with the innocent victims the hurt they are enduring. With them we are suffering the scandal, shock and sadness that has been perpetrated upon them. We pray for them, for their healing and guidance.

As days go by, more reports of accusations are being published in the papers. Great scandal, shock and sadness grip so many victims, their families, the faithful and good people everywhere.

A small group of priests got together in our area several times to discuss what was happening in the church with molestation. These are some of the ideas and opinions expressed. It is the slaughter of the innocents all over again. A priest should be the most trusted one, he is a father image. A priest who molests a child is a wolf in sheep's clothing, trying to destroy a child's innocence, harming the child psychologically and spiritually and in some cases causing the child to lose the faith. He hurts the whole family and all of us. He causes damage to the child so hard to repair. We hold children so dear that we are angry with the molester who violates them and hurts them for life. Christ showed a holy anger when he said, "If anyone scandalizes one of the little ones . . . it were better for him to have a millstone tied around his neck and be cast into the sea."

> Michael, the archangel is looking in,
> Saying holy men fell into sin,
> Like when the holy angels fell
> And God said, 'cast them down to hell!'

Dear Lord, "Your mercy is above all your works."
Being holy means being Godlike. Holiness has always been a hallmark of the church. That holy image is now defaced by the very ones who are called to teach holiness by their lives, priests of God. They have exchanged their halos for horns.

> When a priest is a wolf in sheep's clothing,
> the sacred trust then turns to loathing.
> I cannot fathom the depths of despair,
> for victims damaged beyond repair.

A lady came to me crying over what is happening in our holy church saying, "All priests will now be looked on with suspicion by people with suspicious minds: we know the vast majority of priests are good, devoted servants of God's people."

> We priests love the people whom we serve,
> we are with them in good times and in bad.
> We share their joys and their sorrows,
> maturing with them for all tomorrows.

Love is not love 'til it's given away.

ACKNOWLEDGEMENTS

I thank all who helped and motivated me to write this memoir, the members of my family, neighbors where I grew up and friends in the many areas in which I studied and ministered. I have a special feeling of gratitude for Arthur and Iphigene Sulzberger of the *New York Times*, and George Woods, then Chairman of the World Bank, and his wife, Louise. The Sulzbergers and the Woods enabled me to come to the United States. They remained lifelong friends and encouraged me to write. I acknowledge Nikko Lavey for his encouragement and research.

Apart from the names of members of my family and some close friends, the names in this memoir are fictitious.

CHAPTER 1

How I Got Here

The family sat around the fire and talked of their dire situation and when the eviction might happen. The fire gave some comfort. It was alive and it had never gone out for so many generations since the house had stood from time immemorial. The heat and the flames gave hope. The fire was on the flat hearth. The peat cut into sods from the bog in the summer gave out a pleasant aroma. The housewife, the mother, was the keeper of the hearth. Life support emanated from the fire. It was a sign of her warm motherly love and endurance, her dependability, constancy and stability. The fire on the hearth welcomed everyone who came to the house. "Here's a chair by the fire; it's cold outside. The kettle is on. You'll have a hot cup of tea."

As the family and friends sat around the hearth the fire was the focal point. Stories were told and retold. The flames fired the imagination as the soft glow of light reflected its color on their faces. Friendships budded and blossomed. Battles were fought and won. Cattle were bought and sold. Romances were sparked, enkindled, glowed and flourished. Weddings were planned and marriages grew stronger. Bread was baked and water boiled. Bacon was fried and meals were cooked. The cat and the dog slept by the hearth and the cricket sang. The fragrance of the peat filled the air. The tongues of fire kissed and danced. The leaping flames were like free human spirits leaping up in hopes and dreams, planning for their family's future and ranging high and far like birds soaring out of sight into the heavens. At night the family knelt on the hearth round the fire to pray. Then the fire was covered with ashes and put to sleep like the family but did not die. The first one up fanned the coals into tongues of flame which licked the kettle into singing, "I am ready to make the first pot of tea to brighten up the new day." On and on it went this way, day after day and night after night as the years came and went. The fire was the one constant that wove a thread of amber through all the family members of succeeding generations sitting there together as stories were retold and memories relived. It was a symbol of the warm love that bound all the members together and never died out as they talked about and prayed for the loved ones who sat by the hearth before them. They never let them die.

Uncle Pat was twelve and Aunt Marcella eleven when the eviction took place. The traveling minstrel, or wandering fiddler, came periodically, traveling through the countryside, providing entertainment, telling stories and bringing news from other parts. He was given food and lodging. The neighbors came and joined in the singing and dancing. The hat was passed around at these gatherings to help support him on his way. In those days the traveling minstrel brought many stories of evictions. The reason given was they could not pay the rent to the landlord. It was the post famine years and there was widespread poverty in the country. The land which formerly belonged to the native farmers was taken by the crown and given to the landlords who were known as planters. They in turn leased the land back to the farmers who then became tenants, paying rent to the landlords. If the rent was not paid, the landlords could take the land and evict the families who were now only tenants. In many cases all the land was taken. Some poor families tried to survive by digging into the ground on their own land and making shelters, burrows which they thatched with straw to keep the cold out. The landlords' men, riding horses drove them off the land cursing and beating them with horsewhips. The McGuires paid the rent but an agent of the landlord, who lived on the next farm, was being rewarded. Most of the good land was taken and given to him. Some of the good land and the land down by the river with a bog adjacent and another bog on the other side of the river in the County Longford were left with the McGuires, still as tenants, paying rent. They were banished from the good land where there home was to that land by the river.

The rent was always paid on time by the McGuires. The next big move was to get them off the land where their house was. With orders from the landlord this could be done. He ordered it. The official closing or deathblow to a house was accomplished by putting out the fire. This was done by tramping on the fire. When the fire was dead the house was dead and the family had to leave. No provisions were made for where they were to go. Many died of starvation and exposure. Many left the country. Poorhouses were built for the ill and the elderly but these could take only a small fraction of the poor and they had a very bad name. Many died and many migrated.

Pat and Marcella recalled that morning early when the agent and his men arrived on horseback. The family had just cooked breakfast over the fire on the hearth. The kettle and the oatmeal pot were still hanging on the iron crane over the fire. The keeper of the hearth, my grandmother, with her children around her and the suckling baby, Bernard, at her breast, pleaded with the men not to do this terrible thing to them.

Grandfather said, "We won't leave. This house has been in our family for generations. Don't tramp out our fire that never went out. If you do you are tramping on our hearts and the hearts of our children."

The agent, Mr. Abbot, got angry and said, "We'll put you off all the land and leave you with nothing." With that he gave orders to his men to tramp on the fire and put it out. Pat and Marcella had vivid memories of the men tramping on the fire. The size of those big boots they never forgot. They were tramping on something that was alive and determined to kill it. The fire seemed to resist. Puffs of smoke with sparks and ashes kept coming up like dying gasps. The big boots tramped and tramped and there were still signs of life in the fire. There was the smell of burning leather like the fire was fighting back. One man said to another, "My boots are burning."

How do you know when a fire is dead? Can you take its pulse? Do we have to wait 'til it goes cold? There was no running water in the house, but a bucket of water stood there; drinking water which the boy Patrick had drawn from the well in the well-field that morning for the needs of the family for the day. Mr. Abbots took the bucket of water and threw it on the fire.

"This is a matter of form," he said, "the fire has to be put out and then you have to leave." The water caused more smoke and ashes to belch up and fill the kitchen. Everyone was choking with the smoke and ashes. With baby Bernard in her arms and the little ones clinging to her crying, grandmother, the keeper of the hearth, walked out across the threshold, across which she had been carried just a few years before, when the wedding celebration took place with family and neighbors and traveling musicians, when they danced and sang 'til the rafters rang' and the midnight hour seemed early. Now early on this morning they must leave with their loving children clinging to them and crying. Grandfather made a last attempt to stay. "This is not a legal eviction. You could not kill the fire by tramping on it. We are staying." The agent told him he could have him hanged from the nearest tree if he did not leave. The like had happened. He was the last to walk across the threshold. It was raining.

With the help of neighbors, my grandfather built a house nearer the river on the land that was left. One neighbor let him take stones from an eleventh century castle, now in ruins, located on his property. That is the house in which I was born. Baby Bernard was to be my father.

 My mother went into labor with me about midnight. "Bernard, you should get the doctor," she said. Bernard got up, dressed quickly, went out to the stables, put a saddle on the horse and headed out the boreen. It was dark. The silence was broken by the clappedy-clap of the horse's shoes hitting the stony road in pleasant rhythm, waking up Pete Ledwich, a bachelor neighbor and friend who knew everyone's movement. He thought, there goes Bernard McGuire on his way to the doctor, for his wife, Mary Ellen, was really big with child. Bernard moved along quickly past the old school house where he went to school, still in use, past his brother Pat's place, out onto the Ballymahon to Mullingar road, still gravel coated, past Empor Chapel where he went to church since infancy, all the way into the village of Ballynacargy, with business houses on both sides and the owners living upstairs, on out into the country again for another mile, five miles in all, to the doctor's big house. He turned his horse into the driveway, dismounted and slammed the brass knocker on the front door. He waited, slammed the knocker again, thinking of Mary Ellen in labor five miles away. The door opened. "Oh, it's you, Bernard. The missus must be in labor." He had already delivered three babies for her and now she was expecting number four. "Yes, doctor—," my father said. "Can you come right away?" "Right away, Bernard." And Bernard mounted his horse and headed home at full gallop to find Mary Ellen in great labor pain. There were two good women there, Mary Ellen's mother Catherine, and Bernard's older sister, Marcella, who lived there. "The doctor is coming right away," he said.

 Mary Ellen's mother, Catherine Leavy, had everything ready. She gave birth to nine children herself in a farmhouse with a doctor and nurse helping. Doctor Byrne, with horse and trap, stopped in the village of Ballynacargy to pick up the nurse who was a midwife. The doctor arrived with the nurse in his trap. They were the only doctor and nurse serving the village and a large area of countryside. Mary Ellen was so happy to see them. They tried to help but nothing was happening. The grandmother had everything ready, the nightstand with a big pitcher jug of cold water and a basin, the kettle of water boiling in the kitchen. Towels and sheets, napkins and chamber pots and everything else for the new baby. Mary Ellen's labor was intense, coming in waves and spasms, the doctor telling her to push at the right moments. She was in agony and it

DECISION TIME

went on and on. The baby would not come. The doctor was frustrated and so was the nurse. The labor pains were getting less frequent and the mother was getting weaker. Twelve hours passed. It is now early afternoon and the situation is getting worse. Aunt Marcella and the Grandmother prepared food for everyone. Bernard and the three small children, Mary Jo, 6; Marcella, 4; and Brian, 2, were huddled close to the fire in the kitchen. Tension grew in the house. Things were not going well. The situation dragged on. The doctor tried and tried harder and harder but could not get the baby's head out. Bernard and the Grandmother and Marcella were praying. Night came. Everyone was doing their best, working hard and praying hard and hoping but facing a deteriorating situation.

Morning came again and Doctor Byrne was faced with a decision. The most challenging birth in his career, but would not lose hope. If I can't get the baby out they will both die and this was not unknown to happen in the area. He could not do a Cesarean because the facilities were not available. This is a farmhouse depending on oil lamps for light, peat fires for heat, a hand pump in the yard for water. After 36 hours of labor there was no labor any more. The mother was weak and fainting.

Dr. Byrne, a big strong man who trained in obstetrics in the famous Coom hospital in Dublin decided to use all his strength and skills to force this baby into the world. He worked on my mother with the nurse helping. I was inside her womb and could not come out. The doctor used all his strength and all his pressure and force wondering if he would kill the baby or the patient or both in the process. The patient, exhausted after 40 hours of labor went in and out of consciousness. Finally the head came through the breach, pressed out of shape, and the shoulders followed very slowly with strong pulling, the mother groaning in agony. Finally the whole baby was out. Everyone breathed a sigh of relief but the feeling of relief was short lived. Dr. Byrne said, "The baby is a boy and he is dead." What a shame, after all this he is a DOA. Grandmother shouted down to the kitchen. "The baby is dead." Bernard ran up the stairs, Aunt Marcella is taking care of the 3 children. Grandmother is praying out loud. The nurse is attending to the mother. Dr. Byrne said to Bernard, the father, "It's a boy and he is dead." He continued to dip the baby in the basin of cold water and slap him on the back, holding him by the ankles. He would not give up dipping and slapping. Finally he laid him on the cold marble tabletop. As he turned away, there was a cry. "My God, he is alive after all that," the doctor said. The father was silent, the mother was too weak to speak, the grandmother thanked God. It's a miracle. The nurse took the baby from the doctor and cleaned him. He was all red, his head squashed out of shape and he cried and cried that distinctive newborn cry. The doctor said, "He will develop strong lungs." Grandmother said, "Maybe God wants him to be a preacher." The mother came around and was able to breast-feed the baby. This was the fourth one she breast-fed and she would breast feed four more.

It was September 30. The baby was expected to be born on September 29, Feast of St. Michael, and they planned to call him Michael, a name in both families. There were two Uncles Michael. But September 30 was the feast of St. Jerome—no consideration of calling him Jerome. Mary Ellen's father was John and she had a brother, John. Bernard had a brother John. So his name will be John. They agreed for the middle name. Mother thought the baby looked angelic. She wanted to call him Aloysius after an angelic saint. So it would be John Aloysius McGuire but they would not call him John every day, rather they would use a Gaelic form of John, Shane. They had a hard time getting the baby to stop crying. This went on for several days.

Bernard walked out the boreen to a neighbor's house three evenings later. Their casual visiting they referred to as rambling. He went into the house where Pete and his two sisters lived, none of them married. He asked Josie Ledwich to be the godmother and she was honored to accept.

A cousin on my mother's side, Owen Fox, was the godfather. They brought the baby to church as soon as Dr. Byrne said it was safe to do so. He was baptized in the local family church of Empor. Father Swan did the baptism.

After nearly dying and having a baby pronounced dead on arrival by the doctor, Mary Ellen and Bernard went on to have four more children. No birth was as difficult and frightening as number four and it remained in their minds in one sense the low point of all the births and in another sense the high point, because of the relief and joy of life out of death. He was the biggest baby. When the new baby was a few days old, the doctor, after visiting with the mother, came downstairs into the kitchen. Bernard, the father, had his two-year-old son, Brian, on his knee and said, "what do you think of this little man?" He said, "I told you you have your ploughman, but don't make a ploughman of the one upstairs."

And remember: Love is not love 'til it's given away.

CHAPTER 2

Early Memories

I always had a visual memory. Some things that happened in my early life are still embedded in my memory: people, trees, animals, birds and events. Like all small children I could not see the forest for the trees. Those closest to me took up my full attention; first my mother who breast-fed me, then my father and the other members of the family. The older children helped raise the younger ones. I was carried a lot and, was never left alone even while I slept.

I remember a beautiful chestnut horse my father rode. I was only three or maybe four years old. It was long before I started school. This was a tall, fast horse and my father loved to ride him. One day the churn had been left in the front yard by the pump to be washed and the horse was standing there while my father went inside for a cup of tea. The reins were thrown over a post near the pump but he had some leeway. The horse was checking out the churn and caught his bridle in it. Trying to shake loose, he lifted the churn and swung it around, just missing me. The image of the house and the fright were embedded in my memory and are still there today. He was a lovely, elegant horse with a friendly personality and loved to be petted.

One day my father rode out of the yard sitting on the horse, going on some errand. We never saw the horse again. My father was brought back into our yard by Patrick Lynn with his horse and trap. Patrick helped my father out of the trap and he started walking into the house with a stick in each hand and all bent over. My mother was crying. We all started crying. "How are you?" mother said. "I'll be alright," he said, Dr. Byrne fixed up my leg that was hurt. I have to use these sticks for awhile." "Where is the horse?"

she said. "I am sorry but he is dead." We were all crying for my father and crying for Dick, the horse. He thanked Patrick and made his way into the kitchen and sat in his chair. We were all gathered around him and he told us what had happened that day.

"I was on my way to Ballynacargy, had just passed Empor Chapel and was outside Patrick Lynn's house when I saw a big army lorry coming toward me. It was making a loud noise, kicking up a cloud of dust from the limestone road and belching black smoke. Dick never saw anything like this before and he got excited. I got him over close to Lynn's wall and tried to make him quiet down. He pranced and jumped and turned around on the road. The lorry kept coming and there was a collision with Dick, the horse, who fell, trapping one of my legs under him. The lorry stopped. Patrick Lynn came out of his house. They took care of me first. Then Patrick and the army officer who was driving the lorry were saying that the horse had a broken leg and will have to be destroyed. The police, now called guards in the Irish Free State, came. They looked at the whole scene and said I should see the doctor. Patrick Lynn got his horse and trap ready to take me to Dr. Byrne.

While I was still at the scene of the accident, the guards shot Dick in the head and it broke my heart to leave him there." We all felt broken-hearted and kept on crying. We wanted to cling to my father but mother would not let us, saying he had been hurt. She said, "You must be in great pain." He said, "It was very painful but it is easing up now. Dr. Byrne said there is no broken bone but my left knee was wrenched a bit. I should get rid of the sticks in a few weeks." Mother said, "Let us say a prayer and Thank God that Dad is home and he is going to be alright." So she put up an impromptu prayer all in her own words standing there in the middle of the kitchen with us all around her. The crying and sobbing stopped and there was silence except for her words of prayer.

At five years old I started school. We walked the two miles in all kinds of weather on roads often flooded after heavy rains. Mary Jo, Marcella and Brian were already going and I was now the youngest to go. My mother put lunch and a bottle of milk in my schoolbag, as she did for the others, came to our white gate leaving the front yard, kissed me and told the others to "take care of the child." Mary Jo took my hand and had me walk beside her. Being the oldest and a girl, she was like a second mother to the younger ones. Later on when she was a young lady, the boys of her age and older were anxious to be friends with me so that I would introduce them to her. She was very attractive and spirited. Steady company keeping was not allowed by parents unless there was some prospect of marriage. The farming community had very strict traditions.

The school could be all right or a place of terror depending on the mood of your teacher. The schoolhouse, which we always passed on the way out to the main Mullingar—Ballymahon road was familiar from the outside. An old whitewashed building standing back from the road in a field, part of which was used as a playground. It was on high ground with no trees and could be seen for miles around. There were two schoolrooms, one for the boys and one for the girls with separate entrances. There was no water or plumbing, no bathroom, just an outhouse. There was no light except the daylight. We were never there after dark. There was no communication with the outside world, no electricity and no radio and no telephone. There was no heat except a fireplace for which pupils brought sods of peat as they walked to school in the winter. Since there were two classrooms, one for the girls and one for the boys, all the children from infants, for that was what kindergarten was called, up to the 8th grade were in the one room. The lady teacher had one end of the room with the infants; first, second and third classes and the master had the rest of the room with the children from the fourth to the eighth classes inclusive. They were never referred to as grades, just classes. The infants sat on open wooden forms. Some of the infants cried for their mothers. I did not cry. My brother, Brian, was in the same room and he had warned me not to cry or he would kill me. The teacher welcomed us and fussed over us, but she had a cane and slapped some of the older children on the hands when they did not know their lessons. I felt very sorry for them. At lunchtime everyone ate their sandwiches and drank their milk. There was no water. We were shown where the outhouse was. The land around the school was an extensive area. The road went through it without any fencing. Cattle and goats and geese from neighbors' land would sometimes go in there to graze. One day a hissing gander chased me and bit me with his beak on the leg. He belonged to the lady teacher's parents and she just laughed when she saw the gander chase me. It hurt a lot and left a red mark for days.

At three p.m. we were released and started walking home. There were other children from different houses on our road and we were together for a while. But since our house was the farthest away, down by the river, we were left by ourselves for the last quarter of a mile or so. Passing one of the houses I was lagging behind and a little white terrier dog came out barking and chasing us and caught up with me, being the last, and bit me on the leg. The dog belonged to a man who had consumption—a dreaded word. My father went out to the man and asked him to keep the dog in when the children were coming home from school. He said it was my fault because I teased the dog. Word got around the school and they all said I would die of consumption from that dog bite. The man died of consumption not long afterwards. Consumption was the word used for tuberculosis. They never used that word or even TB but always consumption and it was considered incurable. The person wasted away, consumed by the disease. The man who owned the biting dog had consumption and everyone knew it. He would be seen walking around his yard with a big coat on the warmest days and a big scarf around his neck and head. They said it ran in families. If one got it they all got it.

Abbots' old house was vacant. They all died of consumption and their ghosts haunted the house. Pat Burke, who worked for my father at times, is having dinner in our kitchen and the conversation got around to Abbots' old house. "Be God, Bernie," he said, "no one could ever live there. The consumption is in the rafters." Consumption was feared and it always put a stigma on a family if one of the members got the dreaded disease. Children were advised by their parents not to get close to anyone known to have consumption. Children ignored the advice. Sanitariums were built throughout the country to which patients were sent by the doctors to be treated. Bad air was also blamed for the disease. So the sanitariums, with open fronts and verandas were built away from towns. Consumption was supposed to thrive in dark, stuffy places and good fresh air was supposed to kill it. Sitting by the fireside the conversation often came around to consumption and the houses that were affected.

After the youngest, Mike, was born at which time I was nine years old, there were eleven of us in the house, my father and mother and my father's oldest sister, Aunt Marcella, and eight children. Every morning there was a flurry of activity. All were up early. Brian and I helped my father feed the cows and horse and pigs. We tied up bundles of hay and carried them on our backs out to the cattle in the fields. Mother and Aunt Marcella joined us in the milking and taking the milk to the dairy which was a building attached to the house and putting it through the separating machine. This machine was operated by turning a handle. The milk was put into a large container on the top and came out through two spouts, one with cream and the other with skim milk. The cream was kept to churn and make butter. The skim milk was fed with meal to the calves. We kept some whole milk for use in the house. After the work was done we had breakfast; porridge, eggs and bacon, bread and butter and milk or tea. I can still see my mother busy making the lunches for school, slicing the wheaten bread she had baked the day before, buttering it and making sandwiches, filling bottles with milk. Before leaving we would take the milk and sandwiches and put them in our school bags. Then we started for school no matter what the weather. Mother shook holy water on us before we left and told us not to forget to say the rosary on the way. She frequently gave us a container of milk for a needy family whose house we passed on the way to school.

When we came home from school, in the winter we helped with foddering the animals and milking the cows. In the spring the boys helped in the fields, thinning turnips and pulling weeds. In the summer we helped with the hay-making which was our favorite work. At harvest time we helped bring in the crops. After the work was done outside we got down to our homework with kerosene lamps. We sat around the big kitchen table with our books. My father sat by the fire reading. He loved to read. My mother and Aunt Marcella sat by the fire mending clothes and darning socks. The older children helped the younger ones with their homework. When that was finished we all sat around the hearth and talked. Father told stories of the old days, fishing and shooting wild game and going to fairs. Mother and Aunt Marcella told us ghost stories and everyone got scared. Sometimes I thought they were making them up. We danced to gramophone music. Every Sunday we went to Mass in Empor Chapel about two miles away. My father would yoke the horse to the trap and take my mother, Aunt Marcella and the younger children. The older ones walked. The trap was a six-seater but with children it would take more. Aunt Marcella wore a fox fur around her neck with the head and the paws hanging down. In my very young days it was a big distraction to me as I sat beside her in church touching the fur gingerly and jerking my hand back, amusing the other children near me. Many women wore them in those days. When we got home from church Mother and Aunt Marcella would be busy preparing Sunday dinner. Father would sit in his usual seat by the fire and gather us around him.

He would read the scriptures of the Mass that day. Then he would ask who could remember what the preacher said. We could remember the announcements about football games and the other sports but we were not always good in remembering the sermon. Then he led us in a discussion on the readings of the day. We were always impressed at how much he knew and the number of books he had. After dinner father would take us somewhere, depending on the weather and the season of the year. He would take us for a ride through the country with the horse and trap where he knew everyone for so many miles around. He would take us down by the river fishing which we all loved. In season we went bird shooting. We got pheasant, grouse, partridges, wild ducks and snipe. On those occasions he would take only one of us with him and we had to walk behind him all the time. First he started taking Brian. Then when I got older he would take me but only one at a time. He would take all of us to the bog, play hide and seek and collect blueberries and blackberries.

Sometimes on a Sunday we did something different. We would visit our grandparents on my mother's side, John and Catherine Fox in Dysart about two hours away with the horse and trap. Arrangements would be made by letters as there were no telephones. On the designated Sunday we would leave early and attend Mass in Castletown at eleven o'clock. The Fox family would attend the same Mass. After Mass they would lead the way in their horse and trap out to their home three miles away and we would follow in our horse and trap.

We always had a great time there. Grandmother would cook a lovely, big dinner, usually chicken and ham. Our grandparents loved to have Brian and me dance on the parlor floor to music provided by Uncle Johnny who played the violin. They would clap and cheer us on. Johnny and Jimmy would take us through their fields for a walk, looking at their cows and cattle and crops. At four o'clock my father would say, "Well, we should go now. We have to do the milking." We would have a leisurely ride home in the trap, the horse trotting along. Mother and Father between them knew the families that lived in every house along the way. We just talked and talked, enjoying the trip and also reminiscing on what happened that day.

Uncle Pat came often with his horse to help in busy times of the year such as the ploughing season. Usually we kept one workhorse and two were needed for ploughing in the spring and cutting the meadows in the summer. Everyone had dinner in the kitchen together. Pat and Marcella talked often of the old days when they were children and growing up. One of the subjects that frequently came up was their eviction from the old farmhouse and the confiscation of the best part of the farm. The landlord gave that land to one of his agents and banished the McGuire family to mostly bottomland down by the river. If a farm had bottoms that meant some fields could possibly be flooded in the winter. There was some high land called upland that went with the bottomland and that was used for grazing and crops.

In dividing the land the landlord did something calculated to cause trouble among the farmers so that they would fight and disagree among themselves and not unite against him. He divided the land and divided the neighbors in such a way that the McGuires had to pass not through the agent's land but through McNamara's land, a field with no farm road. They were known to everyone as the Macs. To make the situation more complicated the landlord gave one field by the river to another neighboring family that lived a little farther out the road. That family had to pass through Mac's field and cross through our land on their way to their field by the river. No one could dispute the right of way, because it was given by the landlord.

The river fascinated me from as early as I can remember. How I loved to run along the riverbank which was like a lawn, cropped tight to the ground by the grazing animals. I loved to gaze on the river. It was alive and always on the move. There was life on the river; swans, wild ducks, water hens, puffins and coots. There was life in the river; fish of many species. Then the river reflected life and movement, the passing clouds and the flying birds.

We frequently fished in the river. One morning when I went to fish alone and was catching nothing I wandered through the field. The cows were grazing, the mare was grazing and her foal was frolicking around her. The field along the riverbank was carpeted with daisies. I decided to pluck some of them and make a necklace of daisies for one of my sisters by threading them onto a long stringy stalk of grass. As I approached the river I saw a number of fish near the surface. When they saw me they darted away and disappeared. Hoping they would come back, I put a worm on the hook and dropped it into the water. Then I sat down among flowers which looked like wild irises close to the river's edge. My eyes were just above the flowers. I could see the river but hoped the fish would not see me. I took the daisy heads off the stocks and threaded them onto the long, stiff stems of grass. When I had finished I flicked one of the daisy heads that were left over into the river. Right away a fish darted out of nowhere and took the daisy in his mouth and quickly spat it out again. I got an idea. If that daisy had been on a hook I could possibly have caught him. I put a daisy on a hook and still sitting low among the flowers, dropped it to the surface of the water. Right away a fish took it in his mouth and spat it out immediately. I was too slow. So I decided to try again. This time I would keep the line taught from the tip of the rod to the daisy and be ready to lift it sharply as soon as the fish would take the daisy in his mouth. This time I was determined to catch him. As the daisy touched the water the fish darted out and snapped it. In that split moment when he snapped I snapped the tip of the rod up and hooked him. It was such an exciting moment to feel him on the line. He splashed and ran and jumped. Then I could see he was a big trout, the best fish in the river. I had no landing net so when he got tired out I walked him to a shallow part of the river, put my hand under him and threw him out on the bank. He was the best fish I had ever caught, big with all the beautiful colors of a river trout. When I brought him home there were many questions. "Where did you get him?" "What did you use" and on and on. At first they would not believe me. Brian said, "Someone in a boat must have come along and given him to you." When they all saw how insistent I was they stopped asking questions. Then I took the daisy necklace out of my pocket and said to my sisters. "Who believes?" All said, "I believe."

The river was a great joy to me. I loved to walk along its banks, to fish in its water or just sit, look and listen. The next time I went to the same place where I caught the big trout, the same technique did not work. This seems to have been his territory so maybe another one will occupy it and I'll catch him. I sat among the flowers and looked and listened. Looking to my left there were bulrushes and reeds growing on the very edge and some in the water coming up from the bed of the river. The wind blew, the rain fell and the sun came out again. It was a constantly changing scene. The wind and the current stirred the rushes and the reeds. They waved and nodded and whispered. Heavy raindrops fell, each drop forming a crown on the surface of the river, which seemed to be speaking to the passing clouds in gratitude for the extra water. Birds were mirrored in the river. Wild ducks and swans and an elegant long-billed curlew glided and swerved over head as if checking me out, calling, "Curlew, curlew." Stretching onwards the river curved gracefully, reflecting the heavens and watering the earth as it had done for so many generations. My father and grandfather grew up here as did so many of their forefathers before them. They all loved the river. My father liked to quote the poet Tennyson, "Men may come and men may go, but I go on forever."

The facts of life were not discussed in our family. That was the tradition. There were four children younger than me so I was used to babies coming into the house. When we asked where babies came from we were told the nurse brought the babies. That satisfied us and stopped the questioning but only for a while. With my own development and the evidence all around me, doubts came into my mind. Questions were discouraged and sidestepped. I knew boys and girls were made differently as were the males and females of all the species of animals on the farm. We saw copulation go on in front of our eyes: the bull and the cow; the stallion and the mare; the ram and the ewe; the cock and the hen; the drake and the duck and so on. There was no exception as to how the young came into the world. There was vacillation between being sure and being doubtful. One thing that sticks in my mind from that time was when my father and mother were talking about family likenesses. They commented on one family in the area saying "that son is exactly like his father, even the same square head." I recalled my father saying if we take that cow to Lynns' white-headed bull, the calf will have a white head. It was evident all around that the young of animals and people resembled their parents. With my own increasing development and from what I could hear and see I gradually became sure of the facts of life. I was nine years old when the youngest, Mike, was born and I knew where he came from and how he got there. Still the parents didn't say.

At ten years old I was in good health, already as tall as Brian, my older brother, and enjoying haymaking and, sports at school, football and running. That's all that was available. My sisters said my face was like a waterhen's egg—all freckles and that my ears stood out from my head like the ears of a newborn donkey. They flattened out later.

The farm work I liked best was the haymaking, especially when we were all in the meadows down by the river. In the morning I would take a fishing rod with me and drop a line in the river and tie the rod to the reeds so that a big fish would not pull it into the river. This was called setting the rod. Then I went to the hay making with the others. When we were called for dinner at midday I would check the fishing rod. Sometimes I had a fish, mostly river perch. One day when I checked the rod I thought the line was stuck on the bottom. After trying to jerk it loose it was nearly pulled out of my hands by a big fish. I finally pulled him out onto the riverbank. It was a big pike, more than two feet long. I pulled him away from the river to where the land was level. As I lifted him up by the line, he fell off and there was a nice sized perch on the hook. All in the family were excited when they saw the extraordinary catch. Every fish was eaten in our house.

I loved to run along the riverbank to increase my speed for running on the school green. Brian, two years older and Frank, two years younger would run by the river with me. I was tall and light and as such had greater speed. One day as we entered the far meadow by the river we saw a big bird out in the middle of the field. He was a crane or heron. He started running for the river and apparently could not fly. We started running to get between him and the river. I got in front of him and threw my sweater over his head. We then grabbed him by the neck in such a way that he could not peck us with his long, sharp, pointed beak. One wing was injured. We took him home. There were all kinds of opinions as to what to do with him.

"He eats young fish so you should kill him." "Just take him back and leave him where you got him." My mother said, "He is such a beautiful bird you should not kill him." My father said, "We will take him to the barn and see if we can make splints for his wing." We prepared wooden splints and tied them in place with light twine. "Wild birds' bones knit quickly. In nine days or so that bone should be knit together." The break was not too bad. There was no bone sticking out. The string won't last too long. So we took him to where we found him and let him go. We looked for him everyday. He was always in a drain where he could find frogs and other things to eat. When I went fishing I would give him the small perch and tench. He would watch me and when I would walk away he would come out and eat them. Eventually he was flying again and used to come back to the meadow looking for fish which we would give him. The image stays very vivid in my memory; that beautiful, big, blue crane in my hands and the sight of him flying again.

Aunt Marcella used to take us to places with the ass and trap. There was a big trap and cart for the horse and a smaller trap and cart for the donkey. She would take us into our cousins, the McGuires, at the green which we loved. There were eight children in their house, five boys and three girls. She visited there so often that the ass would always turn into their driveway and did not want to go any farther. Sometimes one of the cousins would lead him back out to the road so that we could continue going. She stopped at our cousins, the Foxes, who had a country store and at the shops in Ballynacargy. She would buy us whatever sweets we liked. Our favorite place to which Marcella took us was Barnstown Estate where they had grapes growing in glass houses. The man who worked there knew Marcella well. He would cut big, juicy bunches of purple grapes and hand them to us, and how we enjoyed them. I can still taste them by just thinking of them.

My sister, Marcella, who was called after Aunt Marcella, loved to help my father in the fields. One day she was with him cutting oats and tying the sheaves. He was called to the house and she stayed, continuing to work. As I came she was singing and working. It was such a peaceful scene. Later when I learned this poem by William Wordsworth, it always reminded me of her.

> Behold her single in the field
> Yon solitary highland lass
> Reaping and singing by herself,
> Stop here, or gently pass.

Alone she cuts and binds the grain,
And sings a melancholy strain.
Oh! Listen for the vale profound
Is overflowing with the sound.

At ten I was allowed to drive the ass and cart while working on the farm or in the bog. One day we went to the bog. The ass could go farther on the soft ground than the horse could go. Brian and I brought the peat out to firm ground with the ass and cart, to where my father could come in with the horse and cart. We were approaching where my father was with his first load of peat. Suddenly the ass lay down on his stomach with the shafts of the cart still along his sides. I coaxed him and pulled at him but he would not budge. I got frustrated with him and gave him a smack on the rump with a stick. My father was standing there watching everything. He said, "Don't beat him, he might talk back to you."

"What do you mean, Dad, an ass talking?" He said an ass is mentioned as talking in the bible. I said, "You are having me on." He said, "Balaam beat his ass and the ass talked back to him. Tonight I'll show it to you in the bible." And he did. That night we read from the Book of Numbers, Chapter 22, verses 28 ff. The ass asked Balaam: "what have I done to you that you should beat me." He also read Chesterton's poem to me about the donkey.

The Donkey by G.K. Chesterton

When fishes flew and forests walked
  And figs grew upon thorn,
Some moment when the moon was blood
  Then surely I was born;
With monstrous head and sickening cry
  And ears like errant wings,
The devil's walking parody
  On all four-footed things.
The tattered outlaw of the earth,
  Of ancient crooked will;
Starve, scourge, deride me: I am dumb,
  I keep my secret still.
Fools! For I also had my hour;
  One far fierce hour and sweet:
There was a shout about my ears,
  And palms before my feet.

With so many grades in the one classroom the master had from the fourth to the eighth grades, all the boys could hear and see everything that was going on. One day the master put a mathematics problem on the blackboard for the eighth grade. The fifth graders were sitting at their desks. We had finished our assignment and were looking on. The master said, "Shane McGuire, you keep looking up here. You want to solve the problem? Here is the chalk." I took the chalk and stood by the blackboard. It was already clear to me from watching and listening. So I explained the problem and wrote the answer on the board.

"Right!" said the master and, "you eighth graders should have paid more attention."

Brian was in the classroom with me. At dinner when we came home he told our parents the whole thing as it happened. Uncle Mike who had half a day off had come out from work on his motorbike, as he frequently did. They were all happy to hear what Brian told them. I can recall Uncle Mike continuing to talk about it. He was always encouraging me and asking my father and mother about plans for further education. There were no secondary or high schools in the area. There were no school buses to take students to schools in the big towns. Most children of farmers finished school at the eighth grade or fourteen years old. A few went to boarding schools. This was expensive, especially for large families. There was no government help in tuition or subsidies.

And remember: Love is not love 'til it's given away.

CHAPTER 3

Stricken with Osteomyelitis

Running and jumping both long and high were the craze with the children in the school. I was very thin, and tall for my age. I competed very eagerly and came first in my class in the high jumping and running. It was not easy as there were some almost as good as me and I practiced running a lot to keep up my speed and maintain first place. There was plenty of opportunity to practice running on the farm. I ran through the fields and along the riverbank, sometimes feeling surprised at how fast I was going and thought some day I will fly. At ten years old I could go where I wanted. I knew all our fields and each cow and bullock, also all of the neighbor's fields and their animals. I knew where to find the wild mushrooms and was always very welcome when I came home with hanks of mushrooms, strung on long stems of grass.

I started vaulting in the meadows with a long pole. This was a great discovery for me: how I enjoyed running with the pole and vaulting high in the air and trying to go higher with each passing day. It seemed to me I was getting closer to flying, and even did fly over the trees, but that was in my dreams.

Then there was that pain in my right leg that kept bothering me as it would come and go. Each time it went away, I thought that was the end of it. But no, it would come back again, every few days, and last for only a few minutes. It seemed to me it was getting worse instead of better. The pain made me wake up at night and walk around the house to try and get some relief. My mother found me walking one night and asked me what was wrong. I told her and she got me back to bed, doing everything she could to make me comfortable. The pain went away for a while.

Next morning my mother asked me how the leg was. I said the pain had gone away. She said, "I hope that is the end of it. If it should come back again, let us know and we will take you to Dr. Byrne." I went vaulting along the riverbank which was now my favorite fun in free time. After a while the pain started coming and going. I stopped vaulting and lay down in the shade of a tree. My father came along. He said, "I did not know where you were. Could you help me turn some rows of hay in the next meadow?" I was silent for a few moments and I noticed him staring at me. Then he said, "Are you alright?" I said, "The pain is back in my leg again." He said, "Come back to the house and we will take you to Dr. Byrne. Can you walk on it?" I said, "Yes."

My father yoked the horse to the trap. He, my mother and I trotted off to the doctor's residence, Mom holding my leg on her lap and caressing it with her hands to ease the pain. The doctor examined the leg and shook his head saying, "I can't find anything wrong with this leg." Mother said, "What are we to do? He wakes up at night with the pain." The doctor said, "How long have you felt the pain?" I said, "Off and on for about a month." He said, "You must have hurt it in some way and the pain should go away with time. How much pain do you have now?" I said, "It's not too bad, but it gets worse at times." He said, "I can't do anything right now. It should go away."

That evening around the hearth, all the family discussed the pain I was having in my leg. Mother said, "The doctor thought Shane might have hurt his leg." Brian said, "It must be the vaulting. That vaulting is dangerous." Frank agreed with him. All advised I should not vault anymore. I said, "It was not the vaulting and I did not hurt the leg."

The pain kept on coming and going and it was getting worse instead of getting better. Neighbors who came into our house were all giving their opinions and their advice, each one offering a sure solution. Put a hot poultice on it, hold it in the river stream for a few hours, rub goose grease on it, boil nettles and drink the nettles water, put cow dung on it, go to the quack doctor, go to the bone-setter, the regular doctor's don't know as much as the quack doctors and bone setters because it was handed down to them from olden times and they have the secrets.

The pain kept coming and going, some days worse than others. Brian wanted to put a shovel full of cow dung on the leg to just try it and see if it would cure it. Marcella thought the river stream sounded good and that I should try it. Aunt Marcella said I could have some of her goose fat which she used for her rheumatism. My father and mother decided, since Dr. Byrne said he could do nothing, to take me to a Paddy Muldoon who was highly recommended by a neighbor as a successful quack doctor.

We set out one morning to go to Paddy Muldoon. My father said it was going to take a whole day, so mother packed a lunch. After a half hour or so, I did not know where we were. My father had enough directions but he had been in the area only once or twice in his life. We kept going and going, up and down hills through quiet countryside, with farmhouses and cows and sheep in the fields. Finally, my father said Paddy Muldoon's house should be just about here. Mother said, "Eliza Mac told us he was always shouting and if we go slow we should hear him. That's how she found him when she took her sister Maryann to see him." We were slowly passing a little thatched house, down in a hollow, near the side of the road. We heard someone shouting and listened. We heard it again, a man's voice. As we turned into his yard, we saw him walking around. He came over and welcomed us. My father told him why we were there and he took us inside. It was a small square room with a fire burning in the fireplace. He sat us down and got down on his knees in front of me. He felt my leg up and down asking where the pain was. I told him the whole leg was painful but the worse place was in the shin, down near the ankle. He said, "It's the ankle" and reached away into a hole in the wall beside the fireplace. He pulled out a lot of stuff. Mother said, "What's that?" He said, "It's pigskin and a secret ointment." He proceeded to rub the ointment into the ankle and cover it with the pigskin, which stuck to the ointment. My father offered him some money and he refused it. He said, "The secret was handed down in my family and if any of us takes money we will lose the secret." He said the ankle should be all right in a week. We thanked him and headed home. This time my father took another route around a beautiful lake. When we got to the top of a hill, looking down on the lake, we stopped and ate lunch. I can still see us there sitting in the trap with the horse, eating the luscious green grass that grew along the side of the road, and we eating the delicious lunch mother had packed. My father asked me if the leg felt any better. I said, "No, it is still painful and I don't like not being able to wear a shoe with all the pigskin he put around the ankle. Four beautiful white swans flew over us gliding down to the lake. My father said, "They are the children of Leer."

A week went by. The pigskin came off and the pain was still there. My father and mother were very disappointed and kept saying, "What can we do? Dr. Byrne said he could do nothing and the pain would go away. Paddy Muldoon tried his cure and it did not work. We have to do something." Another neighbor, Pete, told us about a bone-setter down in Longford County who helped everyone who went to him. So we set out on another day looking for the bone-setter Jim. We traveled for miles through farmland and bogs. The last stretch of road through a bog was sunken and flooded and we almost did not get through. In the midst of that bog there was a cluster of trees and a little thatched cottage in the midst of them. My father said, "This has to be it".

A man was sitting inside, looking out over the half door. That was an arrangement in some country houses to keep the chickens from walking into the kitchen and at the same time let in some fresh air. My father said to him, "We hope we are at the right house." He said, "If it's the bone-setter Jim you are looking for, you are in the right place. I have been setting broken bones for people for twenty miles and more around here, all my life. Come inside." This house was even smaller than the other one, but had the fire burning on the hearth. My father explained the pain I was having in the leg and how desperate we were to have it cured. He was very gentle examining my leg, having me move it up and down, from side to side, bending the knee and the ankle and feeling it all over. Then finally he said, "I feel something on the shin bone. It does not feel like a real break." Then he said to my father and mother, "Children of this age don't have bones as hard as in older people. Sometimes when the bone breaks it can be what is called a greenstick break. The bone breaks half way and then the bone splinters down the middle like what happens when you break a green stick". He put splints on each side of the leg after rubbing in ointment and wrapped a bandage around it. Now, he said, "Don't put any weight on it for at least ten days. Meantime you can just hop around on the other leg." My father thanked him and offered him money. He said, "No, I'd lose the family gift of bone-setting if I took money." We all thanked him and headed home. When we came home all the family was curious to know what had happened and if I was feeling better now.

Before the ten days were up to take off the splints, the pain in the leg got so bad I could not bear it. I cried day and night. No matter what I did, hopping, sitting, lying or crying, there was not relief. The leg swelled up from the ankle to the knee. We took off the splints, Jim the bone-setter had put on and, my father and mother got me into the trap and we went to Dr. Byrne.

My father stayed with the horse and trap. Mother knocked on the door. The doctor's wife answered and opened the dispensary door for us. This was an annex at the side of the big house. We sat and waited. We heard footsteps coming. Dr. Byrne was a big, strong man.

He burst open the door and asked, "What can I do for you?" He looked at the leg. He shook his head and said, "You should have come sooner." He took a knife from a sideboard and held my heel with one hand and stabbed the knife into the leg with the other hand. I screamed in pain. Mother held my shoulders and cried. Yellowish puss poured out like water from a kettle spout. He kept cutting and squeezing to get all the matter out and the agony continued as I squirmed and screamed. When he had finished he wrapped the leg in a bandage and said it should get all right. When we got home all the cows and calves were standing in the field by the yard looking through the gate at us. I was sure they were feeling sorry for me on crutches that Dr. Byrne gave me to keep the weight off the leg. Mother told the whole family about the lancing. They were all sorry for me and tried to be very kind. They always referred to this problem as "Shane's sore leg."

After the lancing, the swelling in the leg went down, the pain eased and I hoped that was the end of the trouble. But I was not that lucky. Within a week the pain and swelling came back. The temperature went up and my parents took me to Dr. Byrne again. My mother and I waited in the dispensary. It was one room with a door going into the doctor's residence. We sat in the same chairs and waited for the doctor to come. Every sound startled me. I was waiting to hear his footsteps, fearful and silently hoping he would not come. Then the sound of steps and the door opened. He looked at the leg and shook his head. "I did not expect it to come back like this." He picked up the lance again.

My mother stood behind me holding my shoulders with both hands and pleaded, "Doctor, please don't hurt him." He made no comment but quickly stuck the lance into the leg as I watched and screamed with shock and pain. The puss came out like before. As he cut and squeezed, it seemed to hurt forever. My mother was leaning over me and trying to comfort me. Her tears fell on my face. She was shaking. I felt she was sharing my pain and that gave me comfort. The doctor finished the lancing and bandaged the leg. He said to keep the weight off it by using the crutches. It should be all right this time. It would not get all right this time. He did not know the lancing could not cure the leg because the trouble was in the marrow cavity of the bone. This is why the pain was so bad and so persistent. The bone was rotting. The disease was known as osteomyelitis and also called Brodi's abscess having been discovered by a Dr. Brodi of Edinburgh. It was caused by an infection that lodged in the marrow cavity of the bone.

This time I had several weeks before a reoccurrence. The whole family was hoping and praying it would go away but it kept on returning, usually after several weeks or even more. Each time I had to go through the ordeal of waiting fearfully for the doctor and watching that same lance being plunged into my leg and feeling the agony of pain and screaming. During the periods when I was feeling good I attended school and did mostly everything that I had done before. I had been missing a lot from school and told the master why. He had no comment.

The leaders of the newly established Irish Free State were determined to restore the Irish language which had been replaced by English during centuries of domination. It survived in remote areas in the west and the western islands. Now it was compulsory in all the national schools from the first day children went to school. The intent was to bring it back so that it would be spoken in the homes. The problem was that parents did not speak it. A bigger problem was the language was often forced on the children with pressure and beatings. The punishments often made the children dislike the language and greatly upset the parents. There was no incentive to speak the language in the home. My father and mother discussed the matter often. They were deeply offended when the minister of education said he was certainly not going to consult with the parents. Parents were greatly disturbed and frustrated by the move to teach everything through the medium of Irish. The master punished the students for not giving the right answers to the questions in Gaelic.

He used a cane on the hands. "Hold out your hands," and he came down hard, one or two strokes, on each hand or more, depending on how many strokes he decided the boy deserved and how angry and frustrated he became. Because all were in the one classroom all could see what was going on and all were terrified. If one day a cane broke the next day he would arrive with a new one tied to the bar of his bicycle. That sight sent fear through all of us. We kept on standing up to see if he was coming. Occasionally, he did not come. Then we were in heaven for that day.

The master went on an Irish crush. We were behind in Irish, he told us and he was going to bring us up to standard. The Department of Education wants us to do this and parents have no say. They wanted us to speak Irish at home. So the master got going on the Irish. He ordered us out of our seats to stand in front of him in a semi-circle. He questioned us in turn and ordered us to answer in Irish. I had a fever and great pain in the shinbone. I was too slow to answer. "Shane McGuire, you have a good brain. Why don't you answer?" He said, "Hold out your hands," which I did and he gave me four strokes of the cane, two on each hand. Again he asked a question in Irish and again I was too slow for him in answering. He got angry with me and said, "What are you doing to me?" He ordered me to stretch out my hands again. He gave me several fierce strokes on my hands. He questioned me again and again I was too slow. My sore leg was throbbing and my hands were throbbing and I was deeply humiliated as the master grew more frustrated. I stumbled and he hit me over the back with the cane. It glanced off my back, hit a desk and broke in two parts. He grew more angry and when I got steady on my feet again he slapped me with his hand on my face. He asked the question again and again and again, not giving me time to think. With the unbearable pain in the sore leg, the fever temperature elevated and my brain shaken with the slapping, I was too slow for him in answering and he continued to slap me on the face and ear again and again. He finally gave up. When we came home I felt sick. Mother asked what was wrong. Brian told her about the beatings. She looked at my jaw and ear and they were swollen and discolored, appearing purple. "Oh my God," she said. "The master did that to you." She was furious and angry. "We'll do something about this," she said. She called for my father and showed it to him. He, too, was furious. "How could he do this?" Mother said, "You are not going to school tomorrow and we are taking you to the doctor right now." They yoked the horse and trap and took me to Dr. Byrne who had also brought me into this world and pronounced me dead, and had recently and repeatedly lanced my leg.

He examined my face and said, "This is horrible. There can be no excuse for doing this." My mother asked him for a statement in writing and he gave her one describing what he saw. My mother sent it to the Department of Education, the address of which was given to her by Dr. Byrne. She waited but never got an answer. The Department of Education had declared that parents would have no say and would not be consulted in teaching—forcing—Irish on the children of Ireland. The family lost all confidence and faith in the Department of Education in the new Irish Free State. Mother suggested seeing a solicitor. Father said no.

The parish priest was the school manager and parents were not allowed to go to teachers with complaints. So my mother took me into the sacristy after Sunday Mass to complain to the priest and have him look at the face and ear, still swollen and discolored. Mother also showed him my sore leg and told him of all I was going through. He blessed the sore leg but said nothing about the purple jaw and ear. We never heard from the Department of Education or from the church on the beatings and they did not contact the master. My parents discussed this many times at home. My father said, "That's the way the Department of Education and the clergy treat our children. Don't they realize the children are the future of the country?"

Empor School, built 1833.

When in pain with the leg I would lie on the settle bed in the kitchen. This was a pull-out bed with a wooden frame. When not in use it was folded up against the back wall of the kitchen, providing a place for several of us to sit. When lying there I was part of all the activity that went on. The farmhouse kitchen was the living center of the family during the day. It was where all the cooking and eating and talking took place. When we left we left from the kitchen. When we returned we returned to the kitchen. The dog and the cat would lie in front of the fire that never went out. At times I could not eat much. Whoever went to town brought me oranges which I always enjoyed.

When the weather was good I would sit outside and Lab, the dog, always stayed with me. I loved the sounds of life outside; the birds singing, the swish of the swallows' wings, the calling of the cuckoo and the corncrake. In the spring Brian liked to say: "The bee, the bat, the butterfly, the cuckoo and the swallow, the corncrake put out his bake and bit them all gomorrah."

And remember: Love is not love 'til it's given away.

CHAPTER 4

The Dog and the Birds and More

There was a big sycamore tree in front of our house. One day I heard a cuckoo calling from a tree in the distance. I cupped my hands to my mouth and imitated each call he made. I saw him fly to another tree nearer to us. Each time he called I answered until he finally perched on the top of the big sycamore tree right above my head. Mary Jo was watching and listening. She said, "He thinks you are a cuckoo."

Of all the birds, and there were many, the two best songsters were the blackbird and the thrush. Who said, "The thrush is for the summer noon, the blackbird for all weather"? I loved to listen to birds sing, especially in the early morning when all birds sing. This is called the dawn chorus. It never ceases as dawn moves around the world. The bird I loved to listen to most around the house was the blackbird. He always perched on the top of the highest branch of a tall tree. Nothing stopped his melodious voice from traveling all around and filling our ears with the sound, uplifting our spirits from all the trials that can be our lot in life. He is happy spreading happiness and telling us how good it is to be alive. The quality of song comes from his heart. I can hear this quality and feel it. It is comforting, inspiring and relaxing, promising better things, blaming no one, happy with everyone, soothing and inviting to stop and listen or walk gently by. I loved the blackbird and told him so. He responded by singing sweeter, I was sure. The pain is easier to bear because of you. I cherish the blackbird, he enjoyed singing and all enjoyed listening. The joy of all creation comes through his voice.

His favorite perch was the top of the big sycamore tree in front of the house. One day I sat in a chair with Lab, the dog, at my side. Aunt Marcella had said the sun will dry out the sore on your leg and cure it. So I sat there with the sun shining down on the leg. The blackbird came and perched on the top of the sycamore tree. He sang and sang. It was a relief listening to him. Then I slipped away into a deep sleep. As I awakened the blackbird was singing and there was the feeling of something soft as velvet touching my leg. It was Lab's tongue. He was licking my sore leg where the doctor had lanced it. Every time the leg healed up and I was feeling better we all thought that would be the end of it and the problem would not come back anymore. That would not be the case.

Lab had some interesting characteristics. When we were playing he played with us. If we got into a fight he would jump on us and separate us. He hated fights. When mother was alone in the house, he stayed around. His favorite perch was on top of a stack of peat turf from where he could see anyone coming in the distance. He would sit there, very prominent like a statue. When someone appeared coming in the distance, he would start barking and would keep turning his head toward the house to see if anyone was paying any attention to him. Mother always knew when someone was coming. If there seemed to be a delay, it meant the person was afraid of the dog. Mother would go out to see, Lab would join her. Some would say, "I was afraid of that big black dog." Mother would say, "Look at him walking in front of you wagging his tail. He just came out to wag you in."

Lab had the habit of going around finding things and bringing them back to us. While we were fishing at the river this day Lab was roaming around and sniffing the air as was usual with him. After one of his little search and find efforts, he came back with an egg in his mouth. It was not broken. Labradors were noted for their soft mouths. When they retrieved game they never left a tooth mark on it. He kept roaming around while we were moving along the riverbank, fishing. When it came time to go home I went to pick up a jacket and the egg. To my surprise there were more eggs there, twelve altogether, all of them identical. When we came home, Dad said, "Those are wild duck eggs. Twelve is the number the wild duck lays before beginning to hatch them. There may be young ducks inside those shells. We should try and get them hatched."

There was an extra clocking hen in the yard that was not needed to hatch eggs. We put the wild duck eggs under the clocking hen and hoped we would have little wild ducklings. It takes four weeks for duck eggs to hatch but we were not sure how long these were going to take. It would be a waiting game, checking them every day. We had learned a lot about incubation and gestation. From observing the nests we knew that small birds like blackbirds and thrushes took only two weeks: chickens took three weeks and geese took four weeks. The larger the bird, the longer the period of incubation. We also knew the length of time of gestation for animals on the farm: sheep and goats took four months, cows nine months and mares eleven months.

We had no goats on the farm until Brian got a gift of a kid goat from a boy in school. The kid grew up to be a nice friendly nanny goat. In time she came into season, that means she was looking for a puck goat, because she was lifting her head in the air and bleating loudly and would not stop. Brian and I took our goat across a mile of fields to a man called Bill who kept a puck goat. It was the only one we knew of because they were very hard to control and would wander everywhere. This one was tied on a long tether to a post in a field beside his cottage. We left our nanny goat there and went back in the evening. We paid Bill five shillings, which was the fee. He thanked us and said she should have kids in four months. We came home and wrote on the calendar, "4/4 kids due." On that very date, after school we ran down to the field where the cows were. Right enough, the goat was not grazing with the cows, so she must be having the kids. We searched around and found her in the shelter of a tree with two little kids, white in the body with black faces and feet, a combination of the colors of the nanny and the puck. We had more goats every year. They were very playful, jumping and running, bowing their necks and threatening as if they were going to ram us. We all experienced a charge on the bottom when we were not looking.

The clocking hen hatched the wild duck eggs faithfully until one day we noticed one of the eggs beginning to crack at the thick end. Anyone who eats a boiled egg knows one end is thicker than the other. When you take off the thick end you can see a pocket of air trapped behind a filament. That is the end where the head of the baby bird is positioned so that when he is ready to peck his way out of the shell, he has some air to get started. I lifted the egg that had begun to crack at the thick end and held it to my ear as I had done before with hen eggs. I could hear the pecking inside and with the egg filling the ear, it sounded like a little drummer inside. In a short time, he broke through and put out his head with a distinctive little duck's bill. By the end of the day, all twelve little ducklings were out and the hen was a proud mother. In a short time she is strutting around the yard with her twelve "chicks". In a few days she had them, with the other hens, down below the yard by the small pond at the beginning of the long field. Dad told us if the ducklings got near the pond they would go in, not like chickens who would never go into water. We were watching when the ducklings found the water. First one swam in then one by one they all followed: They swam and splashed and ducked their heads. The mother hen disapproved. She cackled and jumped and flapped her wings frantically. She kept this up as other hens joined her and the cock began crowing and crowing. The whole yard seemed in an uproar of cackling and crowing. The ducklings continued to enjoy the pond. They were where they wanted to be.

Brian and I decided we wanted to become altar boys. We asked the priest, Fr. Murray. He said yes, but you have to learn the Latin and pass a test. My father made arrangements with Mr. Ward, a retired teacher, to teach us the Latin. We got the Mass servers' booklet and went to Mr. Ward after school for several weeks. Then Fr. Murray gave us a test and we passed. Mother had the uniforms made.

We were to start at the Mass on Ash Wednesday. We got to the sacristy early. There were ten altar boys there dressing to serve. They were pushing and arguing over positions at the altar and about who would ring the bell during Mass. It was a big, dome shaped bell on its own stand and was rung by striking it with a gavel at several specified times during the Mass. The harder you struck it, the louder the sound which reverberated through the church. One of the older boys, Mick, bullied the rest and told them what to do. He said he would ring the bell. The priest came. We were nervous but all went well.

On Ash Wednesday after Mass the priest would sign the forehead of each person with the blessed ashes and say the words, "Remember, man, that thou art dust and unto dust thou shalt return." After Mass we came back into the sacristy. Fr. Murray took a dish of ashes and was ready to go to the altar rails and give the ashes to the people kneeling there. At that moment a lady burst into the sacristy and said, "We have an urgent sick call." Fr. Murray said to Mick, the oldest altar boy, "You give out the ashes. Just rub it on their foreheads and say the words. Here it is." "Oh, Father, what do I say?" Fr. Murray rushed out the door saying, "A day older, a day worse." Mick went to the altar rails where the people were kneeling. He stuck his thumb into the ashes and rubbed it on the forehead of the first person, saying, "A day older, a day worse," and continued on down the line.

The barn was a work center and a social center. When farmers and workmen visited they met us in the barn. We employed workmen from the laborer's cottages in the spring to cut the turf and plant the crops and again in the autumn to save the crops. We had the local carpenter, Jim Murphy, put a new wooden floor in one of the bedrooms. He was busy at a bench measuring and cutting timber. A severe thunderstorm came. The lightning flashed, the thunder roared and the rain came down in torrents. The boys closed the door.

Jim shouted, "Open the door or you'll trap the lightning in here. It has to get out or it will kill us." We opened the door. The lightning flashed. Jim said, "Now you are alright, the lightning can get out." My father had the following written on the wall. He said these words were found on a sundial, author unknown:

> When as a child I wept, time crept.
> When as a boy I laughed and talked, time walked.
> When I became a full-grown man, time ran.
> And daily as I older grew, time flew.
> Soon I shall find in traveling on, time gone.

My father would give us lessons on astronomy, taking three turnips of different sizes to represent the sun, the earth and the moon. Our first understanding of what caused day and night and the changing of the seasons came from him. He would also stand outside at night and explain the waxing and waning of the moon and many of the constellations, especially in the winter sky.

Big Mick Burke would help my father with threshing the grain in the barn with a flail. They used a fan to blow the chaff away from the grain. By the time they were finished it was impressive to see all that grain piled up in a big heap on the barn floor. It all came back to my mind when I read John Greenleaf Whittier's poem.

> Heap high the farmer's wintry horde,
> Heap high the golden corn!
> No richer gift has Autumn poured
> From out her lavish horn.

One day I am with my father down in the far meadow by the river. We had finished some work and were just sitting there looking up at clouds floating by against a background of blue sky. A skylark jumped up from the ground and began to sing. My father said, "Keep watching him because he will disappear into the blue." We watched as he went up higher and higher, singing all the while. He was more and more difficult to see until he finally disappeared into the blue. We could not see him any more but we could hear him singing. My father knew the lines from the poet Shelley in his ode to a skylark,

"Ode to thee blithe spirit, bird thou never wert,
who from heaven or near it, pouret thy full mirth."

While alone one day a skylark that my father had watched and listened to before came running along beside me, as I sat in the irises by the river bank, so that the fish would not see me and come close and take my worm. Delighted with the beautiful bird so close, I could see the color of his eyes, the beautiful feathers and very noticeable, elegant legs, so long for the size of his body and thin as silk thread. His back was brown, streaked with black. His underneath was brown streaked with yellowish white. He paused for a moment and then sprung into the air effortlessly and held in one place too high for man or animal to reach him, and he sang so joyfully the whole river valley overflowed with the sound. He continued to sing and spring higher, held aloft in mid air with quivering wings and singing so sweetly, he thrilled my soul. Again and again he sprang higher and higher, singing melodiously all the time and becoming more difficult to see. The lark sprang higher into the blue and sang. I could still hear the singing but could not see the bird.

Looking up into the blue sky, listening to the melodious singing, and seeing nothing, was an experience not easily forgotten. In a sense, the bird took me with him on his flight from earth into the heavens. There was an ecstatic sense of being transported with this bird into a singing enjoyment of the celestial. I cannot see the skylark, but I can hear his singing, singing from heaven and filling the whole earth around me.

Suddenly, the singing ceases and the bird appears in descent, and lands on the ground beside me, pauses a little, then runs a little, with head stretched up and looking around. I was so happy to be in the company of my skylark. I felt he was my friend. He sang for me, and he trusted me.

Next morning I went to bring home the cows early for milking. I was on the crutches, but would not let that slow me down. The cows were in the skylark's field by the river, and I went to his territory. There he was running and picking something off the grass. I kept my distance, and just watched. After a short time, he jumped into the air and began to sing. I was so happy watching him and listening to him. He resumed his pattern of singing and soaring to higher levels, and pausing while his wings held him motionless at each stage on his ascent. Finally, he entered the blue sky and soon could not be seen, but could still be heard.

I was enraptured motionless, leaning on the crutches and looking up into the heavens. Then there was a voice calling me. It was Brian: "What are you doing? You went to bring home the cows." Together we brought home the cows for the milking. The skylark lived on in my mind. "A thing of beauty is a joy for ever." The skylark was brought from Europe to North America and survived only on Vancouver Island.

And remember: Love is not love 'til it's given away.

CHAPTER 5

Parents Romance and Backgrounds

My father was born to the land and loved nature and the environment. He learned from his father and older brothers, he being the youngest boy in a family of ten children, 6 boys and 4 girls, with one girl younger than him. His mother died when he was eight. The oldest girl, Marcella, second in the family after Pat, the oldest, became the second mother, taking care of the family for many years. After the father died there were three left at home, Marcella, Larry and my father, Bernard. The two men worked hard at the farming and draining the bottomland and turning it into meadows which produced good crops of hay. The years went by and none of them married. They saved carefully. Larry was planning to buy a farm and marry. Their philosophy of life was such that no man in the community would enter marriage unless he had a house and farm to take care of and support a wife and family. Larry died of pneumonia, leaving Marcella and Bernard in the home.

During the many years of his bachelorhood, Bernard did a lot of reading and had many shelves of books. They had a boat on the river and he loved to fish in season and continued the great family tradition of bird shooting with dogs in the winter. He had many stories to tell and we heard them many times around the fire at night. There were many people who heard of him and came down all the way to him at the last house at the end of a long winding road which became a boreen and then across a field. He was like a free guide who made time for anyone who wanted to go fishing or bird shooting. They did not say hunting because hunting always involved a chase with dogs.

One of the stories he told went like this. "Fr. Smith, a priest in the parish, liked to fish and go shooting. He would meet me after church and say, 'Bernard, can I come down one day this week?' Of course we always made arrangements. One Sunday after Mass he said, 'Bernard, I have a few priest friends who would like to come to your place on Thursday for a day of fishing.' That was fine. They arrived and I took them down the river in the boat. They wanted to troll for pike and I took them to the best places. They caught several pike and kept the largest one weighing about twenty pounds. The others they released. When they began to feel hungry they said, 'We will go ashore and eat lunch.' As I rowed the boat to our side of the river, the side in the Diocese of Meath, Fr. Smith said, 'Bernard, pull over to the other bank of the river because that is the Diocese of Ardagh and Clonmacnoise which does not have a suspension for clergy drinking alcohol like the diocese of Meath does.' The Bishop's jurisdiction is territorial. The long arm of the Bishop of Meath reached from the Irish sea to the river Inny but was not long enough to reach across the river. They sat on the grass and took out their sandwiches and bottles of Guinness and knew they could 'eat, drink and be merry for tomorrow we go dry!'"

Fr. Smith and his friends discussed, among other things, the bicycle replacing the horse. Up to the early nineteen hundreds, when my father was a young man, there were no bicycles and everyone rode a horse. The priests rode horses and sometimes, when priests became handicapped or aged, they used jaunting cars drawn by horses. As bicycles became available, they became popular. They were more convenient and cost nothing to run. A horse cost much more than a bicycle and then had to be fed and shod and stabled. After buying a bicycle, the cyclist used his own energy to push it. It did not have to be fed or groomed. Men, women and children could use bicycles and it would be easier to have many bicycles in a household than to have that many horses. The bicycle also gave each person a better sense of freedom and independence.

As some of the clergy began to use bicycles, some bishops found it difficult to adjust to the transition from the horse to the bicycle. It seemed to them to be unbecoming for the clergy to be swinging their legs over the saddles of bicycles. Heated debates arose in many dioceses. What a sad time for Ireland to let the noble horse be replaced by the nondescript bicycle. To see the clergy, ministering to their flocks, instead of coming as masters on horseback, now pushing themselves on bicycles.

The bishops of the country decided to settle this important matter at a synod in Maynooth to which all bishops would be summoned to attend. Then came the day the synod would begin. Then the bombshell, the Archbishop of Dublin arrived on a bicycle!

Now another problem had been created. What about the annual oats collection when each household brought a sack of oats to the church to feed the priest's horse for the year? They certainly were not going to stop the oats collection. So it was decided to continue the oats collection and call it the oats collection but money could be given where priests did not have horses.

By my time, and when I was an altar boy, the priest announced the oats collection even though no priest had a horse. By that time they all had either bicycles or cars and all the people gave money in the oats collection.

My father was tall, of athletic build, with chiseled features and wore a mustache. He did not use alcohol. He was never a patient in a hospital. He grew up and lived his life on the farm that had been in the family for many generations. There are records in the parish archives of the McGuires of Empor on that same farm from the early seventeen hundreds, records of baptisms, marriages, and funerals. His father was Bernard McGuire and his mother was Marcella Hogan. Their names are on the family tombstone in Milltown graveyard. I never knew my grandparents on my father's side of the family. They had died before he married my mother.

My mother appeared short compared with my father. She had brown, curly hair, a pretty freckled face and an engaging smile. She was athletic and well proportioned in appearance. Her father was John Fox and her mother Catherine Leavy. I knew my grandparents on my mother's side of the family. We enjoyed visiting there and they made us feel they enjoyed having us. John Fox spent several years in the Argentine as a young man, working with his uncle on a sheep ranch before returning home to Ireland and getting married. I remember the deep sorrow of the family at the time of my grandparents' funerals. Their names are on the family tombstone in the Castletown graveyard.

Father was the ninth of ten children, six boys and four girls. Mother was the fourth of nine children, five boys and four girls. Uncle Johnny, who was two years younger than my mother and remained on their home farm, took me through the fields one day where father and mother walked during their time of romance. "Your father would come into the front yard on horseback in time for Sunday dinner. He was a fine young man. We loved to see him come and we would talk to him and admire the nice horse he was riding. He would sit in the saddle until Mary Ellen came out of the house. Then he would dismount and she would greet him and take him inside. Her father and mother and the whole family liked him. We always had a great dinner and everyone joined in the conversation. My father had many stories from his days in the Argentine and even spoke a few greetings in Spanish which he learned from Spanish workers there". After dinner, Jimmy and I would pressure your father to come down through the fields to the bog and go shooting grouse. Your mother, Mary Ellen, would say, "Don't be long, Bernard came to see me and we want to have time to go for a walk when you come back." We always succeeded in getting him to go with us, promising we would be back soon. So we would take the shotgun and walk all the way down through the fields to the bog. Your father was far more experienced with the gun than we were and a very good shot. Most of the time we succeeded in getting grouse and came back very proud. Afternoon tea would be ready. Afterwards Bernard and Mary Ellen would go for a walk through the fields. The children would want to go with them. My father and mother would say, "No, they have to go on their own. They have a lot to talk about." We used to think they were a long time in coming back. Some of the younger children would say, "We were waiting for you. What kept you?" My parents would say, "Keep quiet." Bernard would say, "We were watching the sunset. You get a better view of it in the fields." Then Bernard would say, "I am sorry but I have to go and get back to Marcella before it gets too late." Then he would say goodbye, mount his horse and ride out of the yard, waving to us as he went.

Eventually Bernard and Mary Ellen decided to get married. Mary Ellen's parents approved wholeheartedly. Her brothers and sisters were very happy Bernard was joining the family. When Bernard came home he told Marcella. She said, "It's about time you brought a wife into the house. I thought we'd never see any new life around here." So they started getting the place ready for having the new bride carried across the threshold. They got married in the church in Castletown and had the reception in Mary Ellen's home. They went to Dublin by train for their honeymoon. A week later Bernard carried Mary Ellen across the threshold into a house she had never seen. Now there were two keepers of the hearth. They began their new life together. Father introduced Mother to the river where so many McGuire grooms has introduced their brides for so many generations. One day she went with him and they walked along the riverbank looking for wild ducks. Ducks came flying overhead and he dropped two of them on the river. They had no dog with them so mother said, "I'll bring them out." The ducks drifted into shallow water. She waded in and brought out the ducks. Tom Reilly was fishing nearby and was watching what was going on.

That night in the pub he told all the boys, "You should have seen what I saw when fishing today down by Bernie McGuire's farm." They were curious to hear. He continued, "Bernie McGuire got himself a retriever." Tim Kelly said, "I know he got a young wife. What kind of retriever did he get?" Tom said, "That young wife's the retriever. I saw her bring ducks out of the river today."

They had their first child within two years and then one approximately every two years until there were eight of us, Mary Jo, Marcella, Brian, Shane, Frank, Vera, Celine and Mike. Dr. Byrne delivered all of us in the master bedroom upstairs in the farmhouse.

From my earliest years I can remember my father reading to us around the fire on the hearth, We had a family bible and he read from it, not only passages on Sundays which were read in church, but also on one evening during the week when the homework was finished. Commenting on what the priest said in church he often emphasized the dangers of materialism, giving us the impression he was speaking primarily of himself but not excluding us. "Materialism can weaken one's faith," he would say. "We are body and spirit and must cultivate our spiritual lives."

When old enough we took our turns in reading bible stories. One night the three boys, Brian, myself and Frank, were reading about Joseph being sold by his brothers and taken to Egypt. We were allowed to stay up extra late because we wanted to finish the story. We just could not stop. Frank was bothering Brian who was reading. Brian said, "Francis Joseph, if you don't keep quiet I will sell you to the Egyptians," and Frank began to cry.

My father had several shelves of books. He loved to read to us. He had an old dictionary and taught us how to look up words before they got round to teaching us that in school. Among his books were old ones that had been handed down. Others he had purchased. He had books on husbandry, works of Dickens and Scott and Chaucer and others. He loved to read poetry. He had many books of poetry. We liked some of the poems so much that we memorized lines or verses from them and I can remember them still. *The Lady of the Lake,* by Sir. Walter Scott was one of my favorites. I learned most of the section on the chase by heart, beginning with:

"The stag at eve had drunk his fill where danced the moon on Monin's rill". Among the lives of saints his favorite was St. Francis of Assisi. *The Farmers Almanac* was always within reach. We consulted it for seasonal weather forecasts. It also gave tips on farming and other pieces of wisdom. Part of his daily reading was *The Imitation of Christ* by Thomas a Kempis. It was always on the windowsill of the back window in the kitchen where he could reach it from his chair.

He was an excellent reader. His voice was pleasant and no matter how long he read it did not sound monotonous because of modulation and cadences in his style of reading. Sometimes I would be upstairs in bed with a fever because of the leg. In the quiet of the evening the sound of his voice reading downstairs by the hearth was soothing and would help me relax. He read the newspapers and kept us up to date with what was going on in the world. There was time to discuss everything around the hearth. Radios were not available in the country. We did not have one until I was in my late teens.

Mother read to the younger children and told them bedside stories as they went to sleep. The older ones helped in putting the little ones to bed. We would tell stories. You could not make a mistake for the child would correct you. As soon as the younger ones we were responsible for, fell asleep we would slip away and come down to the kitchen to sit by the fire and listen to my father reading or telling stories.

My father was out in the fields or at fairs a lot of the time and we would all be in the kitchen with mother. When any of us got out of hand she would call us by name in a low, firm voice. I was called Shane but if I was not giving her my full attention, she would call me John Aloysius and I knew this was serious. The kitchen, which was usually peaceful around the hearth, became an uproar at times with heated arguments. Mother, in her low, firm voice would appeal to us to be quiet. When that did not work she would come and stand in the middle of us and call each of us by name slowly, firmly in such a calm way that each one felt respected and each one went silent. Mother was in charge without raising her voice or shouting. It amazed us when in some of the other families we visited, as things sometimes got out of hand, the mothers were screaming at the children, the children were screaming and nobody was listening. Over and over again mother would quiet us down by her quiet presence and respect for her grew. As the younger children came along they learned from the older ones how to respect and listen to mother who had such a charism of love and respect for each of us. She taught us to have the same love and respect for each other. In this way she drew us closer together as a family.

There was no refrigeration. There was no place to buy milk and no milk delivery. Everyone was self-sufficient. The farmers produced their own. Each laborer's cottage which had been built by the government, was on an acre of land to enable the family to have a cow and vegetables. Some of the men in the cottages worked full time while others were employed only in the busy seasons on the farms. We always had enough milk and butter and eggs. Mother baked every day. We had our own grain which was milled and stored in the barn. We grew all our own potatoes and vegetables. When poorer people were in need, the neighboring farmers helped them out. Mother never refused anyone. She gave where she knew the need was so that they would not have to ask.

There were many beggars and tinkers in those days. When any of them came to our house mother would give them something to eat. Then she would share with them whatever we had plentiful at the time; milk, butter, eggs, meal and some of our own fresh pork. Frequently it would be a mother with a shawl over her head and a baby in her arms. No one was ever turned away. Sometimes stories were so entertaining they were hard to believe. Tinkers who were tinsmiths would camp on a wide grassy area by the crossroads. They made kitchen utensils out of tin. The little clay container they used to heat the solder was called a tinker's damn. When finished they left it there and made a new one at their next stop. So, we have the expression today: it's not worth a tinker's damn. The tinker would walk from house to house selling his wares with a string of these shining tin utensils hanging from his shoulder.

And remember: Love is not love 'til it's given away.

CHAPTER 6

Two Years Away From Home

The leg swelled up once again and my temperature went to 104. I could not sleep, just raving all night. My father and mother got the horse and trap ready as they had done so many times before and took me to Dr. Byrne's house. How I hated to go but knew I needed help. When we got there Dr. Byrne was away and Dr. Stanley from Mullingar was taking his place. I had never seen this doctor before and wondered what he was going to do to me. He looked at the shin and shook his head. Then he said it is in the bone and he will have to go to the hospital and get a plaster of Paris put on so that the bone does not break. Take him into the Mullingar infirmary which is under my care and I will see him there. Use the crutches and keep the weight off the leg. "Will he be in the hospital for long?" my mother asked. "It's hard to say," replied the doctor. "We will have to put that leg in a plaster of Paris to prevent the bone from breaking because it is weakened and could break easily and that would be very serious. The leg might have to be amputated. Also it could cause the disease to spread to other parts of the body." Mother told my father and the rest of the family what the doctor said, that my leg might have to be amputated, and the disease could spread to the rest of my body. I had to go to the hospital.

The next morning after Dr Stanley told us I should go into the Mullingar Infirmary, mother packed a little suitcase for me. I said goodbye to the family. I was crying. Tears ran down my father's face, the first time I saw him cry. I was leaving home for the first time and had no idea I would not see home again for nearly two years. I was ten now and would be twelve when I would come home again. We took the bus into Mullingar and walked to the infirmary, about a mile out on the Dublin road. I moved along well on the crutches. There were very big gates and a long driveway up to the building. It was a large two-storied slated gray structure with the entrance door at the center. A nurse took us upstairs. The men's wards were to the right and women's wards were to the left. The nurse took us through a large ward with a lot of beds and into a smaller ward with four beds. She stood by an empty bed and said, "this is your bed". She left us there. Mother and I talked for a little while. Then she said, "I'll have to leave now." She kissed me. We both cried. She walked out the door wiping the tears from her eyes with one hand and waiving back to me with the other.

A nurse took my temperature and said I had a fever. She also said that I had to have a plaster of Paris put on my leg to keep the bone from breaking. That night the fever got worse. I was in great pain and could not sleep. The next morning a nurse took my temperature and said, "It is one hundred and four, just stay in bed." I was suffering. I knew no one. This was my first time I had spent a night away from home. I was homesick and it was depressing. I felt trapped. Outside my window there was a very high wall and big trees. I could hear children's voices coming from the other side of the wall, but I could not see anyone. They were talking and laughing. They seemed to be passing by in groups. I was day dreaming, imagining I was with them. Then I'd look at my bed with a cage over my leg to keep the weight of the blankets off the painful leg. It had the shape of a tinker's tent. A little hole had appeared on the front of the shin and matter was coming out. This occurred without a lancing.

A man came in carrying a bucket. There was a nurse with him. She said, "We are going to put on the plaster of Paris now." He proceeded to put it on and the nurse instructed him on leaving a window in the plaster at the right place to allow the bone to drain through the hole in the front of the shin. "Now," she said to me, "You are safer walking and putting your weight on that leg."

After a few days the fever left and I was told I could dress in my own clothes and walk around. I had one jacket and short pants, to the knees. The pain was always there, sometimes severe and other times more tolerable. When very severe I would involuntarily shake my leg to ease the pain. One patient saw me sitting in a chair and shaking and contracting the leg. He noticed and asked, "Why are you doing that?" I said, "It helps me bear the pain." My leg kept jerking around and contracting, keeping me awake at night. A nurse gave me a couple of sandbags to keep my leg in place.

There were four patients in my ward and six in the big ward with a large sitting area and a fireplace. That was the center of the social life of the infirmary. Everyone in those two wards was permanent, some in bed all the time, some able to get out into a chair and some able to get around with help or with crutches. There was a third ward out of sight to us, with two beds. Only very ill patients were in that ward and no one was there very long. They went home or were transferred to another hospital or died. There were only three wards in the men's end of the hospital. There was also a general hospital in town.

The daily round began with being wakened up early and washing. Nurses or maids helped those who could not wash themselves. There was a very small staff, so anyone who could move around was expected to help. I helped in carrying basins around and emptying bedpans and urinals. Breakfast was bread and butter and tea. In mid-morning Jack with one arm, a bookie's runner, came in and brought the daily paper that had a section on the horse racing of the day. Those of us able to get up from bed sat around the fire. Those in bed listened as Tom, one of the patients, read out the names of the horses and jockeys in the different races. There were discussions, questions and arguments; they talked about each horse, how many races he had won before, the jockey's name and weight and winning record, the trainer and his record and on and on. There were as many opinions as there were men in the room. The arguments got hot at times some going quiet as two or three kept going trying to show who knew it all. The discussions came to an end when Jack said, "Give me the bets. I have to bring them to the bookie by twelve o'clock." Then they huddled into small groups some around beds where patients were confined. Jack went around each group, picked up the bets and left. As soon as the races were over the results were given on the radio. Then the bet makers would know if Jack would be coming back with the winnings. This did happen sometimes but it was rare and never a lot. This went on every day. The men were always ready and waiting for Jack to come with the daily paper. I learned a good deal about studying form. Names of horses and jockeys and trainers became familiar names. I was surprised at the importance they put on the weight of the jockey. With all the other information the weight of each jockey was given. This one is eight stones, six pounds. This one, nine stones, 12 pounds. One commented, "too heavy for that horse."

They spent a lot of time playing cards. They taught me card playing which I had never done before. Sometimes they played for money and I had no money. When visitors came they got money. Most of the time they played cards for fun. Two of them played chess for long periods of time. Austin, who was confined to bed, was an expert chess player. He spent time patiently teaching me the game. He used to say, "Playing chess is like life. You should think for a while before making the next move and be sure it is the right move you are deciding on making." I liked Austin; he was so patient with me. I felt sorry for him being in the bed all the time. He looked to be in his thirties and was a victim of polio. When no nurse or maid was available he would ask for me and I would take care of his needs.

The matron had a room at the top of the stairs. She was there all the time, day and night. Everyday she came around and spoke to each patient. I used to like seeing her come. She was a very tall strongly built woman with a cheerful smile except when she had to correct one of the staff. Then she could be stern. I think she pitied me being the only boy with all those men and not yet eleven years old. She always spent a minute talking to me and asking just how I was doing. She always listened. I kept on asking if anything could be done for me. She kept on saying the doctor will decide.

Dinner was served at noon. There was always soup, meat or fish, vegetables and potatoes. I ate except when I had a fever which came back every two or three weeks. When the draining of matter from the bone stopped and the opening closed up the leg would swell and the temperature would go up very high. On this occasion another opening started higher up on the bone indicating the infection was spreading. No one said anything about what was going to happen. I was thinking, am I going to spend my life here?

Dr Stanley was the doctor who decided I should come here when he saw me at the time he was covering for Dr Byrne in Ballynacargy. He did not speak to me even though he came to the hospital once a week. He did some surgery. The operating room was on our floor, off the landing, across from the Matron's room. During surgery he used ether as an anesthetic. The smell of ether came out of the operating room and all through the hospital. Our ward was filled with the smell and we hated it. The smell was so strong it made me feel sick and hoping I would never have to get it. It seemed Dr Stanley was in charge of the infirmary. There was a hospital in Mullingar and at the time they were building a new one, all white.

One day the matron came around and told the staff and patients the doctor in charge of the whole county, Dr O'Neil, was coming to inspect the infirmary tomorrow. The last time he came he said the place was too stuffy, had not enough good, fresh air and was a hot bed for TB (consumption). This disease was to the forefront of everyone's thinking on health. What we all needed was good fresh air. The sanitariums built for patients with TB were open in the front with verandas onto which beds could be wheeled out so that the patients could breathe the good fresh air. In preparation for Dr O'Neil's visit the place was thoroughly cleaned. On the morning he was expected, the windows were all opened and the good fresh air was coming in, assisted by a good, fresh breeze. Dr O'Neil arrived and the matron brought him into our ward. He was tall and thin. He looked around at all of us. Then he looked at the windows and said, "You had better close those windows or the patients will get pneumonia." He left. I was very disappointed because he did not talk to me.

After I was a few weeks there, Mother came to visit me. I was in bed with a temperature when she arrived. When she walked into the ward I was surprised and delighted to see her. She leaned over and kissed me and gave me chocolates. She said, "Why are you in bed?" I said, "A nurse told me to stay in bed because I have a temperature." She felt my forehead and said, "You do feel hot." Then she sat by my bed and talked. The baby, Mike now two years old, is getting more active everyday, running around. The rest are doing well except for Aunt Marcella. She is still confined to bed since she had the stroke. When they lift her out to put her on the commode they notice she is getting weaker. "What are they doing for you here," she said. "Nothing" I said, "except to take my temperature everyday and tell me to stay in bed if it is high. I hate the smell of ether which they use in the operating room when the Doctor is operating on someone. Some of the patients seem to know a lot. They tell me one of these days the doctor will operate on me to scrape the bone and I will have to be put to sleep with ether. It frightens me to think of it and I am hoping this will not happen." Only the patients told you all this. Yes. And what do they know? Pay no heed to them. She told me they all missed me and were praying every evening when saying the rosary asking God to make me better and bring me home soon. After a nice talk she said, "I'll have to go now and walk into town and catch the bus." She kissed me, said, "Good bye." Tears ran down her face and she walked out the door. I was alone.

Uncle Mike, my mother's youngest brother worked in Mullingar. He came to visit me regularly. I enjoyed his visits very much. He was always encouraging but seemed very concerned that so much time was passing and I was not improving. He discussed school with me. What was going to happen missing all this time from school and being taught nothing here in the hospital. He also visited home regularly and discussed these matters with father and mother. They all felt helpless and hoped I would get better soon. Sending tutors to teach children in hospital was not heard of in those days. It was never mentioned except by Uncle Mike.

The only other visitor I had was Larry McGuire, one of my cousins who lived near the school in Empor. He was the same age as my oldest sister, Mary Jo, six years older than me. He was a great football player and often played in Cussack Park in Mullingar. After the game he would cycle out to the infirmary to see me. He always brought me a big juicy orange which I enjoyed eating then and there. He said he always ate an orange at the halftime break in the game. Larry would bring me up to date on the football games that were being played in the area. He was a real breath of fresh air and I was impressed that he would remember me and go to the trouble of coming out to see me before his long ride home.

Mother came to see me often. She kept me up to date with everyone and everything at home. They were all very busy, the children going to school, Dad working in the fields, sometimes with help. The cows had to be milked twice a day and all the animals had to be fed. Dad was the only one able to lift Aunt Marcella out of bed which needed to be done several times a day. When mother came, sometimes, I was in bed with a fever and sometimes I was up and feeling better. I looked forward to her visits and did not want to see her leave. Because we had no telephone I never knew when she was coming until she appeared. She was the only one in the family I was able to speak with and I missed them all.

After several months the cast, which was very tight from the beginning, was now becoming more and more uncomfortably tight. I told a nurse and she said you need it to keep your leg from breaking. One day shortly after this the cast broke at the calf of the leg at the height where the window was in front of the shinbone. I showed this to a nurse. She said that was not important and it would take sometime to find someone to cut off the cast and put on a new one. At the time I was able to get up and walk around every day. I could feel the cast moving where it was broken, still very tight and uncomfortable. After a week walking around like this the cast began to pinch the calf of the leg where the cast was broken into two parts. The muscle was growing and was restricted. This got worse every day. I told the matron when she came around on her visit, I could not walk around because the cast was broken and pinching my leg. She said she would get someone to take it off and put on a new one.

The next morning a man came into the big ward where we were sitting around the fire studying form. He was carrying a long metal shears. He said he had come to cut the plaster off Shane McGuire's leg. I put up my hand. He started to work right there in front of the fireplace. The plaster was very tight, pressing into the flesh of the leg. He tried to insert one blade of the shears between the plaster and the leg. He tried harder and harder. It was hurting. He got one blade of the shears in flat. It was a wide blade, so when he tried to turn it into position to cut, it hurts so badly I shouted, "That hurts."

He shouted back, "Keep quiet." He continued using all his strength trying to cut the hard cast. I shouted, "It hurts me." He shouting back, "Keep quiet." It was taking so long the patients were all watching and making comments I could not hear too well. Finally Tom on the crutches, shouted to the cast cutter, "You don't know what you are doing." He shouted back, "What do you know about cutting a cast?" Tom shouted something back to him. Other patients joined in. There was shouting back and forth. All the while I was being hurt badly. The man with the shears went silent, finished the job and ran out of the ward with the shears and broken cast in his arms. The matron came in and said, "What happened here?" Not waiting for an answer she continued, "That poor man said he is not coming back here any more." When she left Tom said, "Good riddance." They were all consoling me for having suffered so much. The calf of the leg had shrunken compared with the other leg. Later that same day a man came in with a bucket and put on a new cast. He made it tight to keep the leg from breaking and left a window in front to allow for the drainage from the rotting bone and dressing.

Studying forms and putting on bets went on everyday as did the arguing about horses and borrowing from one another to bet. I was part of it when I was not in bed with a fever. Jack with the one arm and the other sleeve, empty and tucked into the pocket of his jacket, came everyday to chat and pick up the bets and take them to the bookie. When Jack brought back the winnings they tried to straighten out their debts. Austin, who was in bed all the time was ahead of the rest of them in winnings. He even had a daily double which paid very well. I had never bet on a horse. For one thing I did not have the money.

Excitement grew every day as we approached the biggest and most important race of the whole year, The Grand National. The newspapers were giving advance information about it for weeks. The patients discussed and argued about The Grand National, morning noon and night. They knew the names of all the horses and jockeys. They knew the history of each horse and jockey and trainer. Each one was sure he was going to "win big". They also listened to the radio for the horses everyday. There were endless reports and discussions. Experts were giving advice and tips. As the day approached the excitement grew. Some were planning what they'd do with the money they felt they had already won.

As the day for the Grand National drew near, excitement mounted. The more they got excited the more certain they were of winning. Jim, in a wheelchair, kept telling me you have to put something on a horse for the Grand National. He was betting on a sure thing. This horse had won so many races he ran in. The jockey is only eight stone and this is a big horse. His trainer has a great record for training winners. A shilling is the smallest bet the bookie will take. If you don't put a shilling on him you'll be sorry this evening after he has won. He is paying a good price. Think of that. Then his name sounds great, Golden Miller. I said, "I don't have a shilling." "How much do you have?" "Sixpence." Pat, who rarely bet was listening and said, "Shane, lad, I'll put my sixpence to your sixpence and we'll have a shilling which we can give to Jack to place on Golden Miller and we'll be rich." So my last sixpence went on Golden Miller. Jack, the one armed man, took all the bets including my six pence and took off on foot for the bookie.

That afternoon the Grand National was at three o'clock and all were glued to the radio, those who were up and those in bed. Michael O'Hare, the commentator had everyone excited, shouting out the names of the horses and their jockeys. Golden Miller he mentioned more than once and then, "They're off and running!" He kept shouting names of horses. This one is leading, now that one is leading. Golden Miller is not mentioned yet and the race is half over. Then Golden Miller falls and is out of the race. Good bye, sixpence. At ten years my first bet and my last penny. We are all broke! Now each thought he knew why he backed a loser. Some blamed the jockey, some blamed the horse, some the trainer, some the weather. They would not stop talking. Each one was an expert.

The next day they were still discussing what happened at the Grand National.

> The more they talked the more my wonder grew;
> that no one won in spite of all they knew.

One of the patients, Tom, was on crutches. He got around pretty well. He was about thirty years old and had a bad hip. He was there several years and they could do nothing to help him. He spent the day like the rest of them, listening to the radio, studying form, backing horses and playing cards. Sometimes I used to think, "Will they keep me here all my life and do nothing for me." "Will I be spending each day like he is doing and grow old doing the same old thing?"

Tom was getting more and more friendly with me. He was always asking what he could do for me, especially when I was in bed with a fever. He would sit on the side of my bed and talk for hours on end. One day while he was sitting on the side of my bed, my mother came in to see me. After kissing and embracing me she asked, "Who was that sitting on your bed?" I told her it was Tom, one of the patients. She said, "It is not good for you to be here, the only boy with all these men and no one of your own age." "Have they done anything for you yet to help you get better and get out of here?" I said, "No. The only thing they did was to put on a plaster to protect my leg from breaking and the cast itself broke and they waited over a week to replace it." She said, "The cast to keep your leg from breaking, itself broke and they waited for more than a week to put a new one on?" I said, "Yes, and the broken cast pinched my leg and left a raw sore." She said, "Ill try and find the matron before I leave and talk to her. We could sue the Board of Health for neglect." The matron was not available.

Tom kept coming and sitting on the side of my bed. If I were able to be up during the day, he would come at night after everyone went to sleep. If I were asleep, he would wake me up to talk to me. Sometimes I would fall asleep again while he was still there sitting on the side of my bed. One night I woke up and he was molesting me. I asked him, "What are you doing?" He said, "I'm making you feel good." I said, "Stop, it's a sin." He said, "Don't worry about that." I said, "It is a bad sin and I'll have to go to confession." He left me and I felt very guilty and impure.

Next day I still felt guilty and wished I could go to confession. No priest came to the infirmary to hear confessions while I was there. The only priest I saw was Father Mick from the parish who came to visit a wealthy bachelor farmer with whom he used to fish and shoot game. He passed by the end of my bed and recognized me as one of his altar boys. He looked at me, put his thumbs in his ears and waved his fingers and walked on. I was so disappointed he did not stop and talk to me, and shocked with what he did. That picture remained with me and will probably never go away. The feeling of guilt from the night before stayed with me. I was able to get up, dress and go to meals. Tom asked me how I was. I said, "Very worried, and don't come near me tonight!" He said, "You'll get over it."

I kept thinking of all I was taught at home and in church about the virtue of holy purity. Impure thoughts and actions were very sinful and the only way to get rid of the sin was to go to confession and receive absolution. This teaching was kept to the fore and emphasized all the time. The positive side was the beauty of the soul in grace and free from sin in the eyes of God. Now, with Tom touching me sinfully and trying to rouse me, I felt sinful in the eyes of God and very unhappy. I wanted in the worst way to go to confession and be relieved from this terrible feeling of being sinful and unclean. We were also taught not to consent to bad thoughts and feelings. One had to consent to commit sin. Sometimes it was not easy to know whether there was consent or not, and touching another's private parts was always sinful and offensive to God when done to get pleasure out of it.

I felt very frustrated, the leg not getting better, my classmates going into higher levels and I learning nothing and being left behind: Tom trying to lead me into sin; the happiness I used to have, gone away. At ten years old, from being a happy kid, I have become miserable. Have I lost my innocence? I dream of being back vaulting along the riverbank. I have lost that too. I think of running away, slipping into town and getting on the bus to go home.

That night I woke up again. Tom was sitting on the side of my bed molesting me. I took a swing at him and hit him on the face, then he slid off the bed and fell on the floor. He made such a commotion trying to get back on the crutches that other patients woke up. One of them threw on the light and saw Tom struggling to get on his crutches. He said, "Tom, what are you doing in here at this time of night?" Tom did not answer, but made his way out of the ward. I felt I had committed sin again and decided I was going to get out of here. If they don't let me go, I'll leave on my own.

Next morning I got the courage to go to the matron's door. I stood there thinking of what I was going to say. The door opened and the matron was standing there looking down at me. She looked so tall and I felt so small. "What do you want", she said. I started to cry. She took me inside and sat me down. "What is wrong?" she asked. I did not want to tell her about Tom, so I said, "I want to go to confession." She said, "I cannot hear your confession; you have to go to a priest." Then there was silence for a few moments. I knew she was wondering what happened that I was so upset and crying and wanting to go to confession. She started talking again and said, "Father Murphy has not been here in a while. He always comes when he is called and hears the confessions of anyone who wishes to go. I will call him." About an hour later she came around the wards and told all the patients Father Murphy would be here at four o'clock this afternoon for anyone who wanted to talk to him or go to confession. I was waiting for him to come, looking forward to talking to him and still a bit afraid of what he was going to say to me. I was going over in my mind what I was going to tell him about the sins and if I should ask him to help me get out of here and go home.

Just a few minutes after four o'clock Father Murphy came. He was tall, beginning to turn gray and very friendly to everyone. When my turn came I went into the room provided. He was seated in a chair and pointed to another chair in front of him and said, "Please sit here." He was chatty, asking me a lot of questions, how old was I, where did I come from who was in my family and why was I here. While he was talking I was thinking, I cannot tell him about this terrible sin, and started crying. He reached over, put his hand on my shoulder and said, "You are upset about something; please tell me whatever is on your mind. I am here to help you." He was kind and made me feel good. I told him about Tom and exactly what happened each time he touched me and tried to arouse me, telling me I was going to like it. I told him how I stopped Tom but still felt sinful. Father Murphy's face became very serious looking. I knew what I was telling him was really upsetting him. He said, "I am not going to say anything until you have finished telling me everything." I went over it all again, filling in anything I had left out. I said I just wanted to be forgiven and clean again in the eyes of God, because I felt very sinful since this happened.

He said, "This is a very serious matter. I am pleased you told me all about it, because you are suffering greatly and you are going to feel much better about it after getting it off your chest. You were brave to tell me because many boys won't talk about these things. If you have any sin it is forgiven, but I don't think God is holding you guilty. The guilty one is Tom. He tried to lead you into sin, to scandalize you. You know what the Lord said about this, 'If anyone should scandalize one of these little ones, who believes in me, it were better for him if a millstone were hanged around his neck and he were cast into the depths of the sea.' The Lord sounded angry with such a one and I feel angry with Tom for doing this to you." He then gave me absolution and a blessing. I was feeling free from sin and much happier. Father said, "Can we talk about this a little more?" I said, "Yes."

He said, "As we can understand from what the Lord said, this is a very horrible sin, to scandalize a young person, to lead him into sin and away from God. The older person deserves to have a heavy millstone hanged around his neck, but he puts the weight of a millstone of guilt around the neck of the young person. This Tom will try to do it again, so I want you to tell the matron what happened. I cannot tell her because you told me in confession but you can tell her. You are not bound to keep it secret." I said, "I'll tell her and I also want to tell her I want to go home. I am here eight months, they are doing nothing for me, I am not getting better, I'm learning nothing but how to bet on horses and play cards. I am missing a year from school. Can you help me to get out of here and go home?" He said, "You should not be here. It is no place for you. I can talk to the matron, but only about how badly you want to go home. On second thought, I think it would be better if I don't speak to her after hearing your confession. When you tell her what happened, she will be smart enough to get you out of here. If she doesn't, then write to your parents and ask them to get you out of here." He patted me on the head and said he would pray for me. I thanked him and he left.

I felt good, greatly relieved now that the weight of the millstone had been lifted. I felt determined it was not going to happen again. I went to my ward, sat on my bed and said the three Our Fathers and three Hail Mary's Father Murphy had given me as a penance. I sat there for a while thinking of just how I was going to tell the matron everything and ask to go home. After speaking with Father Murphy I felt really strong and had no hesitation about speaking with the matron. I'll soon be eleven. I am a young man.

I knocked on the matron's door. She told me to come in and gave me a chair and said, "sit down." I sat down. She said, "Are you alright now?" I said, "I am much better but I have to talk to you and tell you what happened." She said, "Go ahead and tell me." I told her all about Tom and what he did to me. Her face was getting red and I could see she was getting angry. She said, "Why did you not come to me right away when this first happened?" I said, "Because it was a sin. I could not talk to anyone about it except the priest. Father Murphy told me to tell you. He could not tell you because he heard it from me in confession and priests can't tell anyone what they hear in confession but he said I could tell you and should tell you." Again, she said, "You should have told me right away. I'll tell Tom to stay away from you." I said, "I don't want to stay here any longer. I want to go home." Then I told her how I was there so long and I was lonely for my family and missing school and learning nothing. She said, "The doctor had you come in here and have a cast put on because there was danger of breaking you leg". I said, "Well the cast broke and my leg did not break even though I had to wait more than a week for a new one. Now I want to go home. I don't want to be in this place with Tom. If you don't let me go, I'll run away." She said, "I can't get over what Tom did to you. I'll get you out of here." I left her room feeling sure I was going home real soon.

Next morning she came to me and said, "You are leaving here today." I said, "I am going home?" She said, "No, you are going to Coole Hospital." I said, "I told you I wanted to go home!" She said, "Get your things ready. The ambulance will be here at twelve o'clock to take you to Coole."

I had heard many stories of Coole Hospital. People used to call it a cripple's home where boys went who had incurable bone disease. That is exactly what the other children in the school, the mean ones, taunted my brothers and sisters with when they heard where I had gone. They would say, "Your brother is in a cripples' home." I was so disappointed I was not going home because I was sure I would be home soon after what the matron told me yesterday. "I'll get you out of here." Last night and this morning I had been thinking of the joy of going into the house and seeing all my family again. Now I am going to that cripple's home and I don't want to go. I don't know anyone there. I'll be a stranger and probably won't be happy at all.

I packed the little suitcase mother gave me when leaving home and, carrying it in my hand, went around on the crutches and said goodbye to the other patients. They wished me well. Tom shocked me by saying, "If you stayed here I would change you." I said goodbye to the matron. She told me to stand at the entrance door and wait for the ambulance.

I stood outside the door, leaning on the crutches, with my little suitcase at my feet and realized I was all alone. There was no one around. The thought came to me, I could go now, the short distance into town and get on the bus for Ballymahon. Then I realized I was broke. I had lost my last sixpence on Golden Miller. Still the thought of taking the bus would not go away. I knew the bus driver, Mr. O'Hanlon and he would take me. I would tell him we would pay him tomorrow when he stopped at 'the foot of the Green' where we always got on and off the bus. Then I thought of meeting my father and mother and telling them I really ran away from the infirmary instead of going on the ambulance to Coole. I knew they would not approve, so I stood my ground alone. The ambulance arrived. The driver said, "Are you Shane McGuire?" I said, "Yes." He said, "Get in. I am taking you to Coole."

The ambulance drew up in front of a small white building. The driver said, "This is the Coole Sanitarium." Sanitariums were built for patients who needed constant fresh air, like those with consumption and rotting bones. They were long buildings open along the front with just a roof and a back wall.

A lady brought me inside. "Did you have your dinner?" she said. Dinner was always at noontime and it was now early afternoon. "No," I said. She took me into the kitchen and gave me a plate of cold ham and potatoes. When I was finished a nurse in a white uniform took me into a bathroom and told me to take a bath, and "Don't get the plaster of Paris wet." I sat in the tub with my leg with the plaster of Paris resting on the side of the tub. When finished the nurse took me to the ward. It was very long with a row of beds with boys in them. It was open in the front with columns supporting the roof. Between the beds and the columns there was a good space to walk, push beds and wheelchairs and do whatever was needed for the patients. Outside the columns there was a wide cement veranda the whole length of the ward where the beds with patients in them were pushed out in the good weather. There was a low wall about a foot high along the edge of the veranda and then a big field with a few tall trees and some cows grazing. The nurse took me to a bed about half way down the ward. There was a door in the wall at the back of the beds that led to an area of treatment and an operation room. The nurse said, "Here is a bed shirt and short underpants. Wear them and put your own clothes in the bin under the bed. You are to stay in bed. You are not to walk around because you could break the bone in your leg."

I am eleven years old and among total strangers. It was so difficult leaving home and going to the Mullingar Infirmary where I knew nobody. Now, instead of going home, I have been taken from the Mullingar Infirmary where I knew so many to the Coole Sanitarium where I knew nobody. A Sister came walking through the ward. The first thing I noticed about her was that as she walked her white headgear waved up and down like the wings of a butterfly. She stopped at the end of my bed, all white from head to foot and said, "Are you Shane McGuire?" I said, "I am." "Well, I am Sister Ita and I need some information." She asked me more questions and jotted down what I said in the notebook that hung from her belt. "How old are you?" "Eleven." "Are your Mother and Father living? How many brother and sisters?" When she finished I asked her "Do my parents know I was brought here?" "I don't know" she said, "The Mullingar Infirmary will let them know you've moved." "I would like to write home, could I have a writing pad and a pen?" "Of course," she said.

After Sister Ita left the boys began to talk. There were only three or four feet between the beds and the beds were narrow single beds so it was easy to have a shared conversation with five or six boys without shouting. The first thing they told me was their names. To my left was Willie, then Mike. To my right were Craig, Matt and Jim. "The six of us were good friends," Craig said. "Kevin who was in your bed died yesterday," Mike added, pointing to my bed, "and you're lucky to get in with us." "We are the best bunch of friends in this whole hospital." They were all from eleven to thirteen. Craig was in an iron frame because he had the disease in the spine and could not move. He lay there on his back looking up at the white ceiling. He could not even see the field and the trees. When we were pushed out onto the veranda in good weather he could see the blue sky and the clouds and the birds flying by. He enjoyed looking up when out on the veranda and this put him in much better form. He loved to talk. He was very smart and very friendly. My heart went out to him. I was wondering if he could ever get better. Jim had two bad hips which had to be tended to every day with a change of dressing. Everyone had running sores, the matter coming out from the marrow cavity of the infected bones. There was a bad smell from this which was a good reason for open wards, as otherwise the stench would be unbearable.

Willie had five bones in his body with running sores. Mike had iron calipers on both legs from the ankles to his hips, because his leg bones had deteriorated so much. Matt had two affected hips with sores. They were all there for several years and were told they could not be operated on. I was thinking how long am I going to be here and is this going to be my life now? They told me they were not getting many visits from their families. The visits were becoming less and less. Some patients were from orphanages. Each morning early the nurses and maids came on the wards. We were washed, sores were cleansed and dressed and then we were given breakfast; buttered toast and milk. At noon we had dinner, small portions of meat or fish, vegetables and potatoes. At five o'clock they served us tea and bread and butter. At 8 o'clock we had night prayers and then the lights went out. We were supposed to keep quiet and go to sleep, but we never did. We talked a lot and sometimes laughed. Then a night nurse would come and tell us to go to sleep. Some patients cried with pain and they would be wheeled off to another area. During the day there was constant traffic up and down the ward, nurses and maids taking care of patient's needs, some visitors and some observers taking notes.

After a few days I was wheeled through the doorway beside my bed to the treatment area. They proceeded to remove the cast from my leg. It went from the ankle to the knee with an opening about three inches by two in the front where the matter was coming out in two small holes. They called this opening a window. When the cast was removed Sister Ita looked at the leg and she said that the cast was on for too long a time without being replaced and it was too tight on the leg. You can see how the muscle in the calf of the leg is shrunken. Just compare it with the other leg. The nurse who was helping her kept nodding her head. They put on another cast, leaving a window in it where the holes were on the front of the shinbone where it could be cleaned and dressed. I was wheeled back to my place in the ward where my life could continue as usual after that big event of the day.

DECISION TIME

A real obsession with the boys was sports, football, hurling and boxing. The newspapers, especially the Monday papers, were very popular because they gave out not only results but also information about upcoming games. If anyone wanted a paper he had to pay for it. The six had an agreement whereby one would buy a paper each Monday in turn and then pass it around to all six. That seemed to work well until my turn came. I had no money. What do you mean, you have no money? *The Irish Press* or *Independent* cost only a few pence. I lost my last sixpenny bit. "Where did you lose it?" "I put it on a horse." Jim said, "You must know a lot about horses." Willie said, "He didn't know enough about that one." "What happened?" "He fell going over a jump and threw the jockey. And my sixpence went down with him." "Where did you learn about horses?" "I went to school for it." "Where?" "In the Mullingar Infirmary." "Who taught you?" "All the men. They bought a paper every day and spent a lot of time studying form. They were teaching one another everything about horses and jockeys and trainers and I learned a lot." "But you are broke now." "Yea, but I'll catch up with my share when my family comes to see me."

They cut out pictures of footballers and hurlers and boxers from the newspapers and pasted them onto cardboard. They frequently took them out from the drawers under the beds and admired them and trimmed them and passed them around and discussed them. One final in football was between the Caven Slashers and the boys from the kingdom. Craig was from Kerry. He said, "Kerry is going to win." "You know we are the only county called the kingdom. When I went to school the teacher told me there are only two kingdoms, the kingdom of God and," they all chimed in, "the kingdom of Kerry." The world top boxers at that time were Joe Louis and Max Schmelling. Everyone tried to get pictures of them in action.

There was no radio except when a provincial or national final was being played. A radio would be brought into the ward and turned up high so that all could hear it. Michael O'Hare would be the commentator. He had the ability of communicating the exciting moments of the game. He would get excited rising to a climax or anti climax as the footballer scored or shot the ball wide. The patients joined in the excitement, cheering and waving hands and clapping. Boys got so involved and excited, especially when their home counties were playing, that they sometimes shouted at one another and even threatened to get out of bed and settle the whole matter there and then on the floor.

Several weeks before my twelfth birthday an announcement was made that the Bishop would be coming in the spring to confirm all boys who were eleven or older and had not yet been confirmed. A Sister would instruct us in preparation for confirmation. The Sister's name was Sr. Maryann. She came through the ward, stopped in front of each bed and asked, "Are you due for confirmation?" Then she wrote down the name and age. She stopped at the end of my bed and I was looking up at her. She was tall and slim. The butterfly headgear seemed much too big for her. It must have been three feet across from the tip of one wing to the tip of the other. I was surprised she looked so young, really like a teenager, especially when she smiled. She was very attractive looking. Most of us in our group were candidates for confirmation and she gave us a catechism and told us the lesson to learn saying she would be back. Later that day she came by and stood by my bed. After talking for a little while she reached under the mantle that was over her shoulders and took out some chocolate and gave it to me. I was embarrassed that no one else got any. The others gave me a hard time. They called me her pet and laughed. I shared the chocolate around, saying, "I don't know why she did this." They were happy to get the chocolate, which was delicious. That eased the teasing a bit. Every couple of days Sister Maryann came with chocolate just for me. I was shy and deeply embarrassed hoping she would not do this. "Here she comes" Matt would say, as she walked along quickly, the butterfly hat flopping up and down. It looked like a puff of wind would take it and her out into the field. One day the wind blew up and she held onto it with one hand to keep it from taking off. The boys laughed. "Here's your friend, she is going to lose her butterfly hat." Each week she came and stood by each bed for a few minutes and asked questions from the catechism. She always told me I was very good before she walked on to the next patient.

I wrote a letter to my father and mother. Mother answered right away. She was good at writing and explained everything going on at home. While I was in the Mullingar Infirmary, she was the only one from the immediate family who visited me. The bus from Ballymahon to Mullingar passed a mile from our house and stopped at the "foot of the green" beyond the school. She would leave her bicycle at Biddy Graham's cottage there and take the bus. In good weather she would cycle all the way, fourteen miles to Mullingar. My father and the rest of family were too busy everyday, eleven people in the house and ten while I was away. There was all the work on the farm, school and all the children's needs and Aunt Marcella now confined to bed from a stroke. I got the impression they all felt I was gone for good and would spend the rest of my life in some kind of a home for cripples. My Mother's visits gave me hope and the feeling that they would never forget me. Now in her letter she explained there was no bus or train that would take her to Coole. Also it was much farther from home. They were praying for me, saying the rosary every night and adding the prayer to St Jude for me. He is the patron of hopeless cases, as well as many other trimmings to the rosary. The children walking to school in the mornings were praying another rosary for Shane to get better. Her letter gave me a lift, knowing they were all remembering me everyday and hoping I would get better and come home. I read her letter several times and kept it under my pillow. My Mother reminded me in her letter that my 12th birthday was coming up. She said they all felt bad I as spending my 12th birthday in bed in the hospital and sent me best wishes from all. There was not a tradition of sending cards or giving gifts on birthdays.

 I did not say anything to anyone in the hospital about my birthday. Being very shy I did not want to draw any attention to myself. It was a very nice day and we were wheeled out onto the veranda. Some of the boys were reading and others were just looking out at the field and trees and sky. Craig was very happy because he did not have to keep looking up at the ceiling with his head resting in an iron frame, but could see the sky and clouds and the birds. There were great numbers of pigeons and crows that kept circling around, some sparrows that dared to fly onto the veranda and pick up crumbs and a blackbird that sang from the top of a lone tree that stood in the field, not far from the veranda. I was kneeling on my bed looking at it all, and listening to the blackbird and wishing I could leave the bed and run out into that field. There were nurses and maids and other people including, some visitors walking behind our beds because we were now out on the veranda. While living with my thought I heard a women's voice behind me say, "that is a very nice boy, can he be adopted?" I looked around and saw Mother Cecilia and a man and woman well dressed. When they saw me look at them, they walked on and I heard Mother Cecilia say, "I'll look into this for you." Most of the boys were from poor families and some were from orphanages and could possibly be adopted. My friends gave me some teasing. It seemed they would never stop.

 The next day after my 12th birthday Sister Maryann came around teaching. She stood by my bed as usual but this time her face was serious. She said, "You are getting no more chocolate, let me hear you answer the question." She proceeded to question me and I answered. Then she began asking questions that were not in the catechism. As I tried to answer she got furious and reached under her mantle and took out a blackthorn stick, about a foot long with knobs on it. "Hold out your hands" she said. I held out my hands, palms up as we did for the master in the school at home. "No," she said, "turn up the backs of your hands." She lifted the blackthorn stick and hit me on the back of my hands, first one and then the other. The pain was terrible. I could hardly bear it. This was much worse then getting the cane on the palms of the hands from the master. A shiver went through my body and I pulled back my hands. "Put your hands out again, backs up," she said. I put them out again, backs up. She hit me several times on the both hands. I was squirming in pain. She stopped. I looked into her face. She was grinning. Mike said, "Well that's the end of the chocolate." Craig said, "Why did she beat you?" I was silent and in pain. The next time she came around she did the same. I was looking to see if she had the blackthorn stick but I could not see it until she pulled it out. I could not understand what was going on with her. First I was the only one getting the chocolate and now I am the only one getting the stick. The blackthorn is a very hard black bush with long straight shoots with thorns on them. With the thorns cut off leaving black knobs, these sticks were popular for walking and driving cattle to the fairs. The backs of my hands and fingers developed hard knobs from the beatings with the blackthorn stick. It was more then a year before the knobs went away. I could not understand why she had changed. Did she hear about the people who wanted to adopt me? It was very confusing for me and there was nowhere to turn. I was not angry but could not understand her changing in that way and being so cruel.

    Looking to our left we could see another ward which was at right angles to ours. This was for younger boys, some only three or four years old. Behind that ward there was a glass corridor elevated, which led from the sisters' convent to the chapel. The glass was not clear but one could see the outline and shape of anyone going through, especially when it was lighted after dark. Every night at nine o'clock when our lights were already out, the sisters went through the corridor to the chapel for night prayers. We watched for this every night. We could see the outline of the figures, especially the butterfly headgear. The sisters stopped in the glass corridor before entering the chapel, Mother Cecelia in front of them. They were all standing still except that Mother Cecelia's headgear was moving up and down, nodding to emphasize what she was saying. This happened every night and we were asking one another what must she be saying to the sisters. Willie said when Sr. Gabriel took him for an x-ray he asked her what Mother Cecelia was telling them. Sr. Gabriel said Reverend Mother always emphasized that they should treat each patient like they would treat Jesus. They should see Jesus in each patient. Looking through the glass and seeing Mother Cecelia's head nodding emphatically I said, "I wonder if she is telling Sr. Maryann not to be beating her young patients on the backs of their hands with a blackthorn stick." Mike said, "she should be telling her not to use a blackthorn stick on Jesus." I was abused in the first hospital, the infirmary, and felt guilty of sin. Now I am being abused by a nun in this hospital and feel no guilt. I am innocent. The sister should feel guilty of sin for beating a patient without reason. I think she deserves a millstone around her neck.

Sister Gabriel came to me and said, "I am taking you for x-rays." She wheeled me out the door through the wall at the back of my bed and through the treatment area, then down a path to a separate building standing on its own, away from all the other buildings, where she took me. She told me to lie down on a cold bare table and moved the x-ray equipment into place. She went behind a door. "Keep still" she said and pressed a switch. There was a click. She repeated this several times on both legs. This was a new experience for me. I had never been x-rayed before. Sr. Gabriel was older than the other sisters I had met. She was tall and thin with wrinkles on her face and a little bent over. She wore the same butterfly hat. She was friendly and kept talking to me. She gave me the feeling that I was grown up and could carry on a conversation like an adult. She told me a doctor McCawley came down from Dublin once a month on Fridays. He looks at the x-rays and then decides who could be operated on the next time he would come. Not too many can be operated on. "I think you will be one of the lucky ones," she said. Back in the ward the boys wanted to know what happened. I told them of the experience and what Sr. Gabriel told me. Craig said, "None of us can be operated on because of where the sores are, mostly in the spine and hips." Mike said, "I am glad I don't have to go through an operation. Boys who went through it tell me it was terrible. The next morning Sr. Ita dresses the wound. She fills it with salt to kill the infection and the boys scream aloud with the pain. Sometimes you can hear them here because the treatment area is behind that wall at the back. Also, sometimes these operations don't work. The disease and the sores come back again. I know one boy who was operated on three times and he is not better yet, he is even worse than before."

Life continued as usual for the next few weeks including the beatings on the back of my hands with the blackthorn stick. Then one day Sr. Ita came to me and said, "You will be operated on next Friday." The day before, they wheeled me through the door in the wall at the back of our beds, the boys waving and wishing me good luck as I went. I was prepared for surgery. Next morning they put me in a waiting room because someone was ahead of me. It was very warm, too hot, as I lay there alone wondering what was going to happen to me. The sun was shining through the window beside me. It had tinted glass so I could not see out. I was thinking of my family. What are they all doing now? Mother is in the kitchen with the small children, the older ones are at school, my father is out on the land and Aunt Marcella is in bed. None of them know what I am doing. They have no idea I am lying here, fearful and waiting to be taken into the operating room. I knew they prayed for me last night and this morning and will pray for me again tonight. As soon as I get over this operation I will write and tell them about it because, I don't think anyone here let them know. No one asked me anything about my family. I was getting more feverish and the time seemed very long. Then the door opened. Two nurses came in wheeling a stretcher, moved it along side my bed and told me to get onto it. Now on the stretcher they wheeled me down a corridor and into a big room with lights hung from the ceiling. They wheeled my bed alongside a long narrow table, covered in white and told me to get onto it. I knew this was the operating table. After I got onto the operating table, Dr. McCawley, whom I had not seen before, stood over me. He was a big man dressed in a blue coat with a white mask over his nose. The mask on the nose struck me as very strange. I had never seen that before. He spoke to me and asked, "How old are you?" I answered, "Twelve." He said, "Lie on your side." This I did. "Now bring your knees up to your chin." This I did. I felt a needle go into my spine. I prayed in my heart. They straightened me out on the table, lying on my back. The feeling had gone from my waist down and at this point I did not know what they were doing with my leg. Someone put a wet face towel over my eyes. I could not see but I could hear everything. The Doctor giving orders: a hammer, a chisel, hold the basin here. Then my whole body started shaking with blows of the hammer on the chisel. I could hear each blow of the hammer. I could hear pieces of bone falling into the basin. It went on and on sometimes hard loud blows and sometimes lighter ones that I could still hear and all the time each blow shaking my body. All the while I am lying there praying silently in my mind, saying Our Fathers and Hail Marys without words. Eventually, the hammering and shaking and noise stopped. It took a little time more and then they put me back on a stretcher to wheel me into the recovery room. I did not see Dr. McCawley after the surgery or ever again, but often thought of him and saw the image of a surgeon with a white mask over his nose and heard his voice asking my age and telling me what to do.

As they wheeled me into the recovery room I saw another boy there who had surgery that some day, just before me, while I was waiting. He was in bed with his feet tilted almost straight up and his head down against the head of the bed. They lifted me off the stretcher and onto a bed, then tilted the bed so that my feet pointed up nearly vertical with my head pressing against bars at the head of the bed. I told nurse the bars were hurting my head. She got another pillow and put it between my head and the bars. It helped. She explained that I had to stay that way overnight because of the type of anesthetic they gave me in the spine. Gradually the feeling came back into my legs and I could feel pain where the surgery was done. They kept me in the recovery room that night.

In the morning my feet were lowered and they wheeled me back into the operating room where I was the day before. They put me on the operating table again. This time Sr. Ita stood over me. She was of medium height, dressed in white with the usual butterfly headgear. "Now," she said, "we have to clean out the wound and put on another plaster. This may hurt, but it is necessary that we do it." I could not see what she was doing but I remember what the boys had told me about the salt. Right enough I felt terrible stinging and the pain was unbearable. I felt I was a man and should not cry. The tears rolled down my face and my whole body shivered, but I did not say a word or emit a cry. It was torturous. The pain eased. I presumed they had washed the wound out. They put on a new plaster cast. This time they left no window, as the abscess was removed.

I wrote a letter home telling the family about the surgery. Mother wrote back saying they were all relieved and happy that the operation had taken place. She said they would come to see me soon. There were very few cars in the countryside in those days. The first to get cars were the doctor and the priest. Matt Slevin in Ballynacargy got a car and used it for hire. My father talked to him and arranged with him to take the family to Coole on a Sunday. I was expecting them to come someday but did not know the exact day they were coming.

It was a very happy moment when I spotted them walking down the ward towards me, being led by a nurse. As they came near, tears welled up in my eyes. There was my father and mother, my sisters, MaryJo and Cissie. Mother was first to the bedside. She kissed and hugged me, tears running down her face. My father shook my hand and put his other hand on my shoulder. Fathers did not embrace or kiss their sons in our tradition. My sisters hugged and kissed me. I was wiping the tears from my eyes. Then everyone wanted to talk at the same time, my mother asking about the conditions in the hospital, the food and so on, my father apologizing for not visiting me sooner, saying they were under a lot of pressure with Aunt Marcella having to be lifted out of bed onto a commode several times a day. He was needed all the time. Of course he did not have to tell me how they were tied down with a house full of children and milking cows twice daily, foddering animals and the many other chores all day every day.

A maid put a tray before me with my dinner. My Father looked at it and said, "That would be no good for Brian or Frank." Then he said, "I have some bad news to tell you. Aunt Marcella died last week. We buried her in the family plot in Milltown." I began to cry again and everyone went silent. Finally I said, "I will miss her. She was very good to me." Then they talked of her long confinement since she had the stroke and how her life came to an end. I felt a big void in my life. My sisters brought me up to date with the news from school and the young people. They were upset with the mean children who frequently taunted them about their brother Shane who was in a cripple home and who would never come home again. Mother and Father both said, "Don't bother Shane about that." "It really does not matter. We have more important things to talk about."

"We will have to go now," my father said. "There are things we have to do before it gets dark." They still stayed another little while. My mother took my right hand between her two hands and began rubbing my hand gently and caressing it with her hands. It felt very soothing. Then I could sense her feeling the knobs on the back of my hand and on the knuckles. She looked at the back of my hand and said, "Let me see the other hand." She saw and felt the lumps and knobs on the back of the other hand. She looked at me and said, "What happened to your hands?" I was silent. "You must tell me," she said. So I told her. She jumped to her feet with fire flaring from her eyes. "I am going to get to the bottom of this," she said. A nurse was nearby. She spoke to her and said, "I want to see Mother Superior." The nurse showed her where to go. My father said to my mother, "We will go together." After some time they came back. Mother said, "We saw Mother Cecilia and she is going to take care of this." My father said, "The sister had no right to beat you like that. You must tell us everything that happens to you. We will stand up for you and protect you." Then my father said again, "We must go now." He shook my hand firmly saying, "Come home soon we miss you everyday."

My sisters kissed me saying goodbye. My mother kissed and embraced me. I could feel her tears on my face. I cried. Mother lingered in the embrace with her face pressed close to mine and her tears running down her face and mine while the others walked slowly away. She joined them and I watched them go. Halfway down the ward Mother turned, looked back and waved. I waved. Before going through the door at the end of the ward, mother looked back and waved again. I waved back and my father and sisters waved. Then they were gone.

A few days after the surgery, the plaster cast, which had no window in it for draining as the sores were gone, showed a big red and yellow stain down the part where the operation took place. A nurse explained that this was normal draining after this kind of surgery and that the cast would be replaced in a few days. After another cast was put on there was no stain for about a week. Then a faint yellowish stain appeared. There was no pain now and I felt like I could run. They kept me in bed, fearing I could fall and break the bone which was greatly weakened now since so much had been chiseled away during the surgery. Life continued as usual in the ward. That was our world except for the Monday morning papers with all the news about the weekend games and the pictures of the athletes. Sister Maryann did not beat me any more. I prayed for her.

The whole area we were in was L shaped with the other ward jutting out from the end of our ward. Because the fronts were all open, we could see what was going on. There was always plenty of activity. The boys were younger in that ward, some as young as three years. There were plenty of visitors there and very few where we were. One very young boy was admitted. When his parents left he cried out loud for his Mommy for hours until he finally fell asleep. They needed much more attention then we did, so that ward was the center of activity. There was another ward at the back of ours, but we could not see it. There were older teenage boys there. One called Harry sneaked over to us after dark and talked to us telling us about his ward. They could stay there until they were sixteen. Then if they were not able to go home they were sent to a place in Dublin. He was supposed to stay in bed but he was able to hobble around. He brought us his collection of footballers and boxers, all glued to cardboard. He was very proud of them. We looked at them by flashlight and we were very impressed. We liked them so much that he gave us some of them.

About seven or eight beds down from us there was a boy in an iron frame. He had sores all over his body. He suffered great pain at times and moaned a lot. This got so bad that they moved him. We were told he was taken to a regular hospital and, later we were told he had died. The boys were reluctant to talk about him, they felt so bad. There was no heat in the ward, so they gave us an extra blanket in cold weather. The front was open at all times except in severe weather. We would wake up in the mornings and see the sun rising and hear the birds singing. They sang more in the mornings than at any other time of the day. I looked forward to hearing them.

Between the posts that were supporting the roof there were heavy blinds that looked like tent material. In stormy weather the blinds were pulled down and secured with ropes. One day there was a fierce thunderstorm. We could hear the claps of thunder and they were getting louder. We could see the flashes of lightning and they were becoming brighter. That meant the storm was coming towards us. There was a flurry of activity. The blinds were all pulled down and fastened. Some of us, including me, were excited and watching everything gleefully, while others were fearful and pulled the blankets over their heads. The storm came directly to us. The thunder gave such a loud crack right over us that we thought the building was hit. The heavy rain came down and the strong winds blew. We watched the blinds shudder and flap, swaying in the wind which was getting stronger by the minute. As the winds got stronger and the storm grew more violent, Jim shouted for all to hear, "We are taking off and going up into the sky. Hang on!" The storm passed and we were all still there safe in our beds.

During their visit to me my parents asked Mother Cecilia about Mary Jo, my oldest sister becoming a nurse. The Revered Mother spoke to Mary Jo and realized she was very enthusiastic about nursing and said she could come to Coole for a period of orientation and then attend their nurse's training school in London. Mary Jo followed up on this and came to Coole shortly before I left. She was not assigned to our ward but came around to see me regularly. I was so happy to have a member of the family near. It took away a lot of the loneliness and isolation. She wore a nurse's uniform and looked very nice. She was too young looking to be a nurse. She was six years older then me. Later she went to London to continue her training.

It was now six months since the surgery. The cast had been changed several times. This time the nurse said it was healed. It was dry but there was an ugly scar. "You do not need another cast but be careful", she said. I was allowed to walk around. My friends were happy to see me walking. I said, "Am I walking very fast?" They said you are walking very slowly. Then is this fast? Not really. I thought I was walking very fast but they said I was walking normally.

A couple of weeks later a nurse came to me and said, get ready, you are going home today. The ambulance is waiting. I was stunned with joyful anticipation, said a hasty goodbye to everyone and got into the ambulance. He took another way to Mullingar, and then headed for Ballynacargy. As we arrived in the area I had been familiar with I recognized everything. We passed Dr. Byrne's house with all the painful memories, the repeated lancing of the sore leg. I could not believe it could ever get better, though I prayed and prayed for years. The family prayed the rosary every night for me and adding the prayer to St. Jude, patron of hopeless cases for me as part of the trimmings to the rosary. Mother prayed in the kitchen doing her work. Father prayed in the fields doing his work. My brothers and sisters said an extra rosary on my mother's instructions, as they walked out the long boreen on the way to school every morning. Mother would remind them as they left the house with school bags filled with books, lunch and bottles of milk and a sod of peat under the arm, "remember now, say the rosary for Shane's shin that he will get better." We passed Empor Chapel where we went to Mass every Sunday, turned right off the main road, up the hill of the green on a gravel road with loose stones and limestone dust flying up into the air. There was the schoolhouse on Empor green situated on high ground and painted white. I remembered the friends I went to school with. I could not forget the beatings and the terror of waiting for the master to arrive each morning. I remembered my father telling me how my grandfather had gone to a hedge school nearby when the Irish Catholics were not allowed to be educated. When the penal laws were abolished their school was built in 1830 and my grandfather and father went there and learned the three Rs of reading, 'riting and 'rithmatic. Each house was familiar as I guided the driver to take every correct turn until we arrived at the gate into the front field. There was no gravel road beyond that gate, just a grass field and our house could be seen across the field with white gates and the farmyard buildings and the big sycamore tree in front of the house. "That's our house", I said to the driver. "Well", he said, "you get out and walk across the field. I am turning around and going back with the ambulance."

The family had not been told I was coming home. The sound of the ambulance could be heard a long distance in that quiet countryside. I saw my mother coming out the gates and across the field to meet me. We were both crying and we embraced in silence for a long time. The other members of the family were quick on the scene. They all shook my hands and welcomed me home. My father came into the house, held both my hands with his and said,

"Welcome home. Are you alright now?" He put his right hand flat on top of my head and pulled me close to him as if measuring my height. "Shane," he said, "you must have grown a foot since you left home." Tears ran down his face. This was the second time the family ever saw him cry. The first time was when I left home. Brian, two years older than me, is looking up at me staring and realizing how much taller I had grown.

He said, "No wonder you grew so much, spending so much time lying in bed. That's where you grew. I had to work hard and there was no time for me to grow."

And remember: Love is not love 'til it's given away.

CHAPTER 7

Coming Home After Two Years

Returning home from Coole was a great joy to me after being away for nearly two years. The biggest change was Aunt Marcella was not there any longer. She had died. I missed her and we talked about her and the memories we had. There were more changes also in my brothers and sisters. The youngest, Mike, was now three years old, talking and running about. Next to him coming up the line was Celine, now six and going to school. Vera was eight and in the second grade; Frank, ten, was in the fifth grade. Brian, fourteen, was in the eighth grade. They had all grown but they said I had grown the most. Cissie, sixteen was at Ardagh convent and Mary Jo, eighteen, was beginning to study nursing in London.

I returned to school. My classmates who were in the fifth grade with me when I left and went to hospital were now in the seventh grade. They welcomed me back. "It is so good to have you in our class again." I sat with them. The school had become co-ed. There were girls in every class from the fourth to the eighth grades. When the master came into the classroom he looked at me and hesitated. Then he reached out his hand to me and said, "Shane, you are welcome back and you grew big." At the lunch break he asked me to stay while the others went out to the playground. He asked me if I had any schooling while I was away. I said, "Nothing in Mullingar Infirmary. In Coole I received instruction for a short time in preparation for confirmation but I was not confirmed because I was discharged before the time of confirmation." He asked me if I thought I could fit in with my old friends in the seventh grade. I said, "yes." He said, "We'll give it a try and see how you do." I got the impression he had changed for the better; more relaxed and treating me more like a grownup.

As the days went by it was obvious there was competition between the girls and boys. Some of the girls were bright and scoring better. I felt happy with having the girls in our class. The whole atmosphere in the school had changed for the better. The master did not punish anyone anymore and he did not even have a cane. I paid full attention to everything being taught in all the grades and worked very hard to make up for the lost time. Fortunately I was gifted with a very good memory and could retain what I had learned very well. The master was encouraging and told me I was doing even better than he had hoped.

Confirmation was coming up. The parish of Milltown and Empor had so few candidates that the Bishop came only every three years. Those to be confirmed had to be over ten years of age, so Frank, who was now ten, and I were due for confirmation. All teachers in the national schools had to teach religion, so the master was preparing us for confirmation. He called himself the pope because he said he was teaching religion just like the pope. He would repeat this humorously quite often. The diocese had a priest with a full time job going around to the schools examining students to see if they were ready for confirmation. There was intense preparation prior to the time he was expected. The catechist was very strict. At the end of the examination which was verbal, he gave out cards to the candidates, a white card to those who answered all the questions, a green card to those who failed some questions but otherwise did well and a yellow card to those who failed. Students whose parents helped them at home did best. The children in our family always got white cards.

Then came the day of confirmation. We all piled into the trap and with my father up front driving the horse we went the six miles to the parish church in Milltown. The residence for priests was by the church. They also served the church in Empor which was called the chapel and there was no residence there. The bishop stood in front of the altar. Those to be confirmed were called up to stand in front of him. He asked us questions to see if we were ready for confirmation. Each one in turn had to answer a question. It all went well until he came to the last one, a boy who was not very smart. The bishop was standing there with the crosier, which is the shepherd's crook, in his hand. Now he said, "The people are the sheep and the children are the lambs. So what am I?" Well, there was a long silence. There were no shepherds in Empor. The word shepherd was certainly not in daily use. The boy was stuck for an answer. The church was packed. The teachers and parents were tense. They all wanted to prompt the boy but were afraid to do so. Again, the bishop said, stamping his shepherd's crook on the floor, "The people are the sheep of the flock, the children are the lambs. What does that make me? What am I?" The boy finally answered the bishop and said, "You are the ram."

He held his hands over us in prayer for the Holy Spirit to come upon us. Then he anointed each one on the forehead with the holy oil of chrism and gave each of us a stroke on the cheek with his hand to remind us that we must be ready to suffer for the faith. He told us we were now strengthened by the Spirit to live our faith for the rest of our lives in spite of trials and temptations of every kind. The priest assisting the bishop asked us to make a voluntary pledge to abstain from alcoholic drink until we were twenty-one or for life. He read the pledge and we all repeated it after him phrase by phrase. I remember on the way home feeling, I am stronger in my faith now because I am strengthened in the Spirit. The younger members of the family kept talking about the bishop's big hat, and why did he put it on and take it off so many times. When we passed Empor church on the way home, the Bishop's car was there. He and the parish priest were looking at the church. My father said, "Every time the bishop comes to a parish for confirmation he inspects all the churches in the parish."

I was the eldest walking to school now with Frank, Vera and Celine. Brian had stopped going when he was fourteen and had finished the eighth grade. After the morning work and breakfast, mother sliced the bread she had baked the previous day, put the sandwiches and bottles of milk in our school bags and sprinkled holy water on us and sent us on our way with the reminder not to forget to say the rosary on the way to thank God that Shane is home and well. There were no children in Mac's or Mulderry's, so we had no company until we reached Halions. By then we had finished the rosary. There were all boys in the Halion family, five of them, some in our classes and they joined us on the way. As we got nearer the school children from other families joined us. We always arrived before the master. The first to the school got the key from a house nearby and opened the door. Students from the older classes had to take their turns in sweeping the floor and locking the door after school before going home the previous evening. The only light was daylight. There was still no electricity, no plumbing or running water, no heat except from a turf fire in the fireplace in the winter. We had to bring a sod of turf (peat) every day from home, one per family for the fire. As I was the eldest in our family going now, I would put a sod of turf under one arm and the schoolbag over the other shoulder as we started for school.

Some families brought a sod of turf and some did not. We built a fire and lit it before the master came. We got down on our knees and blew the fire with our breath to get it started. You had to be careful in doing this. If you held your mouth close to the fire while drawing in your breath you could inhale the smoke and get dizzy. So you learned to turn your face away from the fire while drawing in your breath. It was common for a boy to inhale the smoke and feel faint and turn pale. One day Nick was blowing the fire and he inhaled so much smoke he fainted and was lying on the floor as white as a ghost. The others were trying to revive him by slapping him on the face and shouting at him. The master arrived.

"What's going on here," he said. Then he saw Nick lying on the floor. "What happened?" he asked. We said he was blowing the fire and fainted. He patted Nick on the cheek, "Get up, get up," he repeated. As he patted Nick you could see the contrast of his yellow fingers, yellow from constantly smoking and Nick's white face. The lady teacher in the other end of the classroom had just come in. We were all around Nick. She came over to see what was going on. The master told her. She said, "Don't you all be standing around him. Take him outside to get some fresh air." There was no phone so we could not call for help. We carried him outside and tried to make him stand up. While we were struggling to get him to stand he came to and began to talk. "I'm alright, I'm alright. What are we doing out here, it is freezing." We all came in and sat down. The master said, "Now don't try to light the fire again. We can do without a fire for one day." We were sitting there freezing with no other source of heat but the master's cigarette which he smoked constantly in the classroom.

At lunchtime I always went into our cousin's house, McGuires of the green, we called them, and ate my lunch. My father's oldest brother, Uncle Pat, was dead by now. I remember him well from my younger years. He came to our house a lot to help my father. He was not as tall as my father but stouter built. He loved to talk and tell stories of his early days when they were evicted and so much of the good land taken away from them. He had spent several years in the Argentine working on a great Uncle's ranch. He saved his money and came back home to Ireland and bought a farm near the schoolhouse. He married Brigid Tyrell and they had eight children, Mary Ann, Paddy Joe, Johnny, Bernie, Larry, Jimmy, Cella and Brigid. Aunt Brigid made me feel very welcome and always offered me some of the food she was cooking. My mother told me to eat only my lunch because I would have dinner after coming home. Their three youngest children, Jimmy, Cella and Brigid attended the same school during my time. When the weather was really bad and the boreen was flooded, father and mother would tell us to take the ass and cart and leave them at our cousin's place during the day. We never forgot to say the rosary when we were in the cart.

The parish priest, known as the P.P., was Fr. McCaffrey, He had a curate, Fr. Murray. Fr. McCaffrey was a bit on in years and did not come down to Empor church. My father was very friendly with him for many years. He went to see him now and discussed the children bringing the sod of turf to school and how some days the fire went out and the children got cold. My father offered to give a horse cartload of turf to the school for the winter. Fr. McCaffrey approved and thanked him. That was the end of the sod of turf.

And remember: Love is not love 'til it's given away.

The old home and family
Front: Michael 3, Celine 6, Vera 8, Frank 10
Back: Shane 12, Brian 14, Marcella 16, Mother and Father
(Mary Jo away at nursing school)

CHAPTER 8

Life on the Farm

When not at school or working I am down by the river fishing, running, walking or learning to swim. My father loved to fish and often spoke of his father and how he loved to fish. The biggest trout he caught was the day he saw this big trout jumping for flies. He caught one of the same kind of flies along the riverbank, took it home and tied to a very small hook, went back to the river and in a short time came home with the trout. We were all so happy to see that beautiful fish. My father always emphasized small hooks for trout. It does not make the fly or even the worm look unnatural but light and free moving. He had a big supply of small hooks, some from my grandfather's time. We used them and never had to buy any because there were so many. My fishing skills improved and I kept the family going with fish a lot of the time during the season starting on St. Patrick's day, March 17th. The Lenten fast and abstinence was strictly observed. It was Palm Sunday, the beginning of Holy Week. I caught forty-five fish; pike, perch and trout. Mother was happy to see all the fish, especially with all the fast days coming that week. The children were growing bigger and eating more. Also, she was baking more but how were we going to keep the fish fresh? There was no refrigeration in those days. We gave some to the Macs, our nearest neighbors. Eliza Mac said the best way to keep them was in a basin of cold water. My father said not to keep them in water but to keep them dry and in a very cool place. Everyone enjoyed them. Pike grew very large in the river. The big ones lived mostly in the deep areas. My father and grandfather caught them weighing over forty pounds. The biggest one I landed was twenty pounds. He had a large head and big mouth with a lot of sharp teeth. I mounted his head on a branch of the sycamore tree over-hanging the entrance gate, putting a stick in his mouth to keep his jaws wide open with all the teeth shining. Many who came into the front yard would ask, "what is that," and each of us kept adding to the story. My youngest sister, Celine, told her classmates it was a shark that attacked me and I shot him.

I told my father, "You and grandfather lived by the river all your lives so I may catch a pike bigger than yours." Some people think a big pike is tough to eat but the traditional family recipe was so good everyone enjoyed it. Sometimes I caught an eel. I would bring it into the house holding it behind my back, go up to my sisters and suddenly hold it up squirming in front of them. They would scream and also refused to eat an eel. The rest of us thought they were delicious when fried with eggs for breakfast. The eel skins were dried and used to tie the two ends of the flails together. They were very flexible and would never break. George, from the other side of the river used to come by in a boat. He had a net in the river. One day he said to me, "You are catching more fish with that rod in your hand than I am getting in the net."

I am enjoying the skylark more and more. He seems more trusting when I am sitting quietly. He will come closer and sing more often. The moment he jumped off the ground he had my full attention. The greatest thrill was the moment he disappeared into the blue sky out of sight, but still could be heard. This continued to fascinate me. Where did he learn to do this? Why does he sound so joyful? Can he not see me because I can't see him? The time he sang best was after a shower of rain and the sun would come out again. The air is fresh and clean. The wet grass is shining in the sunlight. The sky is a deep blue. While these thoughts are going through my mind I feel he is singing from heaven. Then suddenly he appears in descent and in seconds he is on the ground beside me. Every time I see the skylark and hear him from the blue sky, unseen, it thrills me as a brand new experience as if I had never witnessed it before. I am so happy to be in the presence of this beautiful bird and to have the privilege of seeing and hearing him.

The river remained fairly cold all summer. There were small rivers that flowed into it. These tributaries were fed mostly by springs which kept the water cold. Some people did swim in the river especially during a heat wave. My father said he could swim but he was always too busy making hay in the good weather. When we discussed swimming he would say the best way to learn was with a sheaf of bulrushes. I was determined to learn to swim and cross the river without a boat. So I made a sheaf of bulrushes, tied it at one end, divided the other end by hand and put the front under my chin and half under each arm. The bulrushes would keep me afloat while learning to swim. My brothers saw what I was doing but did not come along with me. Was it that the water was too cold or did they consider it a waste of time or were they just not interested? I went to the river every day and learned to swim with the bulrushes. In about a week I was swimming on my own. When my brothers saw me swimming in the middle of the river they made sheaves of bulrushes and began learning to swim. They did eventually swim but just about enough to stay up. They did not seem to relish it. They seemed to like the work better. I used to swim across the river and run along the bank on the other side.

Occasionally boys from neighboring farms would come to our land by the river and join us swimming. The boys did not wear swimsuits. One day while we were swimming a group of girls came down to the river on the other side. We picked up our clothes and ran out through the field among the cows. The cows stopped grazing and were looking puzzled, staring at us. We dressed quickly, just pants and shirts and went back to the river. The girls were gone. We stripped off and jumped in the river. The girls stood up. They had only been hiding. They began daring us to come out of the water. We would not come out but stayed submerged with only our heads up. They kept daring us to come out but we stayed. We were turning blue with the cold before they finally left. After that experience I got my first swimsuit but did not wear it.

The sheep were sheared every year in the summertime. The wool was sold at an auction priced by the pound. If the wool was washed it fetched a higher price per pound. Some buyers would not buy wool that was not washed. They said wool could be washed and dried better on the sheep's back. Before shearing we would take the sheep down to the river and take them in until only their heads were up. They could swim but we held them in there rubbing the wool with our hands until clean. Then we would take them out of the river and let them go. They would run wild through the fields. I helped with the shearing and was always surprised at how fast the sheep ran away looking clean and shiny without the fleece that would be left on the ground at our feet. Then the wool would be sold. The farmers used to say ewes were very profitable. They gave you the lambs and the wool every year and you got money for them when it was time to sell. At times we sent some of the wool to the mills in Swinford to be made into tweed from which we would have suits made by the tailor.

I looked for the blackbird. He was not to be heard singing. My father told me, because it is now winter he does not sing much, but you can see him eating grain by the barn door. I looked and saw him with his mate and lots of other birds scratching for grain. He had a lovely, shiny, black color. The female was not as bright in the color. In the month of March birds could be seen flying around with pieces of withered grass and other materials in their beaks. We knew they were building their nests and soon there would be baby birds. The blackbird took up his position again on the top of the sycamore tree and sang to his heart's content, sharing his joy of living with all who listened.

    The churn we had for churning cream to make butter was called an end over end churn. It was in the shape of a small barrel made of wood and mounted on a wooden stand with four wooden legs. It had a handle attached about the middle. When the handle was rotated, the churn rotated. This was done as quickly as possible until the cream turned to butter. We would take turns at this for a few minutes each until finished. The whole procedure would take about a half hour. There was an old, unused dash churn in the barn. My father explained to us how it was used. It was also the shape of a small barrel, but standing up on one end. There was something similar to the handle of a brush going through a hole in the lid with a dash-board attached to the end of it. The operator moved the handle up and down quickly causing the dash-board to dash the cream up and down until it turned into butter. He told us that when they bought the end over end churn they felt they had become very modern. Back in those days a boy named Willie from the neighborhood whose family were not farmers loved to help on the farm. After his first day churning Aunt Marcella made potato pancakes. He ate all he could heaped with butter. He felt so full he lay down in the field behind the house until the full feeling went away. He went home and told his family, "There was butter in the middle and butter running through and to tell the truth of it, my face was buttered too." Being back home was like starting a new life. The suffering, the hospital and the hopelessness were now behind me. I am back with my family, back at school, back on the land with all the animals, the delightful birds and the lovely river. I can run free along the riverbank again and feel like I have been reborn. I can vault higher and feel I am flying free. I thank God in my heart and there seemed to be no limit to life.

    I sit by the riverbank and watch the flowing water. Up to my right as the river comes from a distance and curves gently, it is calm and silent. Downstream to my left it is shallower water with rocks. There the river runs fast and babbles. My father always said it was like people. The silent ones think deeply while the shallow thinking ones babble a lot. I am thirteen years old. I feel I am a man. Girls are very attractive to me. The feelings and movements of my own body want to assert themselves and get away from control. Thoughts and memories flood my imagination. Our family has been here a long time. We survived the famine years, the landlord years and now we have our own free state and we are surviving the efforts of the ministry of education to beat a language into our heads which our parents do not know and on which they are evidently not consulted. We own our own land without paying rent to a landlord. I am a survivor and I have a freedom that no one can take from me. Some are saying a country without its own language is without a soul. The soul is not in the language. There is no soul except in the people. If they want to speak the language they will speak it. Parents said the Department of Education could facilitate whole families to speak the language instead of forcing the children to learn.

That evening as we all sat round the hearth with a warm fire burning I told them what I was thinking about our family as I sat on the riverbank today. My father said his father was a young man at the time of the famine. He always said there was no need to have a famine in Ireland. There was plenty of grain and meat in the country when the potato failed. The landlords took the grain and meat out of the country in payment of rent on the land. The land had been taken by the crown and given to the planters. The farmers were then the tenants who had to pay rent to the landlords. The native farmers rose up in some areas of the country and tried to stop the wagons of grain and cattle on the way to the ports. The crown ordered the army to ride alongside the wagons and protect them so that they could arrive safely at the ports. On route they frequently passed people dying on the roadside, too weak from starvation to reach the ports to leave the country.

"My father," he said, "used to emphasize that the landlords kept on promising that plans were in progress to bring food to the hungry people." Later it was discovered that no plans for help were made at the time help was promised. The people were deceived and many landlords were happy to get rid of the people. In some cases it was an attempt at deliberate genocide. Grandfather had told his children the McGuires always had enough to eat because they had mixed farming of cattle and grain and enough to pay the rent. They also took in some poor people and fed them during the famine. The potato was not native to Ireland. It was brought by the British and was unsuited to the Irish climate.

Two of Uncle Pat's sons, Paddy Joe and Larry, were visiting us to help with harvest work. My father took them with us to the old farm from which the family was driven and which my father was now renting to graze cattle. After looking at the cattle and counting them, he showed us where the original house stood before the eviction. The stones were gone but the foundations were left, now covered with grass and raised enough above the ground level to see the outlines of the house that was there. We had seen it before, but the cousins were seeing it for the first time. They were angry and asked a lot of questions. The more they heard the angrier they grew about the evil that was done to their father's family. They would take back the land from the present owners who were descendents of the landlord's agent who carried out the eviction. My father told them we cannot blame the present owners and we are living in a peaceful relationship with them.

Members of our family in every generation enjoyed fishing and hunting wild game. The knowledge and skill was shared with each rising generation. Brian and I were eager to learn and do our share, enjoying the family tradition of fishing and shooting game. It was challenging and the skills had to be learned. It took a lot of practice and observing the older members perform. My father was a real expert in taking the flying bird and running hare. He knew when we were doing it right or wrong and instructed us every time. He was encouraging and we became very successful in using the gun and fishing rod. The gun was also referred to as, a fowling piece, and there was never any thought of using it for any other purpose.

Brian got a Kerryblue Dog from a friend and we were training him to the gun. His long hair was blue and hung down his face in front of his eyes. It was a wonder how he could see at all. The previous owner told us not to cut the hair over his eyes. That's the way he is supposed to be. The county Kerry, known as the Kingdom, was the only county that gave its name to two breeds of animals, the Kerry Cow and the Kerryblue Dog. We called him Finn. He was with us all the time, at work and at play. He was a natural swimmer and loved to retrieve anything thrown into the river for him. He was rugged and hardy and did not hesitate to go into the water, no matter how cold, even when there was ice at water's edge along the riverbank. He had a good nose for picking up scent. When we went through a field or any area with him we felt sure he flushed out all the game that was there and found it after it was shot even in the heaviest cover. My father was very busy and went shooting only on a Sunday afternoon. I asked him if I could take the gun out on my own. He answered, "One of these days I'll give you some lessons on safety and then you will be able to take it on your own." He never had a loaded gun in the house. When going shooting he would not load it until he was down in the field away from the house. On the way home he would unload it before he got to the house.

DECISION TIME

There had been guns in the family for generations. There was one old muzzle-loading gun there from my grandfather's time. My father used to speak of the energy and skill of grandfather when eighty years old. One morning he saw ducks raising from a pond on the other side of the river. He expected they would come back before dark to feed there again for the night. So he took his single barrel, muzzle loading gun and the dog. He got into the boat and rowed across the river and set up a blind by the pond. In due time the ducks began to circle around, preparing to land. He waited until he saw two come into range and crossing in line. He fired and took the two with one shot. The dog brought them out. It was dark when he got home but he was very proud of himself and his dog. My father used a muzzle-loading gun for years. In a cabinet in the parlor he kept everything he used when going shooting; the gun, the ramrod, which was clipped underneath the barrel, the measuring pouches for the powder and the shot, and a pack of wads. I never used a muzzle-loading gun. It seemed to be a very slow process reloading after firing a shot. In my time we had a breach-loading gun and used cartridges. You bought the cartridges with the different sizes of shot according to the size of birds you were going to shoot. My father bought the different sizes in bulk. It was all still there in that cabinet. The smallest grains of shot he called snipe shot. It was number 8 and looked nearly as fine as powder. The first time he saw a breach-loading gun was down by the river in the winter when a man opened his gun at the breach to reload. He said to him, "You may as well go home now as your gun is broken." Having examined the convenience of it he soon bought one for himself. It was confiscated during the civil war. He got it back when the war was over. That was the gun I started shooting game with.

One morning my father took the gun and said, "I want to give you instructions." He took me to the field looking down at the river in safety and said, "You have been out with me and have seen the precautions I take such as loading only after you are this far away from the house and unloading before you get back near the house. Now I am going to teach you the most important safety factor of all." He pointed to the muzzle and said, "every shot leaves the gun there so you should never point the muzzle at yourself or anyone else or any living thing, even if the gun is unloaded. You point it only at game you have decided to shoot." I followed his instructions exactly all my shooting days and never had a problem. In all the years guns had been in the family there never had been an accident.

The first morning I went on my own with the gun and dog I felt very grown up and capable. When I got into the first field I loaded the gun and headed for the riverbank with Finn close by. As we walked along the riverbank we came to an area of marsh and rushes. A duck flew up. I pointed the gun, took steady aim and fired. The duck fell on the river. Finn went in with a leap, swam to the duck and brought him out to me. It was a drake mallard in full bloom. It was my first wing shot and I got the duck. Looking around I saw ducks flying away at the sound of the shot. We headed home, Finn and myself. It was a cloudy morning, the wind was causing a ripple on the river. The reeds and bulrushes were swaying back and forth. It would be nice to spend more time walking along the riverbank but there is school today. My father was proud of me, my mother thought I was great, but, not understanding the gun, she was nervous about it, telling me to be careful. Then Brian and I started going out with the gun and dog together. As we had only one gun we took turns in carrying it, the one without the gun always walking behind. On a Sunday afternoon we would walk for miles by the river and through the bogs. Sometimes we did well and at times we came home with nothing. We got ducks by the river and flooded areas. We got pheasants, partridge and hares in the bogs. We all liked the hare soup that mother made. It was always so delicious. There was sport to be had year round, fishing in the summer and shooting in the winter. After school, when finished with the milking and foddering, we would go down to the river and wait in a blind for ducks to fly by. That was an exciting time as there were always a lot of birds passing, most of them out of range. "When in doubt don't fire" was our instruction because you might just wound the bird and not be able to get it. No one wanted that to happen. When it got dark, which was early in the winter, we came back and did our homework.

And remember: Love is not love 'til it's given away.

CHAPTER 9

Eighth Grade and the Bully

I am fourteen, in the eighth grade and the last year at Empor School. I am having no difficulty with any subject including Irish but there is not one word of Irish spoken in any of the homes. It is required by law to be taught in the primary national schools, a necessity to graduate from secondary school and to enter a university. Parents showed no interest in it. They did not know a word of it and saw no benefit in it for their children's future.

The master gave us a love of poetry, both Irish and English. We had to read out loud in turns. Then he would read it to show us how it really should be read. Put some life into it, he would say. One day he called me aside and asked me what I hoped to do after finishing school there. At that time I did not know, but I would like to continue my education by going on to secondary school and college. He emphasized that there was no secondary school in the area and no busing to those far away in the towns. The only solution would be to go to a boarding school. He said, "I want to tell you something. You can be anything you want to be if you apply yourself. You have the talent." When he read Chesterton's *Lepanto* he made it sound like you could hear the drums of war.

> Dim drums throbbing on the hills half heard,
> where only from a nameless throne a crownless prince has stirred,
> as if from out the heavens or half attainted stall
> the last knight of Europe takes weapons from the wall
> . . . Don John of Austria is going to the war.

Brian had finished school in Empor and was home full time now working on the farm. That's what happened to most country boys in that area. They just stayed at home. Secondary education was not available to them. The same happened with the girls. Some boys and girls went into the bigger towns to serve their time with families who owned businesses and lived there. Others might migrate, mostly to England to look for work. Pat, known as the red because of the color of his hair, was in my class. He talked constantly about the relief and freedom he was going to have when he would leave school. The law required everyone to go to school until fourteen. He said he planned to leave earlier than that and pressured me to leave with him, saying we would be free as the wind and really enjoy life.

All of the others, boys and girls knew of his intentions and mostly ignored him. We were all looking forward to leaving that school. The girls in general were more ambitious than the boys in continuing their education but the opportunity would not be there for most of them. I liked having the girls in the class, the cheerful, bright ones who were fun to be with and tolerated the moody ones who on some days would speak to no one at all. They were not as forgiving as the boys in forgetting about fights and insults. Most of the girls outperformed the boys in the classroom. The boys tried to make up for this by showing off their strength and brash talk and behavior.

There was one girl I found to be most attractive. She was bright and cheerful, athletic and beautiful in appearance and quite sure of herself. Friendships between boys and girls of that age were not tolerated by the school or by families. I did not even tell myself how I felt. However, I became aware of how pleasant she was to me and how she listened if I talked to her, though she did her share of the talking too. I was always very conscious of how people were listening and not just being polite. The girls often made me feel tender and loving. We were walking out the school door. She came alongside me and seemed casual. She said in a low voice, "Do something about the bullying that's going on here. The only way to stop that bully, Magee, is to give him a good trouncing and you could do it."

I had been disturbed with the behavior of the bully and how he made life miserable for so many, especially those younger and weaker than himself. On some particular instances I told him to lay off. He would sneer at me, desist for a while but always resumed his vicious activity. He used foul words and called boys and girls degrading names. They hated being put down by him in front of others. They suffered great humiliation. He would not let up on a boy who was greatly overweight, calling him a fat pig and worse. It was degrading and hurtful. A girl who was very skinny got a lot of revolting words from him. She was a very good singer with a beautiful voice, the most liked member of the choir. While the bully was harassing her she said, "I am a good singer and you cannot sing a note." He sneered at her and said, "Do you think you are a singer because you have legs like a lark?" He had developed a biting way of putting others down, verbally degrading family members. When I was in Coole Sanitarium he would taunt my brothers and sisters. "Your brother, Shane, has a rotten bone in his leg and he is in a cripple's home for life." They suffered from the taunting and told him to stop it, but he would not give up. He would make ugly faces at others, sticking out his tongue at them and sneering. He did these things before and after school and at lunchtime or whenever the master was not present. He would pick generally on one at a time and keep it up for days. He would twist an arm or bend fingers until students cried. This brought on many a fight but he was feared and would not give up. It had been raining this day and there was a manhole with water in it at the back of the school building where we were standing at lunchtime to keep out of the wind. He removed the cover from the manhole, took a long stemmed yellow-topped weed, dipped it repeatedly in the manhole and splashed another boy in the face. I told him to quit. He made a splash at me. I took a swing at him. He stumbled and fell into the manhole, injuring his ankle. He could not walk so the others dragged him into the school. He told the master he slipped and fell, hurting his ankle. He went quiet and eased off for a few days. Then, it started up again. He was back at his bullying tactics. The students would not think of telling the master. It was an area of student life that no adult was admitted into. What could the master do? He would not be present at the critical times. If a victim were to tell the master he would then be despised and would be made to suffer much more than if he had kept quiet.

It was winter and I was wearing a tweed jacket, made from the wool of our own sheep. The boys wore jackets and short pants to the knees. The girls wore a jacket or blouse and skirt. The bully was very jealous of my tweed jacket and he slit the back of it with a razor blade. I did not feel it but one of the boys who had been bullied a lot, told me as we were on the way home. I took off the jacket and looked at it. Right enough, there was a two to three inch slit in the middle of the back. I told my mother. She looked at it and expressed horror. "I will do something about this," she said. "I will talk to his parents."

I said to her, "You don't have to get involved, I will handle it." The next day I challenged him on it. He denied it. I said, "You have been a bully in this school too long. I am not afraid of you. Touch another student and I'll break your neck." He was taken aback with my words and said nothing for a while. A few of the boys and girls overheard us. They said, "Have a fight, have a fight. Say you'll have a fight." They pressured us. "Shane, say you'll fight Nick. Nick, say you'll fight Shane. Who's afraid? Who's afraid?" I said, "I'm not afraid of Nick Magee." He said, "I'm not afraid of Shane McGuire." They cheered, the fight is on. We'll all be in the hollow today after school.

The hollow was a favorite place for boys to have a good fight. Light fights or squabbles broke out all the time and took place right away on the spot where the quarrel began. Ours was considered a very significant fight and would take place after school in the hollow and all the boys and girls from the master's schoolroom would be there. Moira, the girl I liked most came to me quietly and said, "I am happy you're going to fight the bully. It's about time, give him a good beating. We'll be cheering you on." The hollow was in the field across a wall from the school green. The interior sides and bottom were covered with grass. When down at the bottom we could not see the school or the playground, known as the green and no one from there could see us. It was shaped like a bowl.

After school we all climbed over the stone wall and went down into the hollow. We all left our school bags down on the grass. Magee, the bully, and I stood in the middle with the boys and girls standing around us in a circle. I felt I was fighting for all who had suffered from the actions of the bully. They were cheering us on, the girls shouting louder than the boys. Magee rushed at me, ducked his head and tried to ram me in the stomach, flailing his fists at me. He lifted his head and tried to punch me in the face. I fended him off, being careful to protect my face. The bystanders were cheering us on. He kept repeating his tactics trying to rush me in the stomach with his head and thinking my defenses would come down and he would try again to punch me in the face. I kept fending him off and waiting for an opening to give him a really good crack on the nose. That should draw blood and the sight of the blood would frighten him. I got an opening and connected with a strong punch to the nose. He staggered a bit but kept on punching. The blood started flowing. The others kept cheering us on and seemed to be getting a great kick out of watching us fight. The weather was very cold and his blood was congealing on his lips and around his mouth. I got another punch at his nose. The blood kept coming and congealing. His lips, mouth and chin were covered with hardened red blood.

Some of the students started shouting, "Magee, your liver is coming out your mouth." It started with the girls and I could see and hear the nice girl who was so anxious for me to give him a trouncing, shouting even louder than the others. All were joining in now, "Bully, your liver is coming out your mouth." It was loud and clear and I could see it bothered him, but it gave me more strength. He kept on fighting for a bully thinks he cannot be beaten. The shouting and jeering kept coming, the girls much louder than the boys and leading the chant. Then I hit him a strong punch to the jaw. It spun him around and he staggered and backed off. He put his hand up to remove the blood from around his mouth. He got a handful of congealed, red blood that did look like liver. He looked at it, flung it to the ground and walked away.

The students continued shouting in unison, "Magee, it's your liver, Magee, it's your liver." I signaled them to stop. He was gone. We lifted our school bags and went home. I was thinking of the time I lay in bed in Coole, while the bully was taunting my family about the cripple in the cripple's home for life.

Next morning it was still very cold. I had just started the fire in the school when Magee walked in and stood in front of the fire to warm himself. We were silent. I took an apple out of my pocket and offered it to him. He took the apple and began to eat it ravenously. There was no more bullying in the school during the remainder of my time there.

And remember: Love is not love 'til it's given away.

CHAPTER 10

Economic War, Depression and the Ninth Child

The 1930s were depression years for the people of Ireland. The treaty signed by the two countries, Britain and the twenty-six counties of Ireland, made Ireland, except for the six counties in the northeast, a country in the British Commonwealth. This required the government of the new Irish State to take an oath of allegiance to the crown and pay land annuities. When DeValera came to power in 1932, he proceeded to take steps to make the twenty-six counties a sovereign free state. He refused to take the oath of allegiance and the paying of annuities. Britain was horrified and struck back where she knew Ireland could be severely hurt, in the world of trade. Ireland's largest income was from the export of cattle. Britain did two things. One was to place a tariff on the head of every animal coming from Ireland, the other was the placing of a quota on the number of cattle accepted from Ireland. She had other markets. Ireland responded by putting a tariff on all imports from England, that included oil, coal, and manufactured goods. Ireland's imports were much greater than exports. The country was being strangled in an economic war. The price we were receiving for cattle dropped dramatically and the price of imported goods went up severely.

Every time we heard our parents talk with neighbors and friends, the topic of conversation was primarily the economic war. The economy was getting worse and worse. There was no profit in cattle. Often they were sold for less than was paid for them at an earlier date. My father depended on selling cattle for income. He raised some cattle on the home farm and rented land from other farmers. He stocked that land with cattle, hoping to make a profit when he would sell. He saved money, especially during the years when he was a bachelor. Now, not only could he not save, but he was eating up his reserves. As I heard him say to my mother, we are heading for hard times if things do not change. Our income has dried up and our reserves are being eaten up. With a large family and all the children getting bigger and eating more and frequently needing new clothes, my father and mother talked about this frequently, not wanting the children to be concerned but we heard it because the kitchen was where we lived, ate our meals, sat around the fire and did our homework by the light of paraffin lamps. Many families in the area had no reserves to fall back on and had no income from their land. Some farmers did not have the money to stock their land with animals and rented it to others at a very low price. In this way they got some money to feed their children. People who owned no land and were not employed got a small dole.

Unemployment was on the rise because of the growing shortage of money in the country. Many farmers helped those in need by sharing the produce of the land. The numbers of young people leaving the country looking for work increased rapidly. It had become difficult to get into America because a strict quota had been established there. Most who emigrated went to Britain to work wherever they could, very often in construction, factories, hospitals and other institutions. In most cases they sent money back home regularly to help their families get through hard times.

When we visited one of my mother's younger sisters, Theresa, and her husband, Paddy Lynn and their children, the foremost topic of conversation was the economic war. How did the government get us into it, and will they be able to get us out of it? The situation seemed hopeless, with no signs in sight of it ever getting better. Paddy Lynn was also a farmer and shared with my father the concern they had in providing for their families in such trying times.

Paddy and Theresa had three sons, Patsy, Sean and Michael. The last time we visited them Theresa was expecting her fourth child. She was much taller than my mother with a beautiful face and smile and a friendly outgoing personality. I remember her coming with two children, cycling the six miles to our house, one boy on the front of the bicycle and the other on the back. Now on our last visit she was near her due date with the fourth child. Being tall and thin she looked really big with child as she worked in her kitchen, helped by my mother, preparing Sunday dinner for all of us. My mother, who had given birth to eight children, was telling her sister Theresa how well she looked, and encouraging her on the upcoming birth. As we got into the trap to head home we waved saying goodbye and best wishes not knowing the terrible time Theresa had ahead of her.

Uncle Mike came to our house on his motor bike to tell us Theresa gave birth to a baby boy. The boy was fine but Theresa was critical and in great danger of dying. He did not know just what went wrong. Mother and father got us all together to pray. Theresa did die. Paddy Lynn was overwhelmed with deepest sorrow. He had lost his wife and the mother of his four sons, the youngest a newborn infant. I remember being at Aunt Theresa's funeral. They buried her in Welshestown graveyard alongside the road to Mullingar so that we could all visit her grave as we passed by. Many a time I got off my bicycle and visited her grave. My mother was grief stricken over the death of her sister, Theresa, and we all shared in the great sorrow.

Paddy Lynn decided he could not take care of the new baby. Without previous notification he arrived one day at our house with his horse and trap and a nurse holding the infant in her arms. He drove the horse into the front yard, took the infant from the nurse, walked into our house with his baby in his arms and presented him to my mother, saying, "Here, Mary Ellen, you are the best person to rear this baby." My mother now had the baby in her arms. She pressed the baby tenderly to her heart and whispered to him. "I love you. You look like Theresa, your mother, and you'll always remind me of her." Paddy Lynn, the father, began to leave. As he walked out the door mother said, "Aren't you going to wait and speak to Bernard? He is out in the fields. I will send one of the children out for him." "No", he said, "I came at this time because I did not want to face Bernard." So he got into his trap and drove off, leaving his baby in my mother's arms.

We brought the news to father at work. He stopped what he was doing and came in from the fields. His rugged appearance made a striking contrast with the frail looking baby who was very quiet through it all and did not cry. Father was tall, his face weather beaten from exposure to the elements in all seasons all his life. He wore a thick mustache and his hair was black, his eyes kindly and he walked erect. Mother, holding the baby in her arms said, "Paddy Lynn was here and he left the baby with us. He took off saying he did not want to see you."

My father looked around at all of us filling the kitchen. Then he reached out his strong, toil-warn right hand and grasped the baby's chubby little white hand gently, looked intently at him and said, "You are welcome to our home." We were all happy. That baby was number nine.

And remember: Love is not love 'til it's given away.

CHAPTER 11

Secondary Boarding School and War

During my last year in Empor school my parents and I are looking for a secondary school (high school). Being so far out in the country and there being no busing to any of the schools it would be necessary to go to a boarding school. My mother's sister, Lilly, was a nun in the Passionist order, teaching in an elementary school in Belfast. She recommended going to their boarding secondary school there. I was accepted.

Leaving Empor School was not marked by any celebration whatsoever. That is the way things were in those days. Some students had quit early and some stopped during the final year to help on their family farms. Those of us who stayed until the last day exchanged good wishes for the future. The girl I liked best said to me, "You did a lot for this school in putting an end to the bullying." There were tears in her eyes. This moved me. Friendships were not tolerated at that age. It was a relief leaving that school. There were many memories, the good ones and the not so good ones. We had a long free summer ahead of us with time to enjoy everything and time to think before leaving home again and going away to boarding school. Every time I thought about leaving home again there was something inside of me resisted the idea. Maybe it was because I suffered in so many ways while being away from home and maybe because I was so happy to be home and free from illness, confinement and suffering. Still, I could not give in and say, "I am not going." Father and mother kept telling us we would all have to leave home and make our own way in life. They pointed out large families where they all stayed around and then were disappointed with themselves later, admitting they should have moved out earlier. Mother was even more emphatic than father. "You all have to move out on your own as young as possible and don't be staying around because there is no future for you here." Representatives from mission countries sometimes visited secondary schools looking for students who would like to study for the missions.

In each diocese some future priests came out of their secondary schools. In each order some future priests came out of their secondary school. It was always a small minority who were able to make that final decision. I was asked if I had the intention of becoming a priest. I answered that I had thought of it but was not able to make a decision.

It was a nice, warm summer. We were out in the fields and down by the river every day. We made hay and fished and swam in the river. On Sundays we had friends from farms in the area who would join us at the river. Our grazing fields had the best access. The ground was firm up to the river's edge and the grass was eaten tight to the ground by all the animals. Sometimes we brought the gramophone down to the riverbank and played records while some danced around and some sat around or fished. It always came time to bring home the cows and milk them. We all helped in all the work, milking and churning, sowing and reaping and every task that every day presented to be done. My father hired some men at the very busy times. I always admired the way they wielded the scythe. There were areas of meadow where the horses and machines could not go. These areas were cut with a scythe. One day while I was talking to the workman, Joe, admiring his skill with the scythe, he uncovered a bee's nest.

He said, "Keep still. Don't move." The bees were all excited, flying up and down and around in circles, buzzing and buzzing and we were standing close by, still and silent. After several minutes he slowly stuck the tip of the scythe blade into the nest and moved away slowly with me following him. I kept looking back, the bees remained circling the area where the nest was. Not one of them followed us. When we had gone a safe distance we stood under a tree. Joe opened up the bee's nest, broke open the combs and sucked out the wild honey. He gave me some. It was delicious.

The time came to leave home and go to the boarding secondary school. I said good-bye to the family. Mother kissed me and cried. Father said, "You'll do well." The school was in Belfast so there were three legs to the journey, an early morning bus to Mullingar, a train from there to Dublin and a train from there to Belfast. The whole journey took a day. By previous arrangement I met some of the students in Dublin so we are together on the train to Belfast. Charlie seemed to be the leader of the group. Among others were Bill, Joe,

Ray and Kevin. They were in the different grades from freshmen to seniors. The school had sports; soccer and tennis and handball. They had nicknames for all the teachers and even mimicked the way some of them talked. After one day of orientation we started classes.

The curriculum included five languages; English, Irish, Latin, Greek and French. It was quite a challenge. Classes went from morning to afternoon. There were four hours of supervised study in the late afternoons and evening. The students who had attended Christian Brothers schools in cities and towns were ahead of those of us from the country. I worked hard to catch up and was fortunate to pass every exam all the way through. Some left because they found the going too difficult. The doctor had recommended I not play football because of the leg. I enjoyed playing tennis and handball. Some of the students were homesick for the first few days. One was so bad he asked to go home. His parents came and got him. I felt homesick and missed home terribly. I did not tell anyone. It went away in a few days.

The Second World War was raging. The master had talked to us in Empor School on how Hitler was persecuting and killing the Jewish people. We were all horrified and my parents prayed for them every night as we knelt around the hearth. Now I was closer to the war because the north of Ireland was officially part of England. So we were at war. What made us most aware that war was going on was the presence of so many soldiers everywhere, British and American. The north of Ireland was designated by the allies as a special training ground for the invasion of France, now occupied by the Germans. There was a strict blackout every night and exercises with sirens sounding in preparation for air raids. There were shelters built and people trained in what to do during air raids. England had been bombed heavily every night but Belfast was spared so far.

Another reminder of the war was the food rationing. Meat and dairy products were very severely rationed as was tea, coffee and sugar. We did not get a straight cut of beef or lamb or pork that could be recognized as such. All meat we got was processed and had other foods mixed in. The first Sunday we were served a slab of processed meat. No one knew what was in it. Some of the students from the north who seemed to know better than those of us from south of the border said it was horsemeat after we had eaten it. I doubted if they really knew. The Irish did not like the idea of eating a horse. Horses were our friends and companions for riding and working.

There was no butter, just margarine. I had eaten only butter, home produced on the farm but never had tasted margarine. This margarine did not taste very good. We were so hungry we ate what they gave us. The bread was white shop bread only. No home baked wheaten bread like what my mother baked which we ate with the delicious butter she made. Breakfast was always the same; white shop bread and margarine and tea, never any porridge or eggs or bacon. Everyone was told to help the war effort. That bad diet harmed my health for a long time.

Christmas holidays came. We were so happy to get away and go home for a break. It was so good to be back with the family. They all welcomed me home, even the dog, Finn, showed his welcome in his own expressive and inimitable way. I brought home the exam papers for the end of the first term. The family was very impressed with the questions in Latin, Greek and French, Brian looked at them and was astounded. "You learned all that in such a short time! I would rather be looking at a bullock than looking at a book." A letter came from the school with a report card. My parents were very pleased with the marks and the remarks. I overheard them telling neighbors outside of church. Uncle Mike came to visit on his motorbike. Mother showed him the report card. He did not just read it, he studied it. Then he said kind words of encouragement, which he always did with me. The holidays passed too quickly and it was back to school.

School life proceeded normally except that there was a war on. The air raid sirens sounded nearly every day. Sometimes they were a practice and at other times false alarms. People would run to the shelters and wait there until the all clear sounded. At the school a concrete storage room which had already been added to the main building was converted to a shelter. Sandbags were stacked up against it all around. That was where we went when the sirens sounded.

On our walks, which were mandatory, we could see big balloons with cable attached moored to bases. These were released and let go up, when the sirens sounded, to prevent the enemy aircraft from flying low over the city. There were troops on maneuvers and camouflaged trucks on the move everywhere. There were transport seaplanes on the large lakes of Lough Erne in the ancient McGuire country. Soldiers on foot crossed farms and hills, stooped down behind hedges and embankments so as not to be seen. Observing from a roadside one day I heard a loudspeaker voice shout out, "Keep down, I can see you silhouetted against the sky."

The industrial cities in England were being bombed almost every night. Belfast was expecting to be bombed and indeed it was. First there were short periods of bombing. The sirens would go off and we would go to the shelter. The first time we did not know what to expect. We could hear the anti-aircraft guns, their shells exploding high up where the planes were flying. Then we could hear the louder sounds of the bombs exploding. It did not last long and we got the all clear. We went outside to look. The school was on an elevated area in the suburbs so we could look down into the city. There were fires burning in the shipyards on the Lagan River. The flames were leaping up into the sky. The main objectives of the bombing were the shipyards of Harold and Wolff. A lot of very significant shipbuilding went on there. Belfast Shipyards was where the ill-fated Titanic was built. It was very strategic to the allies. There were several of these short periods of bombing going on for a couple of months or so. School life went on as usual. Then there was an all night big one. A few of us were walking in the grounds after supper when suddenly a high light like a massive star began to light up the sky over the city, then another one and another one. While we were wondering what they were the air raid sirens sounded. They were flares dropped by the enemy to light up the city in preparation for bombing. By the time we got into the shelter the bombing had begun and the anti-aircraft guns were firing shells. This was an intense air raid. We could hear the planes. They came in waves one after another all night. Every time it eased off and we hoped it was over it started up again. We prayed for the people, especially for the children who were going through this terrible and shocking experience. The quiet inside the shelter could be sensed in between the bombing waves. Some factories close to us were bombed. Next morning an unexploded land mine was found on one of our handball alleys. When it was all over we went outside. There were fires all over the city with the largest concentration in the shipyards. The fires and smoke blurred the morning sky while the first light of dawn on a golden horizon was appearing in the eastern sky. It was a real contrast of horror and peace reflected in the same sky, telling us God's good creation will go on in spite of man's evil efforts to destroy it.

Life was badly disrupted in the city. The authorities decided to close the schools for awhile. We were all sent home. We missed about six weeks of school. I helped on the farm, fished in the river and lived the life I had been used to at home. The bombing of London was very bad. My father gave me money to wire to Mary Jo telling her to come home for her safety. I cycled to Ballynacargy and wired the money to her and she came home. We were all home now except for Cissie who was in the convent in Kilcullen. The Irish Free State remained neutral during the war. Food was plentiful with no rationing. All the surplus food was sold to Britain and they could not get enough.

Germany was now fighting the Allies on several fronts and also fighting Russia. The bombing of the cities in England and Northern Ireland stopped. We went back to school in September and the school life went ahead as if nothing happened. There was a severe shortage of petrol and diesel fuel. Ireland depended on England for its oil which was severely rationed. Public transportation was hard hit. Getting from home to Belfast was now taking me two days. There was no bus from Ballymahon to Mullingar so Brian came with me as we cycled with the luggage on the backs of the bikes. I would spend the night in a rooming house in Mullingar to be ready for an early morning train or bus. Brian would take the two bikes home, riding one and steering it with one hand while steering the other bike with the other hand.

The final year at the school was a time of intense study. Students from that school went to Dublin University to do the final exams. The English teacher who was familiar with the place used to tease me saying the windows at the university were so big I would enjoy looking out through them. When I was thinking, I would look out the windows which bothered him. I told him it helped me to think. He said, "Why don't you go outside and walk around in circles like the Greek philosophers who were known as the peripatetics. You know you will be spending three hours in the morning and three hours in the afternoon doing written exams for more than a week. Don't waste time looking out the windows." I knew it was my longing for the great outdoors where I could always think best.

I am recalling the time in history class as a student when we were listening to a lecture on the crusades. We were told the Pope called on the Christian countries of Europe to go to the Holy Land and take back the holy places from the infidel. The Muslims occupied the holy places. Christians called them the infidel, while the Muslims called the Christians infidels. My imagination was picturing what was happening.

One of the Christian fighting groups formed was the Knights Templar, named after the temple of Solomon. I could see this Templar walking toward what was left of the temple of Solomon, dressed in his knight's uniform, with sword and shield on the ready. Suddenly, a Muslim appears, with his sword and shield on the ready.

> The Templar asks, "Who are you?"
> The Muslim answers, "I am a Muslim."
> The Muslim asks, "Who are you?"
> The Templar answers, "I am a Christian."

The Muslim says, "You are the infidel."
The Templar says, "You are the infidel."
Back and forth they called each other infidels.
The Templar shouted, "I have to kill the infidel, then I'll go to heaven."
The Muslim shouted, "I have to kill the infidel, then I'll go to heaven."
The Templar shouted, "Which infidel is going to heaven first?"

And remember: Love is not love 'til it's given away.

CHAPTER 12

Deciding the Future

While enduring the pressure of study and sexual maturing I was trying to decide on the future. My spiritual director said he discerned qualities suitable for priesthood but emphasized I had to feel the call from within. "Do you take time to listen to the Spirit of God? I can recognize gifts he has already given you; the gifts of forgiving, reconciling, concern and reaching out to others in need; the gift of speaking so that you could preach his word. Even if you are not called you are expected to use the gifts God has given you." He always ended by saying, "Pray for guidance." I had been praying for guidance for years now. At times I felt God was calling me to priesthood.

At such times something inside me would recoil and ideas of other professions which were not as demanding could come to mind. Paddy, a neighbor went into banking. He is a fine man and comes home regularly in his own car and with a girlfriend. He encouraged me to try for the bank, saying I would have no problem for the entrance exams were easy and they give you a good training. Another profession that would come to mind to block out the ideas of priesthood was business. You could be like Uncle Mike. He was a nice man and apparently happy with what he was doing. He drove a motorbike which he preferred to a car. He would get a girlfriend when ready to get married. A very strong case was made in my mind to become a surgeon like the man who operated on my leg. I would like to help all the children in the world who were suffering like I did from osteomyelitis. The hope of becoming a doctor would wane as I was sure my parents would not be willing to pay the high expenses involved. They had the money, but the family was big and times were hard. They felt the best way to spend money was to buy more land. This was a disappointing thought because a doctor can do great things for others and at the same time have a wife and family of his own. Also when I would make money I could help the family in every way possible especially in paying for the education of my younger brothers and sister. Thoughts of becoming a schoolteacher would come to my mind. I would love to educate children without punishment and without bullies. I would be so vigilant that no bully could exist in my school. All this would be possible and still have a wife and family.

While all these ideas about other professions kept coming and going in my mind, the thought of being called to priesthood would rise inside me. I could not find it within my heart to say yes because I was not able to give up a future with a wife and family. I did not have the ability within me to say yes, so I could not do it. The sexual attractions and feelings continued unabated.

Even though our school was in the North of Ireland, we sat our final exams in the study hall at Dublin University. My results were what I had hoped and prayed for. The school was pleased and I was happy. Some did not qualify for entrance to a university and they had to do another year or drop out altogether. I felt bad for them, especially for Joe who was a good friend. He got tuberculosis and I visited him in a sanitarium. He did not make it.

People who entered the religious life, priesthood or ministry would say they answered the call. Who was doing the calling? God, other priests or religious, or the people? Ministry would be to the people, so they should be doing the calling. Any one of them would say God is doing the calling. God called the prophets. When he said, "Samuel, Samuel" Samuel answered and said, "Speak Lord, your servant is listening." After God called them he sent them to bring his message to the people. Christ called his disciples, "Come, follow me." Then he sent them to bring his message to the people. I think God may be calling me, but I don't hear his voice with my physical ears. Those, who claim they know, tell me you hear his voice in your soul or spirit. God is spirit and can communicate with our spirits without the sound of words. If you think you hear voices people will think you are going crazy.

How can I know God is calling me by speaking to my spirit, my soul? Father Herbert came to our parish. I asked him about this. He explained that there are signs to look out for. First there may be an awareness in the mind that God may be calling. The soul or spirit works through the mind. You probably dismiss the thought, thinking this is not for me. If you are able to put it out of your mind and not think of it anymore, then that is that. If the thought and awareness comes back again and again, in peaceful, quiet moments, it may be

God calling. After dismissing it many times over a considerable period of time and it still keeps coming back peacefully, you give it some attention and begin to wonder if it is true that God is calling. Then you begin to consider, if this is so, what is the price to pay here and what is it all going to be like. This is when there is vacillating back and forth. On the one hand, thinking this is a great honor from God to be called by him to come closer, he be filled with the spirit and go to serve his people. On the other hand, thoughts of how much has to be given up occupy the mind and there is possibly a long period of weighing up and indecision. In some, but not all cases, this can go on for years before a final decision is made. Father Herbert told me the priesthood is a life of sacrifice.

Father Herbert emphasized two things. The priesthood is a life of sacrifice and number two, don't try it unless you are absolutely wholehearted about it. He emphasized two words, sacrifice and wholeheartedness. "You will be expected to make sacrifices, to put the interests and good of others before your own. Making sacrifices is the greatest proof of love. See how parents will sacrifice for their children. It is well known for a mother to pray that God would take her instead of her child suffering from an incurable illness. Christ is the greatest model and example of sacrifice. Greater love no one hath than to lay down his life for his friends. Christ was totally given to the father for us. He looked for nothing for himself. He did not marry and he died willingly on the cross as a sacrifice to the father for us. When he calls someone to priesthood he calls him to be like himself, and be willing to make sacrifices. Some are given the grace and are able to do it. Some are not." I said, "Sometimes I think I am able to do it and at other times I am doubtful and would like to run away from it." He said, "Then you are not ready, but God may give you the special grace you will need if he wants you to be a priest."

I said, "The sacrifices I find difficult or impossible to make is to give up the right to have a wife and children. I think I would be well suited for that and very successful." He said, "You are probably right, keep praying for guidance and be true to God and his grace." It was an agonizing time. There was a conflict going on in my mind. What if God is calling me to the priesthood and I turn away and listen to the daily temptation to forget about the possible call and go for some other profession. This back and forth tug of war was going on in my life all through secondary school. One day one was winning, the next day the other was winning. Fr. Herbert was guiding me away from some wrong ideas that were expressed in some writings on vocations. "Marriage is God given and good; a great sacrament. Sex is God given and good. It is the abuse of this gift that is sinful. You are not turning your back on a sinful world. There is more good than evil in the world. The call to priesthood is a call to follow Christ, the priest, and to total dedication in a life of sacrifice. He who gave himself in the supreme sacrifice on the cross will give you the grace to make whatever sacrifices are required to be in his place for others, to be as it were, another Christ. Man and woman were created good. Human nature is not sinful but subject to temptation and under the pressure of temptation which is a trial, human nature which is weak, can strive and overcome or give in and sin. With the amount of sin in the world it is easy to think human nature is sinful. Pray for the wisdom to discover God's call and the grace to be wholehearted in response."

The thought of postponing everything frequently occurred to me. Put it all out of your mind and follow another career. Later on you could decide. While alone and thinking, an awareness that God was calling me would return. Try as I might I could not put it out of my mind. If anything, the awareness was becoming stronger, but I still did not have it in my heart to say yes, I can do it.

The parish priest announced we were having the forty hours adoration in the church. He left a sheet of paper at the back for people to sign up for an hour so that there would be the required number of people there during the entire time of adoration. He also asked parishioners to bring flowers to decorate the altar for the adoration. Mother signed up for an hour and cut flowers from the garden. I was given the job of bringing the flowers on my bicycle. Then when the adoration started and mother's hour was coming up she said she had just put bread in the oven and would I take her place. I cycled to the church and went in. The altar was beautifully decorated with flowers right down to the floor in front. There were a few parishioners kneeling in the pews. The place was silent. I knelt down and prayed and listened. I humbly asked God for guidance to know what decision I should make and what would be most pleasing to him. It was a struggle to pray and keep from daydreaming. God was invisible. I was looking at the Blessed Sacrament in the monstrance on the altar and praying to Jesus. I believed but felt blank. What is happening to my prayers? They seemed to be coming back to me like I was talking silently to myself. I wanted to do what God wanted and indeed to do what would be most pleasing to him. Feeling so dry and empty how was I to know for sure.

As the hour was up the parishioners who were present left one by one and I was left alone. Those who were signed up for the next hour had not come. I stayed there and some time passed and no one came yet. The priest had said not to leave the Blessed Sacrament alone. Parishioners should be present all the time during the forty hours adoration, preferably more than one. Now I was the only one; the Lord and I. No one came and it became evident I was having to do the two hours. I prayed the same prayer over and over again, asking God for the wisdom to discern what his call for me was and the grace to be wholehearted in my response. I thought of Jesus praying in the garden, "Father, not my will but thine be done." There was something comforting about being alone there with the Lord but all I heard was the silence, a silence that embraced my soul but I could not hear any message. I was thinking of heaven. What was it like? The ladies who decorated the altar said it was heavenly. I spoke in my mind to all the members of our family there; my grandparents, uncles and aunts and others and asked them to intercede for me that I might make the right decision. The war was on. There was terrible suffering and killing. I prayed for all the suffering people and for a peaceful end to the war. I looked at the Blessed Sacrament. I prayed and prayed, felt peaceful and comforted but did not feel wholehearted about a decision. The more I prayed the greater the tug of war going on inside me. I reflected on the fact that this had been going on for some time and I did not seem to be getting anywhere. One day I leaned strongly to one side and the next day just as strongly to the other side.

The second hour was up. Three parishioners came in a side door and knelt down. I got up and while walking back to the main door I glanced across to the side aisle. One who had come in was the bully. I was happy to see him and said a prayer. Brian told me later he had changed and had become a responsible young man. They were all waiting for me when I got home and greeted me with many questions: Where did you go? What did you do? What kept you so long?

While struggling in my mind with thoughts and tensions pulling me in different directions I found this well described in the poem on the *Hound of Heaven* written by Francis Thompson.

> I fled Him down the nights and down the days
> I fled Him down the arches of the years
> I fled Him down the labyrinthine ways
> Of my own mind, and in the midst of tears
> I hid from him, and under running laughter
> Up vistaed hopes I sped;
> And shot precipitated
> Adown titanic glooms of chasm'd fears

From those strong feet that followed, followed after
But with unhurrying chase
And unperturbed pace,
Deliberate speed, majestic instancy
They beat, and a voice beat,
More instant than the feet:
"All things betray thee who betrayest me."

I pleaded, outlaw-wise,
By many a hearted casement, curtained red,
Trellised with inter-twining charities,
(For though I knew His love who followed,
Yet was I sore adread,
Lest having Him, I should have nought beside);

This last line summed up just how I was thinking and feeling.

Sitting by the riverbank and watching the water flow gently by, thoughts came to me about what decision I should make. I tried to put them out of my mind and watch two beautiful white swans fly low over the river. A long beaked curlew glided and circled overhead calling out curlew, curlew. The skylark came running on the grass, stopped and then sprung into the air singing. He repeated the familiar pattern of rising in stages and singing until he disappeared into the blue. I walked along the riverbank enjoying the reflection of sky and clouds. The thought that God was calling me filled my mind. I was saying to God deep inside me, I can do it, become a priest. There was no hesitation about it this time. I felt it was for sure. There was a sense of relief and peace and victory. It was kind of unbelievable after going through so much that the struggle and tug-of-war seemed to have gone. I felt that was a most important moment in my life when I could say without hesitation, "Yes, Lord, I can do it." This was a decision God enabled me to make and I thanked him. I felt like a bird freed from a snare. A burden was lifted off my mind. I had clear vision and not in the dark any longer. It was a definitive decision with a strong sense of God's presence.

When I told Fr. Herbert he said it looked genuine. "You are at peace with this decision." I said "yes." He said, "This is only the beginning; there is a long road ahead of you. Don't think all temptations of the flesh and troublesome thoughts will go away. They won't. If this is a genuine call and you cooperate, God's grace will prevail and you will succeed."

I told my mother of the decision to be a priest. She said, "Are you quite sure you want to do this? It is a very serious decision and it is for life." I said yes. In our conversation she gave me the impression she has mixed feelings, she was proud of me and still she was concerned for me in what this decision involved. There also seemed to be something in her mind indicating she was happy to be giving a son to the church when he could have helped the younger children. She was not explicit on this but I somehow gathered it from what she did say.

When I told my father he did not seem to be surprised and said, "If that is what you want I will not stand in your way. It is your decision and I don't want to put pressure on you either way. You are a survivor and brave. I have confidence in you." Talking to a group around my age while visiting at a neighbor's house I said I was going to study for the priesthood. Mike said, "I'm not surprised." Pat who was crazy about girls said, "How could you live without girls?" Bill said, "That's a lot of study for a lot of years. I wouldn't try that." The others laughed at him, where do you keep your brains? I asked about the girl who encouraged me to fight the bully. Her family moved and we heard she went away to be a nun. I felt proud of her that she had made that decision. But there was a silent aloneness deep within me. Why should I feel a void in my life? I hoped she would be happy.

Preparing to leave for the novitiate and seminary, I had a strong awareness that I was leaving the family tradition of farming and embarking on a very different road. I felt lonely, going to miss the family and the daily support the members gave me, the family circle of love and belonging, the strong invisible bonds that knit us all together, sharing work and meals, sitting round the hearth with stories and humor, listening and talking and joking and teasing, enjoying life and laughter together. Taking off from such strong nurturing surroundings was painful. But, I must go. I feel God calling me and He is winning.

Brian and Frank and I worked close together with my father before I left for boarding secondary school and during the holidays home, especially the long summers. Frank was very attached to Dad and preferred to stay with him, always finding something to do, rather than come fishing with Brian and me. Brian, being the oldest boy became very involved in the farming. He liked working with horses and would follow them all day long with his hands on the shafts of the plough with a long reins in each hand to guide the horses ploughing a furrow straight as an arrow, of which he was very proud, and enjoying the natural good smell of the fresh turned earth. He was a true child of nature and wanted to stay close to nature all his life.

While clipping a whitethorn hedge behind the house my thoughts are running free. I am now eighteen, tall and strong. This is a turning point in my life. I love the farm and farming. All of nature appealed to me. I know this world of fields and cattle, horses and sheep, the mystery of growth and crops, the fascinating river, the open skies and the singing birds. Something inside me is saying: you belong here, you should stay on the land, find a way, work hard, save money, Dad will help you buy land of your own.

My thoughts were changed by the sound of the church bell in Legan across the river tolling the call to the evening angelus prayer. The cows having grazed on lush grass all day were heading home with udders swollen full, now lowing for relief by milking. Brian, after following the plough and horses all day, came in from the fields. It all brought to my mind how masterfully the poet, Thomas Gray described a similar scene when he wrote his elegy in a country churchyard,

> "The curfew tolls the knell of parting day
> the lowing herd winds slowly or'e the lee
> the ploughman homeward plods his weary way.
> And leaves the world to darkness and to me."

Since the three of us, Brian, myself and Frank came one after another in a row, three boys, we worked and played closely together. Frank decided to stay at home on the farm with Brian. He had done well at school but did not show an interest in going to a secondary boarding school. He spoke about becoming a priest but did not pursue the idea. I always liked talking with him. He was a good listener and had the knack of keeping a conversation going. He was strong. Work came easy to him. He saw humor in simple things and had a hearty laugh. It looked like Brian and Frank, staying on the farm were following in the steps of my father and uncle Larry who stayed on together on the farm, worked hard and saved, planning to buy another farm and have wives and families. Uncle Larry died of pneumonia and my father was left, the only boy. Brian and Frank bought more farms and both of them married and had families. The three youngest Vera, Celine and Mike and Tony Lynn were all now walking to Empor School every day. I was going to miss them but they did not understand the importance of the step I was taking. Mother and Father showed great confidence in me and encouraged me. At the same time they admitted they were going to miss me and felt bad that I would not get home for the holidays for such a long time.

And remember: Love is not love 'til it's given away.

CHAPTER 13

Novitiate—A Spiritual Year

We knew from other students that the novitiate year started in the second week in September every year. I was expecting to be home up until that time. We all worked at the haymaking all summer. We fished in the river in the long evenings, there being twilight as late as eleven in the evening. The grouse shooting season opened on the twelfth of August. This date was referred to as "the glorious twelfth." Brian and I looked forward to shooting grouse on that day. When it came, we rowed across the river, taking Finn with us and went through the bog on the other side in county Langford. There were plenty of grouse there. They called a lot to one another. We could hear them calling while in the yard at our house. I practiced imitating them and was able to get their attention and have them come near me while hiding in the heather. On the glorious twelfth we had a very exciting day and came home with a nice bag of grouse. Mother cooked them with the traditional family recipe. Everyone in the family enjoyed them and thought they were the greatest.

Uncle Barney, one of my mother's brothers and his wife, Nora, came to spend a few days with us. Barney asked me to take him grouse shooting. He did not use a gun, but just wanted to accompany me. While we walked through the bog, Finn got busy on the scent. He circled around excitedly for a while and then a sudden burst of sound and flutter of wings as a covey of grouse erupted from the heather. I took one with each barrel and Finn retrieved them. Uncle Barney was proud coming home with a lovely grouse hanging by the feet from each hand. As we came into the kitchen, everyone was happy to see the beautiful grouse. Then mother took a letter from a shelf on the dresser where the dinner plates were standing, leaning against the back, and said, "The postman was here a short while ago and delivered this letter for you from the Passionists in the novitiate at the Graan in Ennskillen. I opened it." All letters that came to the house were opened. There were no secrets. She continued as she handed me the letter, "They want you to be there on August eighteenth. That is less than a week from now. We thought we would have you for longer than that before you would leave." I read the short letter and handed it back to her without comment. As I walked up into the parlor to leave the gun back where it belonged, and Finn was at my heels to see that I was really leaving the gun there, I felt disappointed that the Passionist superiors had made this decision and wrote this letter. When accepted to join the order I was told the first year, called the Novitiate year, would begin at the end of September. Now I had only five days to say goodbye to my extended family, the many friends and the world. I found it difficult to leave. Even though it was disappointing not having more time before leaving, my decision was so strong that there was no consideration for any thoughts about hesitating or turning back; but the thoughts and temptations to choose an easier life never went away completely. These temptations grew stronger at this time, while preparing to take this very important first step. Father Herbert was very helpful, praying with me and the family, expressing his confidence in me and at the same time assuring me he would, of course, understand if I should leave the monastery and return home. My father and mother had expressed the same thoughts to me, and at the same time they had assured me that they supported me fully in my decision. While up in the parlor leaving the gun away I overheard Aunt Nora in the kitchen saying, "Shane is such a calm boy, he took it very well, that disappointment and showed no signs of resentment. I am very impressed with him." These words stuck in my mind and never to be forgotten, as I came back from the parlor into the kitchen for dinner.

    The order did not allow the students to go home for the seven years until ordination. Those years included the novitiate year, philosophy and theology. We would be ordained during the final year of theology and finish the studies afterwards. So it would be a long time without getting home and this saddened me. There never had been a priest in my father's family. On my mother's side, there was a priest about four generations back, but no one living remembered him. I went around on a bicycle and visited my relatives and friends to say goodbye. They all seemed impressed with what I was doing and gave me varying degrees of encouragement. Uncle Mike gave me enthusiastic support and had great confidence in me, which was encouraging. All the other uncles and aunts and the McGuire cousins at the green were very positive and helpful. Aunt Angela's husband thought I was making a big mistake and would regret it. My brothers and sisters reported remarks of some who thought it was a waste of a promising young life. I had gone through such a long process of decision-making that I felt quite secure about the direction I was going in. I did have concern about the sacrifices that lay ahead and prayed for the grace to succeed.

The day before leaving home I helped in the fields with the cutting of the oats and the tying of the sheaves. Brian and Frank and I worked together with my father. We finished early and I said I wanted to walk along the riverbank. Brian and Frank came with me. As I recall, they had little to say. The river winding and flowing through the fields looked more beautiful and peaceful than ever. There was a flock of white swans on the river. They were just sitting there watching us. We went to the skylark's favorite place and sat down for a rest. In a little while he appeared and sprang into the air singing as usual, going higher and higher until he vanished into the blue. Brian said to me you always made time to come down here by the river and fish and watch the birds, especially listening to the skylark singing. Frank said we always had too much work to do to take the time to enjoy this, but it is very enjoyable and peaceful.

The day came for me to leave. We all had breakfast together and then it was the time to say goodbye. We all stood in the kitchen. We were all crying, including my father. He choked up as he held my two hands in his and managed to say: remember if you ever want to come back you will be welcome here. My sisters kissed me and my brothers shook my hands. All were emotional. Mother embraced me and kissed me and I felt her warm tears on my face. She walked beside me out to the front yard where Brian had the horse and trap ready to take me to the high road and catch the bus for Mullingar. Mother is anxiously asking me questions. "Do you have the money with you for the bus and train tickets? You remember where to change trains for Enniskillen?" Brian: "We should go or we will miss the bus." A final embrace and kiss from mother and all waved and shouted, "Good luck" as the horse trotted out of the yard. We kept waving back and forth until we were out of sight of one another.

The novitiate house was known as the Graan, located about three miles outside the town of Enniskillen in the county of Fermanagh. I arrived by taxi and rang the bell on the front door. A brother opened the door. When I told him who I was he said, "I'll get the novice-master." In a few moments a middle-aged priest came into the waiting room. He put out his hand and said, "I am the novice-master and you are?" "I am Shane McGuire." "Oh yes," he said, "You are a new novice. I welcome you. We are expecting six candidates and you are the first one to arrive. Let me take you to your cell." At the secondary school we slept in dormitories. Now, as novices, each would have his own room referred to as a cell. It was a small room, with a bed and table. The bathrooms were at the end of the corridor. He said, "you can go outside with Brother Steven and he will show you around."

There was the main building where the professed priests and brothers lived. It was a long, three story, stone building with the novitiate wing of similar structure attached. There was a very nice public church and a private choir chapel, where the community chanted the divine office of psalms, readings and prayers at the different canonical hours of the day. There was a large farm with green fields, rolling hills and clusters of tall trees. There was a land steward who lived in a house on the property, and workmen who came in every day from the surrounding area.

When I looked out my cell window I could see lawns close to the building, and then a large field with cows and horses grazing. It had some similarity to the countryside I had left at home, but there was no river to be seen. Brother Steven told me the river Erne and Lough Erne were not far away, and reminded me of what I already knew very well, that Fermanagh was the McGuire part of Ireland in the olden times, and I must see McGuire's castle on the shores of Lough Erne in Enniskillen.

There were seven of us. Each was given a new name as a sign we were starting a new life. I got the name David. So I was called Brother David and after ordination, Father David. When I transferred from the order to parish ministry in the United States, I went back to my baptismal name, John and became Monsignor John after receiving papal honors.

We went to supper with the whole community. The dining room was called the refectory. The tables were all close to the walls around the room. The members sat with their backs to the walls. This, we were told, came down from the rule of St. Benedict who had all the monks sit with their backs to the wall. In this way no one could stab a monk in the back. There was a rector and vicar in charge of the whole monastery. They sat at one end of the refectory. That was considered the head table. The master of novices sat at the same table. Then the members sat in descending seniority down to the other end of the room. The novices sat at the other end. There were the last in, the last served and the last out.

The next day the master and vice master assembled us in the common room for orientation. The vice master was considerably younger than the master, not long ordained and more of a companion than a superior to the novices. We were given notepaper to write home and tell our families we had arrived. We were told not to seal the envelopes as the letters would be read before mailing and told further that our letters would be read for the rest of our lives in the order. This was the rule of St. Paul of the Cross, the founder, and his rule had to be followed. Some of the novices said nothing about this to the superiors but, among themselves, felt it was an insult for anyone to read a letter to your mother and father. So the letters were handed in unsealed. Letters we received were first opened.

We got plenty of instructions on ringing the bell in turns by the day for all the observances on the horarium, including sounding the rattle (clapper) throughout all the corridors for matins at two o'clock in the morning. We were given breviaries, books for chanting the divine office in Latin, starting with matins and lauds at two in the morning, morning prayer at six, midday prayer, vespers at three and compline at six. There would be time allotted to mental prayer, an hour in the morning and an hour in the evening. Soon we would be given instructions on mental prayer. We were sheltered from the distractions of the world, no radios, no newspapers, silence except at designated time, not even speaking with members of the "professed community", who lived in the main building and whom we joined in choir for prayer and in the refectory for meals. There was silence for everyone at meals. There was reading and all the novices took their turns, one each day. If anyone made a mistake or wrong pronunciation, the master of novices corrected him, and he had to repeat it correctly.

If anyone was guilty of a fault or mistake he had to go on his knees in front of the master at the beginning of supper bearing a black wooden cross on his right shoulder and confess his faults. The master gave him a penance to do. If the fault was not waking up to sound the clapper for matins at two in the morning, then the culprit put a folded blanket over his left shoulder as well as the cross on the right shoulder. After saying grace after supper we processed to the church for more prayers. The culprit would go first and lie prostrate on the floor to one side of the corridor or passageway until all passed by. The master insisted strongly on mortification of the eyes. We had to have our eyes cast down and not look anyone in the face. When speaking with him he told us not to look any higher than the Passionist sign which they all wore on the chest.

The reading at meals on Fridays was from the Holy Rule. The order was started in Italy by St. Paul of the Cross and the rule was written there. Breakfast was to be taken standing, just bread and coffee. All had to wear sandals, all the year round. This was hard in Ireland during the frost and snow. There was an hour for siesta in the afternoon. This was an Italian custom. Later, when living in the mother house in Rome, I found that they served everyone with wine at both lunch and dinner every day. Of course this was not done in Ireland. So we lost our Irish breakfasts and did not get Italian dinners.

We had instructions on the bible and the spiritual life, including the different forms of prayer, mysticism, and the lives of the saints. St. Paul of the Cross had as his distinctive devotion, the passion and death of Christ, hence the name of the order, Passionists. The greatest emphasis during this year was growing in relationship with God through prayer, especially meditation and contemplation. There was little emphasis during this year on mission or being sent to work with people. That would come later. First we had to be formed in a life of union with God. This is what Christ did with His disciples. First He called them. Then He formed them, and finally He sent them to the people. At this point they understood their mission. Some of the professed priests and brothers who had spent time on the foreign missions, told us of their experiences and had many interesting stories to tell. Some who preached missions and retreats in English speaking countries told us of their experiences and shared their stories with us.

Meditation time always began with a call to place ourselves in the presence of God, a reminder that God is always present, but now is the time to concentrate on Him and open ourselves to Him, listening to the Holy Spirit for guidance. There would be a reading of a pre-selected passage of scripture. Then silence and the lights were put out. Sometimes, after the hour of morning meditation, the novice master would call on one of us to give an account of our meditation and how we spent the hour. The rest of us would listen. No one liked to be called. I was always impressed with the response, including my own. Then the master would give some comments and guidance. We were asked to make efforts to live in the presence of God. Part of the daily schedule was time for solitary walk, a half hour before lunch and a half hour after vespers, walking alone in silence, with eyes cast down, reflecting on the presence of God and not saluting others whom we met on the walkways through the gardens. This was refreshing for body and spirit. I learned to reflect on God's presence and His present love for me, not only during solitary walks, but also at other times during the day. Awareness of God's presence would come to me so often that I began to think God was reminding me of His presence. At those times I would make interior acts of love of God and thank God for loving me at this moment. Father, I love You now at this moment and I know You love me at this moment. This is an eternal moment; let it endure. On these solitary walks I would look up into the heavens. This would remind me of the times on the farm when we would rest in the hayfields after having the tea that my mother would send out from the home, brought by my younger brothers and sisters. On one particular afternoon while we lay on the hay looking up into the sky, I commented on the very high thin clouds that looked like goat's hair was strewn across the sky. My father said these were the highest clouds, torn and stretched by high altitude winds until they looked liked goat's hair and not like sheep's wool like the lower clouds. My brother, Frank, wanted to know if God was that high up. My father said, "Yes, and further up." Brian wanted to know what was further up. My father said, "Some heavenly bodies and then infinite space." I asked if there was an end to infinite space and he said, "No." Now, in the monastery garden, I am wondering about infinite space and the infinite God I am speaking to.

Once a week we took a long walk through the beautiful countryside with the vice master. On more than one occasion I tried to engage him in conversation about space and he repeatedly dismissed the idea. My companions also thought it was not practical and had no interest in pursuing such an obsession. On one of these walks we climbed a high hill, by a farm road, to where we could look down on the long stretches of beautiful Lough Erne with so many islands covered with trees. This was McGuire country for centuries. I was thinking of all my ancestors who lived here, looked on this beautiful scene and enjoyed living here. We had walked a long way on that Sunday afternoon. So we sat down on the grass for a rest and an opportunity to talk together. We all talked about the beautiful view and how happy we were to be there. I told the vice master how I was fascinated looking into space. "You are into that space thing again," he said. "What is it that fascinates you?" There were no complaints; everyone was tired and all were listening. I went on to explain that the infinity of space challenged my imagination. He tried to explain that you cannot imagine infinite, because the human mind is finite. I explained that while our mind is finite it can be aware of the infinite. I speak to the infinite God, even though I am finite. Bill said: "We are made in God's image and we all have a spark of the infinite within us. Otherwise we could not even be aware of the infinite." I continued to comment on how we were now looking into infinite space. I loved geometry and had a sense of measuring everything. We cannot measure infinite space. Where is its center? It cannot have a circumference. Does it have a center? And can it have a radius or diameter? It occurs to me that the center of infinite space is me. That is relative to me. Otherwise, for me, where is the center? Does space have a center? And does it have an end? No. What was there before it, before creation? God made everything out of nothing. That is true creation. God fills the universe, but the universe is not God. He is a personal God. Some of the others were now chatting among themselves and making inaudible comments to one another. Father Ned, the vice master, indicated that this discussion was not getting us anywhere and that we should move on. As we walked home we discussed how to live in the presence of God. All things should remind us of His presence, the clouds that float along, the birds that fly and sing, the trees that grow, the animals that graze in the fields, and our walking and talking together. Father Ned said that when we remember God's presence we should thank Him and tell Him silently in our hearts that we love Him. Even without the awareness of life all around us, the thought of God's presence comes to us, we don't know from where. As we strive to live in the presence of God, He gives us the grace to succeed for He gives us the good intentions and the good desires. As we entered the monastery the bell was ringing, calling us to chant the praises of God.

I found great joy and peace in being aware of the presence of God and praying to Him silently for everyone in the whole world, no matter who they were. I felt being called to help build the kingdom of love and peace for all people. I looked forward each day to the solitary walks and to the walks in the country each week for the life of the monastery was confining for a farm boy.

The year went by peacefully, though it was an intense year, with all the times for prayer and instructions each day. There were three fast days in the week. Otherwise the diet was good, much of it coming from the farm. It was hard to get used to just a piece of bread and coffee for breakfast, after the kind of breakfast I had when at home. In the summer we helped with the haymaking and that was a welcome change. On two afternoons in the good weather we worked in the garden. There were a lot of flowers and shrubs. The rose garden was small and the master wanted to extend it. We dug a long trench about three feet deep. He wanted to fill it with peat moss from a boggy area a couple of miles away. Because I had experience with horses I was given the job to go, with a horse and cart, and bring the peat moss back to the garden. This was also a nice change. We also built a retaining wall in the garden. Having worked with my father building walls, this was not a difficult job. All took part in every job. Whether we were inside or outside we were instructed to remember the presence of God, and thank Him for His helping grace.

Coming toward the end of the year Stan developed bad health. He was always very nervous. We were aware he had many conferences with the master. He finished out the year, but was told to take some time off before going ahead any further. We were permitted to write one letter home every month. As mentioned earlier, all letters had to be left unsealed for the master to read them before they would be posted, and all the letters that came to us were handed to us, already opened. My mother always wrote to me. She told me each time how happy they were to receive my letter and to know I was well and happy. She kept me up to date with all that was going on in the family and the home area.

At the end of novitiate year the professed members had a meeting to decide if the novices were suitable to take temporary vows for three years and become members of the order. This meeting was called a chapter. The novice master would give a report and recommendations on each novice. Then the novice would be called in and kneel down by the master at the end of a long conference table. All of the professed were watching and listening as the master questioned the novice on his readiness to profess vows, unreservedly, and become a member of the order. After the questions and answers the novice left. Then there were further discussions and a vote, which had to be unanimous. Later the master called each novice in turn to his cell and told him the result of the chapter. We were all approved except Stan who requested to wait, but did express the intention of continuing at a later date.

We were all given the date for the profession and told to write and invite our families to attend. It would take place in the public church. I received a letter back from my mother saying the diabetes had gotten worse and she was not doing well. Dr. Freeman had ordered her into the Mater Hospital in Dublin for treatment and she would be away at the time of the profession. They all sent their congratulations and best wishes and were sorry they could not come because of mother's illness. I was very disappointed. When I wrote back I did not want to make them feel bad. I told my mother how sorry I was about her bad health and assured her of my prayers and the prayers of the whole community. I thanked all of them for their kind thoughts and good wishes, saying how much I missed them and at the same time how I understood why they could not come.

The provincial from Dublin came for the occasion and gave a very good spiritual talk. He ended by assuring all the families present, that was all except mine, that these new members would always have enough to eat. That created a chuckle which startled him because he did not mean it to be funny. It was a very solemn ceremony and everyone seemed very happy, expressing congratulations and best wishes.

And remember: Love is not love 'til it's given away.

CHAPTER 14

Philosophy and Theology

The order had a philosophy house near the town of Colooney in County Sligo on the west coast. It was an old, brick mansion that had not been built as a school. For some time it was used as a sanitarium with an open ward attached. The order converted that ward into a church where they held public services. When we arrived there, we walked around the buildings. We were on top of a hill and were impressed with the views of farms, hills and mountains. The order had a farm with plenty of trees and a lake with fish. There was a rector and a vice-rector called the vicar, who was also the bursar. We had a spiritual director and professors. There were also other members in the community, some active and some retired. We had two brothers, one was in charge of the kitchen and the other ran the farm.

The daily schedule was similar to that in the novitiate. We got up at two in the morning to chant matins and lauds for an hour. We were up again at six to chant morning prayer and later chanted the other canonical hours of the day. After breakfast we had classes and study time was in the afternoon and evening. We played soccer and tennis and took long walks in the country. One of the professors had a rowboat on the lake. On feast days, when class time was cut short, we went fishing on the lake. Not all were interested in the fishing, but I loved it because of my having grown up by a river and enjoying the water and fishing.

The word philosophy comes from the Greek meaning, love of wisdom. The philosopher is a student of ultimate reality in search of truth. This search dates back to the Greeks of about 600 B.C. They depended on human reason alone and were not influenced by any religion or theological thought or creed. The main divisions of philosophy, historically, have been metaphysics, a study of the nature of the universe and the ultimate meaning of existence; logic which deals with the laws of reasoning; epistemology, which studies knowledge and the process of knowing; and ethics which has to do with right conduct. There are many other interesting areas of philosophical thought and study.

The three Greek philosophers who had the greatest influence on further philosophical development were Socrates, his pupil, Plato and Plato's pupil, Aristotle. It was Aristotle who gave us the syllogism which has two premises and a conclusion. Our professor used this form all the time and had us take our turns in presenting a proposition and defending it in the form of a syllogism. I began to realize these studies were changing my process of thinking. Reason alone was the tool of philosophy. The professor used to emphasize how important it was to be trained in philosophy, saying one is not ready to study theology without philosophy. St. Thomas Aquinas called philosophy "the handmaid of theology." Truth is one. The truth of philosophy cannot contradict the truth of theology or scripture. The challenge to the human mind is recognizing truth, and willingness to accept the truth no matter what its source.

The spiritual formation one had in the novitiate continued. Our spiritual director was Father Ned who had been the vice-master the previous year. He gave instruction and held frequent conferences, both in a group and with each of us individually. He was very spiritual, kind-hearted and well liked by the students. His outstanding quality was his ability to listen. I always got the feeling from him that he liked listening to me, and was not thinking of anything else while I was speaking to him. I tried to learn from him. He continued to tell us how to live in an awareness of God's presence. One of his favorite lines from scripture was "Walk humbly with your God." I enjoyed the solitary walks every day and the longer walks in the countryside. I was intrigued with philosophy and could not get enough of it. We had to read Decartes, then considered the founder of modern philosophy, Spinoza, Kant and others. Philosophy so occupied my thinking that it was difficult to concentrate on the presence of God during the time of meditation.

We did not get home on vacation, but the superiors rented bicycles for us and we cycled with Father Ned to the beaches in Strand Hill and Rosses Point on two days a week during the month of July. We all enjoyed swimming in the Atlantic Ocean. It was relished as great freedom and recreation after having been so confined. We could also have our families visit us during the summer recess. All of the students had families come to visit. My father and mother came and stayed in a guest house in Colooney. They spent the day with me at the monastery and got their meals in the visitor's parlor. I was delighted to see them and have time to talk with them. They asked many questions about the life I was living there and I asked them many questions about everyone at home and about what was going on at school and in the neighborhood. It seemed to me that mother had gotten thin and father had slowed down, but they said they were all right and did not want to talk about their health. Next morning when they were getting ready to leave the guest house, I dropped in to say goodbye as I was cycling through Colooney with the other students on our way to the beach at Strand Hill. My father and mother did not expect to see me and they were delighted. They said they had been worried about the confining life I had. "We saw you only in the black habit. Now you look a lot better in street clothes and able to cycle to the beach." They felt a lot better about me and many of their concerns about me were lifted from their minds.

The only other visitors I had during the years there was when my sister, Mary Jo, married Ned Martin and they toured the west on their honeymoon. They spent a day at the monastery and had their meals there. Mary Jo looked very well and very happy. I had not known Ned Martin. This was my first time to meet him. He was tall, of athletic build, with black hair and pleasant oval features. He was very friendly, somewhat reserved and well spoken. They were a lovely couple together, evidently well-matched and very sure of themselves and their future. I enjoyed their visit very much. By the time I would have come home after ordination, they would have four children including a set of twins, Seamus, Bernard, Edward and Celine. They would be the first grandchildren in the family.

During the philosophy course we had term and year-end exams. They were challenging and demanded a great deal of concentration. Then there were the finals. We all got through and were approved to go to the theology house. We all looked forward to this important step. When the day to go came, we commented among ourselves on how we had looked forward to coming there. We now felt it was time to leave, with no regrets, and look forward to what lay ahead.

The theology house was called Mount Argus, located in Dublin. This name brought to mind the monastery of Monte Argentaro which was established by the founder, St. Paul of the Cross, in Italy. It was a venerable, imposing building, with a student wing at the back and a large public church. It had about thirty acres of land, which was farmed. There was a front driveway and a back driveway. The city buses passed the gates regularly, so it was easy to go into the city.

Because theology was a four-year course, we now joined the other students in the three years ahead of us. We were the bottom of the ladder and supposed to look up to those older than us, our seniors. The daily horarium included prayer, lectures and study. For recreation we had soccer, handball and tennis and long walks into the country. We studied dogmatic theology, moral theology and scripture and there was a professor for each subject. We also had courses in preaching and psychology. The first year after ordination would be devoted to sacred eloquence. We had term exams in the house and we went to the diocesan seminary for exams at various stages along the way. We had teachers for writing and speaking. We had spiritual reading and solitary walks every day. We continued to rise at two in the morning for matins and lauds, and also chanted all the other canonical hours in choir. There was a rhythm to each day and the days passed quickly. Our spiritual director came with us and continued to guide us here. We were all happy to have him. There was a rector and vicar. Since it was the mother house for Ireland and Scotland, the provincial and his two consultors lived there. We attended mass each morning in the choir chapel. On Sundays we attended the last mass at twelve o'clock in the public church. We looked forward to listening to the different preachers because preaching was going to be a big part of our future. The order was founded for preaching. As we shared after the mass, we did not hold back on our criticism. There were many different styles and each student had his own model. We continued having reading at meals and we all had to take our turns. The refectory was a very large room. There were steps up to a pulpit at one end. When reading, we could look down on everyone. Our English professor would publicly correct any mistake in pronunciation and the reader would have to repeat the word correctly. In the course of the year we went through many informative books including, history, biographies and autobiographies of interesting or renowned people.

All the time I was maturing in body and spirit. Emotions and attractions grew stronger. There were the daily temptations and dreams at night, the constant reminder I had embraced a life of sacrifice and had to be wholehearted about the decision every day. While many distracting thoughts and ideas came into my mind I still was at peace with the decision and the conviction that God was calling me into closer union with him and calling me to be his priest, to serve his people.

The average day had time for lectures, study and prayer. The meditation we were taught during the spiritual year was continued, a full hour every evening in a darkened chapel. This required a lot of discipline, training of the mind to stay with the subject of meditation and not drift off with distractions, of which there were always plenty. We always began by placing ourselves in God's presence. When distractions came unbidden we were to recall God's presence again and pray for strength and continue. The distractions were becoming more persistent.

In the final year it was possible to socialize more. My mother became quite ill. She had been diagnosed as diabetic and her condition had worsened. I got to see her in the hospital. My city cousins that I had not seen for years also visited mother and we met again. She had confidence in Dr. Freeman in Dublin, who took a great interest in her, and what was unusual at that time, gave her time to ask questions and give her explanations. She moved ahead with her life as if nothing had happened.

Off and on I met Cathy while visiting the cousins. We talked a great deal. I felt the attraction growing and became concerned that I was becoming unfaithful to my commitment. Her presence gave me a glow all over. I felt a reverence for her. She was a very precious person. I sensed very strongly that Cathy felt the same about me. I told my priest advisor and explained the whole matter in detail. He was very understanding and said I was perfectly normal. "You have to face this now and realize you will be encountering this all your life. You have delayed too long with the relationship even though you have met only a few times and over a short period of time. Also, you won't be able to do it on your own. You will need divine help. You believe God gave you the grace to make the decision to be a priest, wholeheartedly. You must now continue to believe he is offering you the grace every day to renew the commitment as he calls you daily to come closer to him and live the sacrifice you promised. Of course, you could change your mind, but you would have to pray to understand what that would entail. Your ordination to the priesthood is coming up in the not too distant future. That is not going to change how you feel and how you will be attracted. This is for life and you have to be able, with God's grace, to make the sacrifice every day. Some of the saints have called this a white martyrdom. That is to face life alone without a partner and to live in self-denial of the strongest emotions as a sacrifice. This is possible only with God's call and a daily response to his grace."

We were told the strong drive to love you experience, must be sublimated. You must love God and neighbor with even greater energy. Don't stifle your love, direct it to God and neighbor. All of our desires for union with another may not be love. There is love and there is lust. True love is a virtue. Lust is sinful.

Next time I saw Cathy I told her how much I thought of her but felt sure God was calling me to the priesthood. She told me she was sure I was being called and she did not want to make it difficult for me. She encouraged me and made me feel affirmed in my decision. Parting she cried. I tried to hold back my tears.

We had Father Ned as our spiritual director. We could also go to another priest to discuss spiritual problems. I went to one of the older priests and explained the temptations that kept returning to my mind, the thoughts of having a career in the world, the recurring thoughts and feelings about girls. One of the worst times was when trying to go to sleep. Then there were the dreams and sometimes I would wake up embracing a young lady, only to find when fully awake it would be just a dream. He asked me if I had any sport or hobby that really took up my concentration. I said I used to shoot wild game. "What kind of game gave you most excitement?" I said, "When a convey of partridge would bust out of cover with birds, fast as arrows going in all directions." He said, "when you are trying to go to sleep and have these disturbing thoughts and feelings, imagine you are out in the fields with your dog and a covey of partridge bursts out of cover." I tried this. It did not work too well and I did not wake up embracing a partridge.

St. Thomas Aquinas was one of the authors we studied and followed. He loved to define everything with very correct words. He defined the Holy Spirit of God as *actus purus*, pure act. That impressed me very deeply. It meant he was always acting in our lives, always calling us. Our role is to listen and respond. His grace is always sufficient for us, sufficient to recognize his call, bear the sacrifices involved and respond wholeheartedly. *Actus purus,* pure act means he is calling us everyday and at every hour of every day. The better we listen the clearer the call. The better we respond the more grace we get enabling us to grow in union with God. It is not easy to listen with so many other voices calling us from inside and outside, calls that strive to convince us of how happy we could be if we would listen to them. If you give yourself to Christ you can have nothing else besides. I read Francis Thompson again. The call of the world and the flesh was very strong but I felt myself disagreeing with saying the strongest attractions were from the world and the flesh. I felt a stronger attraction to human love in its purity and grandeur. That was the greatest sacrifice asked for in becoming a priest.

We are in the second year of theology. Because some of the final year will be completed after ordination to the priesthood, we are now less than two years away from ordination to the priesthood. The last two years are the most critical period because of the final step in a lifetime commitment. We were all aware from living in the same building with the rest of the students of theology, that some left during the final two years. It was impressed upon us that it would be better not to go through to ordination if we had any doubts about the future. After ordination it would be very traumatic and difficult to leave. We knew some who did leave at that stage, usually a few years later. This was looked upon then as a great disaster for the individual, who had made a lifelong commitment and was ordained a priest forever. Thinking and attitudes have modified over the years, especially since the Second Vatican Council.

A few of us were very close and shared many of our concerns and hopes together. We discussed matters freely and went out together as time permitted and supported one another on the threshold of ordination to the priesthood.

We had an afternoon free from lectures and we took a bus to a swimming area called the forty-foot. The water was forty feet deep, sheer down the side of an extensive rock formation. The entrance to the place was a winding walkway through high rocks to a level area right by the water. It was an exclusively men's bathing place. The swimmers could not be seen from the road or anywhere else. It was a surprise to me on my first visit there to see so many lying around trying to get a suntan and a few with good tans from head to foot for it was a very free place and those who wanted could swim and sunbathe in the nude. There was a thermometer on the side of a rock which gave the air and water temperatures. On my first time there it read, air 64°, water 65°. I felt the water with my foot; it was quite cold. Everyone was jumping in; I did the same. After the initial shock it felt all right. Most of the bathers wore swimsuits. The longer we swam the more tolerable the water became. We felt quite invigorated when we came out of the water. After running around for a while to dry out, we sat on a flat rock to talk.

A young man of about twenty came over to us and started talking. He was a fine-looking young fellow with very nice regular features and a shock of dark brown hair. One of our group said something funny and he laughed. When he showed his teeth I got a very different impression of him from what I got on his first appearance. Two of his upper teeth in the front of his mouth were missing and there was a noticeable gap which looked very ugly. The rest of his teeth were beautiful and white. Every time he smiled or laughed the gap in his teeth was more and more noticeable. The contrast between the beautiful features and the gap in his teeth was very unpleasant to see. "My name is Joe," he said. We told him our names. "What do you fellows do?" he asked. I said, "We are clerical students of theology preparing to be priests." "Priests," he said, "my God, that must be a great life. I think I would like to be a priest. My grandmother always wanted me to be a priest, but I never took it seriously. Now I think I want to be a priest. It must be a wonderful life. I am sure I would not get a punch in the mouth. See where I have my two front teeth missing. I got a punch in the mouth from a bastard who stole my girlfriend and she let me down and is now going with this bastard. I met him in a bar and gave him a punch in the jaw. Then a fight followed and he punched me in the mouth and broke my two front teeth."

"I don't want to have anything to do with girls anymore. They are all the same; you can't trust any of them. You are lucky to have nothing to do with girls and no one is going to give you a punch in the mouth and break your front teeth. So, I want to be like you, no girls and no punches in the mouth. I really want to be a priest."

Rick, who was always the devil's advocate, said to him, "Do you think you deserved to get a punch in the mouth?" He came back at Rick so fast his words were hissing through the gap in his teeth: "What the hell do you mean, did I deserve that punch in the mouth? Are you siding with that bastard? I don't like you one bit, and if you are the kind that's going to be a priest, then I'm not going to be a priest. I have changed my mind and it's your fault. Goodbye." I felt sorry for him that he looked so bad without his two front teeth but he admitted striking the first blow.

Faith always held a great interest for me. Why some believe and some don't believe, some have a strong faith and others are just nominal believers. Many who know the content of faith doctrines still don't believe. Some seem to have the faith and even practice it then fall away and become agnostics or atheists or believe in nothing at all.

Out of love God gave us life; also out of love he offered us the gift of faith. Through creation and revelation he gives us natural life and a share in his divine life. God asks for a response of faith from us, his people. The ability to make the response is itself a gift. God's grace moves the heart to believe. Trying to understand the magnificence of God's gift of himself, we realize he is calling us to self surrender and the complete obedience of faith. We humans are the only part of God's creation that can make a response to God in answer to his initiative in calling us out of infinite love.

Teachers of the faith prepare the ground and help nurture the faith. They do not give the faith. While their teaching is necessary, go teach the nations, only God can give the gift.

Faith can be looked upon as having, as it were, two dimensions, the content of the doctrine of the faith, and the virtue of faith, which is God's gift. Faith is a supernatural virtue which can be had only as God's gift, uniting the believer to God, sharing his divine life as a true child destined to share God's life forever. It is necessary that faith be a free assent of the intellect and will of the believer to the truth that God has lovingly revealed. There are two gifts, the doctrine revealed and the virtue given. As catechists teach the doctrine of the faith, God is present in their words, sowing the seed and offering the hearer the gift of faith.

The grace and inspiration of the Holy Spirit moves the heart and mind of the individual to believe. Faith then is a response to the personal God, who revealed himself and to the truth God has made known through his church commissioned to teach.

Many of our young people who have been taught the faith do not express it in their words and actions. Some do, but most exempt themselves from ritual worship, especially after they finish with formal learning of the faith on leaving the programs, usually after confirmation at age fourteen. They received teaching on the doctrine of the faith. The question naturally arises: Did they really accept the gift of faith, certainly offered to them? Or, if they accepted the faith, were they poorly informed, and, or, was their faith choked by the attractions of the world? Just as a plant needs the right climate to grow, so does the faith need the right climate in which to grow, the support of a home where the members believe and pray together, regular attendance in the worship life of the church, good education in the doctrines of the faith adjusted to each stage of development. If our young people are not receiving the proper nourishment for their faith, they may lose this most precious gift from God.

Our teachers of theology emphasized, over and over again, that we must be prepared to meet this phenomenon in our ministry. They told us many agnostics and atheists today were from Catholic families and raised in the faith. Examples were Joseph Stalin who was raised Catholic, even went to a Catholic Orthodox Seminary and was expelled for following Marxism. And Adolf Hitler, raised as a Catholic and confirmed in the church in 1904 at age fifteen, but rarely went to church. In ministry I came up against this all the time. Young people, after confirmation, falling away from church going sometimes giving their parents a lot of disappointment and grief, and in some cases, just following the example of their parents.

This is a very complicated scene and it is difficult to understand all its dimensions. A mother spoke to me at the church door. She is a widow and is raising her youngest grandson. Her other children and grandchildren have stopped going to church. The boy, Dan, made confirmation a year ago. Prior to that he was very happy to be an altar boy. At this meeting with the grandmother; I asked her how was the boy, Dan, whom I had not seen with her for some time. She said, "Dan does not want to come to church anymore." I asked her, "Why?" She said, "His friends do not go to church." I said, "He always stood to talk to me and I thought he loved coming to church." She said, "He is at that age, his friends mean everything to him and he does not want me to talk church to him anymore." I said, "Please tell him I miss him."

Pat, the oldest of a large family was an altar boy and so were three of his brothers. He was bright, hardworking and very successful at high school and college. Now he had a very good position in business. The family invited me to their home to celebrate his birthday. In the course of a conversation, in which the whole family took part, he volunteered the information that he did not attend church anymore. His father, a staunch church attendant, asked him, "Why?" Pat said, "Being very successful, I did not feel the need for God." The next time I met him, he and his wife had a baby and lived in another state. They were both Catholic, but not attending church. Their parish had a baptismal preparation program, which they were required to attend. There were several sessions which included sharing by the parents present on why they were having their babies baptized and what the faith meant to them. They varied greatly in their understanding of the faith and their commitment to their church communities. My friend and his wife invited me to do the baptism of their baby. They shared with me how the experience of the preparation program had affected them. They felt a new kindling of their faith and a deeper understanding than they had before. Now the faith seemed to be such a precious gift from God. They were grateful for the faith and decided to share it with their precious baby. They committed themselves to their parish community and got to know their pastor whom they admired very much. They made great friends who were involved in parish life and helped them get involved also. They are raising a lovely, large family, all deeply committed to their faith.

Richard was a boy in a church-going family. He was at church with the whole family every week and his parents were volunteers in church programs. While at grammar school he was rather shy, but he did tell me he would prefer to be called Rich rather than Richard. He was not one who stopped often to talk to me leaving church, and it became more seldom as he grew older.

One weekend he stopped to talk to me. He said he did not believe there was any God. He continued to tell me how his science teacher at high school, whom he admired very much, had told the class there was no need for God, that science had the answers to everything in the universe. He continued to tell me how this teacher explained that God was a human invention in order to have all the answers to questions that could not be otherwise answered, and now science can give all the answers. Rich said he did not want to go to church anymore. His parents told him when he is home in their house, he has to go to church and that is why he is here.

I listened well and told him I appreciated his sharing all of this with me, assuring him I was there to help him in any way I could. He had been a bit on the defensive, but now he seemed to relax and got more chatty. As he continued, I got the feeling he just wanted to talk and was not asking any questions. He told me of his plans for college and he looked forward to being a great scientist.

The parents came to me one day and told me that Richard said he had no faith in God anymore, that there was no God. They were disappointed with the science teacher who said things they felt he should not have said in a classroom. They said they were still hoping he would get his faith back. Questions were popping up in my mind: Did Richard ever really accept the faith? Did he understand the faith as a gift from God? How did he grow in his prayer life and relationship with God, and much more. The parents told me they were moving to another state because of the husband's job. I wished them well and assured them of my prayers, especially for Richard. I did not see Richard anymore, but he is frequently in my mind and in my prayers.

Having studied philosophy and theology, it became very clear that our minds get information from two sources: reason and revelation. Everyone accepts reason and all the great accomplishments of reason. Many do not accept revelation claiming it is just mythology and never really happened. Pushed to extremes, the denial of revelation and the promotion of reason alone, led to atheistic communism, which was adopted by some governments, including Russia and China. Karl Marx declared religion to be the opium of the people. Nietzsche declared that God is dead, and hereafter man is completely free.

They taught that religion took away the true freedom of humans and following reason alone liberated them from slave morality enabling them to develop to their full potential. In Russia and China atheistic governments were established. People were deprived and persecuted because of their religion. Churches were closed and leaders were jailed, deprived of freedom and human rights. They were degraded, made to suffer mentally and physically and held in prisons with deplorable conditions for years on end. Religion was outlawed.

Many people who were supposed to be given freedom from religion and told there was no God, no human soul and no heaven, lost spiritual direction, became dehumanized, their spirits broken, with endless problems of depression, corruption, drug abuse, and social degradation.

As the governments of Russia and China continued to persecute and imprison leaders of religion and their followers, many terrible stories of inhuman treatment came through the news media. I met three priests who were released after several years in prison in China. They were ill and emaciated. They told heart wrenching stories of isolation, starvation, deprivation of sleep and false accusations of plotting against the government. Christ was accused of plotting against Caesar.

Properly understood, the truth of reason and the truth of revelation do not contradict each other, because truth is one and indivisible.

And remember: Love is not love 'til it's given away.

CHAPTER 15

The Osteomyelitis Comes Back

Less than two years from ordination to the priesthood and finding great meaning and fulfillment in religious life and the study of theology and debating with my classmates, I began to experience pain in the leg where the osteomyelitis had given me so much pain and suffering as a boy. As it got worse daily and I was losing attention at class, the thought came to me that it was incurable. That word frightened me because the rule said that no one with an incurable disease could be ordained. I went to Father Ned and told him how I felt. He had me see the infirmarian who took my temperature. He said it was elevated and recommended I rest. The leg swelled and next day an opening came in the front of the shin where the old scar was and matter or pus started coming out. The infirmarian dressed the leg and recommended having a doctor look at it.

I told Father Ned my worry about this being an incurable disease and possibly preventing me from being ordained. He tried to comfort me, but said it would be up to the doctor to let us know if it was incurable. He indicated that he was in no position to say one way or the other. He really left me where he got me. I went to see a doctor, a general practitioner and showed him the leg, explaining the history behind it. He decided to have an orthopedic surgeon look at it. He brought the surgeon to the monastery and they examined my leg in my cell. The orthopedic surgeon said I should go into a hospital for surgery. I was devastated thinking of having surgery on that bone again and the apprehension that this might very well be the end of the line for me on my road to the priesthood.

I prayed hard but God did not give me any comfort. He did not seem to be listening. I was grasping for hope but could find none. I felt terribly alone in my suffering of body and mind. My mind was flooded with memories and questions. Why did God, who gave me life and loved me so much, allow an innocent boy, enjoying growing up, running and vaulting in the meadows on the river bank, to be stricken with an incurable bone disease? Is there any answer? Why? I don't have an answer. I don't know why. We prayed so much then. My family prayed early and late every day. We trusted God was listening. I had the surgery and healing and some good years. I thanked God for all that, but now it has come back again. We thought God was listening, but now I am tempted to doubt if He is listening or caring. In my meditations I feel so dry and empty. God seems to be so far away. Dear God, I'm saying, You let all these things happen to us, my sore leg, mother getting diabetes, Teresa dying and leaving four young children. We prayed hard then. I am praying hard now. Is God listening? Is He there? All alone in meditation I feel I am confronting God. Are You there? Where are You? And then, the worst of all, the temptation comes into my mind to ask "Is there a God." "Is God in our midst or not", as the Jewish people said to Moses. My mind is inundated with questions and no answers. Where is God? Is there a God? Signs are, there is no God. I was suffering in the dark night of my soul. There is nothing worse than this. All I hoped in seems to have disappeared. The God, loving Father whom I loved seems to have hidden from me. My mind is being bombarded with apparent evidence that there is no God.

I am taken to the hospital in Jervis St., and prepared for surgery. Waiting to be taken to the operating room, I am thinking of what happened that morning in Coole hospital when I was eleven years old. Now I am twenty-three and going through it all again. I am not as feverish and fearful as I was then, but I have deeper concerns, wondering if this is going to change the direction of my life and what could there be ahead of me. I feel, with these temptations against my faith, and the total lack of any comfort or consolation, I am in the dark night of my soul. Where is the light? There is none.

This time I am given a general anesthetic and don't know anything until I wake up in my room. There is a penicillin drip going into my leg. I have some pain but it is bearable. A nurse bends over me and tells me I am doing fine and that I will be getting injections of penicillin. Dr. Fitzgerald, the surgeon, came into my room. He explained what he did in chiseling away the front of the bone, leaving the marrow cavity open to drain. I would be getting penicillin injections as well as the drip going into the bone where I had the surgery. I asked if this was an incurable disease. He explained that it can be cured by surgery and penicillin. Since the advent of penicillin some of the sanitariums for osteomyelitis patients are being closed. I told him how I was concerned about not being admitted to the priesthood because of an incurable disease. He told me that I should not be held back for that reason and he would speak to my superiors. We became friendly and talked for a while as he made his rounds daily. He had a brother in the Jesuits and he had grown up on a farm where he loved to fish and shoot. He loaned me some books he had on wildlife, including the works of Audubon. I enjoyed them very much. There was no cast this time. He told me they had moved away from that but advised using a cane for a while as the bone was now weakened by the surgery.

    I had written home to let them know I was going into the hospital to have surgery on the leg. Now I wrote to tell them how it went. Mother responded with a long letter telling me how happy they were that I was doing well, giving me all the news and telling me they were praying for me every day. Father Ned came in to see me regularly. I told him what the doctor had said about the future outlook for me and that he would be in touch with my superiors. He said the doctor had already gotten in touch and everyone was relieved and happy to hear that good news. Father Ned and I had some good discussions. I explained to him how difficult it was to pray and how so many disturbing thoughts and temptations kept coming across my mind, even about the very existence of God. He said he recognized I was going through a very difficult time. This was a time of trial for me, and I would overcome it by God's grace and by being steadfast in my faith and prayers. When we are faithful during trials we come out of them even stronger. God permits his loved ones to suffer and they keep on doing His will. The prophet Simeon told Mary, "thine own soul, a sword shall pierce." Jesus prayed on the cross asking, "why have you abandoned me?" You suffer for yourself and you suffer for others.

    The first evening after the surgery a nurse came into my room and said, "I am your night nurse and my name is Sheila." I told her I was studying for the priesthood and why I was in the hospital. She already knew. She said she had just come from the chapel. Every evening she went there before coming on duty. She prayed for her patients and to be guided in doing and saying what was right and best for them. As I lay there in my bed looking up at her, she seemed tall. She had a beautiful face with blue eyes and blond hair. She had a friendly smile and her teeth were well-formed and glistening white. I felt comforted by her presence and knowing she had prayed for me in the chapel. She expressed admiration and respect for the vocation I was following. She had to move along, saying she would look in on me during the night and make sure I was alright, reminding me I had the bell I could use to call for help if I should need it. Nurse Sheila came to my room every evening. She was always cheerful and anxious to help in any way she could. We always talked a little before she moved on to other patients. She was interested in my life as a seminarian. I felt bad on missing out on lectures and study as there would be exams coming up. Psychology was one of our subjects and I had a textbook by my bed. She said the nurses got basic psychology in their training and she was very interested in taking more courses but they were not available. She was nursing two years now since her graduation, still single and very committed to her profession. She always mentioned that she came from praying in the chapel to take care of the patients. She had so many nice qualities she seemed to me to be perfect for her nursing career. I was growing to like her more and more. It crossed my mind that if I went into another profession I would want her as my wife for life. I dismissed the thought and turned to prayer, remembering the presence of God and my commitment to Him. I was relieved, feeling my faith was strong again and the temptation to think there was no God had weakened. This good person was like a messenger from God who helped to banish the darkness I was going through and made me feel more sure of myself again in my vocation. I was being drawn in two directions at once. One part of me was longing to have this beautiful person as my own and belong to her. Another part of me was saying, "God is calling me and she respects this call." Even though my mind was set the feelings remained for a long time. I could not forget her.

I was in the hospital for four weeks. After the first week I could walk the corridors using a cane. There was a rest area with seats where we sat and talked. One young man, Jim, who was a patient, and I talked quite a bit together. He was admitted because he was involved in a road accident, had some injuries and was having tests done. He was studying to be a veterinarian. He was born in the city and grew up with no religion. When he realized I was studying for the priesthood he told me he was an agnostic. He went on to explain that agnostics are the greatest skeptics. They hold the existence of God cannot be proved or disproved by reason. Had I heard of Immanuel Kant. He taught that belief in divinity can rest only on faith. It cannot be proved by logic. He said he had no faith and he did not know whether there was a God or not. I said I had studied agnosticism and had also read Kant who believed in dialectical materialism. Karl Marx believed the same and taught atheistic communism. Jim said that being an agnostic does not mean you have to be an atheist. They are different. I explained that faith is a gift from God. Jim asked how one would know he had the gift. I said he should ask God and he said he would, then added, "How can I speak to God when I don't know if He is there." He asked me if I was trying to get him to pray. I answered that he told me he did not know whether God existed or not and that he was not an atheist. So what was he going to lose by trying? He asked if I thought he was a bad person because he had no faith in God. I assured him I did not think that way, and I respected him. Anyone who lives upright and treats his neighbor right is pleasing to God. He said I looked like a pretty normal person and how was I going to go through life without a woman. I explained that would be a gift from God too. So: "You need more than one gift from God to live the life you are living." I said, "I need God's gifts and graces because I cannot do it on my own." He said, "What do you think of the night nurse, Sheila, who comes around?" I said I was very impressed with her. He said, "She prays in the chapel for me every night before coming on duty. She knows I am an agnostic and she is still very nice to me. When I get better I would love to ask her out, but I don't think someone with her faith and an agnostic would hit it off together." I said, "Well, you could try it and see what happens." "No, I feel unworthy of her," he said. He continued, "You believe God is giving you the gift to live without a woman for the rest of your life. If I were in your shoes, I would have myself neutered." Then he added, "That might not be the best idea. What if I were to change my mind." I said, "One of the fathers of the early church Origen had that done. The church condemned it as it does all mutilations except to save life. That is why he was never canonized as a saint. When the church canonizes someone that person is presented as an example of heroic virtue to be followed. The church could not recommend the members to follow his example in what he did." "Well", he said, "that seems to be out of the question then." He continued, "Why would you enter this kind of life anyway?" I said, "For the sake of the kingdom, to give my life building the kingdom of God, on earth for all peoples." Jim: "What kind of kingdom is that? I never heard of it." I replied, "It is a kingdom of love and peace where all peoples of all nations can live and work together in harmony as God's family of mankind. The kingdom will reach its fullness when all peoples will enter the kingdom of heaven to be happy together for all eternity." Jim: "How did this start?" Shane: "When God sent His Son, Jesus, into our world He proclaimed the kingdom of God has come for you and gathered followers to build the kingdom. All would be reconciled to one another and to God, and all would work together for the common good." Jim: "It sounds like a wonderful idea, but I don't think it is ever going to happen. There is too much hatred and selfishness and crime in the world and there are not enough people like you." Shane: "Sounds like you might want to join me?" "Oh, no, they would not have me, I am an agnostic." Shane: "So was St. Augustine before he was converted and he became a saint." "As an agnostic, you say the existence of God cannot be proved by reason. What about St. Thomas Aquinas' five proofs of the existence of God from reason? The first one from motion shows there has to be a prime mover." Jim: "I have not read St. Thomas. I would consider that to be in the realm of revelation" Shane: "St. Thomas was also a philosopher and he knew if one could conclude from reason alone that God exists, that is not faith. To believe in Gods revelation one must get the gift of faith." Jim: "Where would I get proof of God's existence from reason by St. Thomas?" Shane: "You will find the works of St. Thomas in any good library."

Every morning Sister Catherine came around to see the patients. I think her order was the Sisters of Mercy who ran the hospital. She was a tall, nice looking lady, dressed in white and appearing to be in her forties. She showed a great interest in the patients and wanted to be sure they were all well taken care of. I liked talking to her and she would spend a little time with me, which I felt she could scarcely afford in her busy schedule. I remember telling her how concerned I was in missing so much time from lectures and study. Father Ned refused to bring the books to the hospital except for the one on psychology. Sister Catherine advised me to try and remember the outline of study for that time and think about it each day. Some of the reading we were doing at the time was by a French spiritual writer who claimed it was very difficult to communicate with God, saying one had to annihilate oneself before the Almighty, using such words as inaccessibility, incommunicability and the like. I shared this with Sr. Catherine and she did not go along with it at all. We talked and discussed the matter somewhat like this. Since God calls us into a spiritual and intimate relationship with Him, He bridges whatever distance we may think there may be between the infinite God and a finite person. His call unites us and give us the grace to be spiritually intimate with Him. Since everything about God is infinite, all His attributes are infinite, He can be infinitely intimate in so far as He knows this is possible with His children, made in His own image and likeness. When she came around the next morning we talked again. She told me she shared our conversation of the day before with her sisters in the community when they got together. She said they all liked the expression that God could be infinitely intimate and should not be thought of as far away. I often thought of that and it seemed to fit in with Christ telling us to call God, our Father, and Abba, which could be even more familiar. Our scripture teacher said Abba could be translated as Daddy.

After a month in the hospital I was discharged and had to see the surgeon periodically for a while. I slipped easily back into the daily round of prayer, lectures and study. Within the last year we would be ordained, subdeacons, deacons and finally, priests. Father Ned was very helpful. We discussed all I had gone through with the osteomyelitis, both while I was a boy growing up and now as a student. I told him I felt a lot better about everything. Even though God permitted me to go through all of this, I was keenly aware that all healing comes from God and that He never leaves me but is always calling me. I was so grateful for this and for not having to worry any more about possibly having an incurable disease. The road was open before me. Father Ned assured me I would be stronger and more mature in the faith because I had suffered trials and overcame them.

And remember: Love is not love 'til it's given away.

CHAPTER 16

Before Ordination

I became more aware of the presence of God in my life, and what we know He has done through the history of the universe. The two great actions of God were creation and revelation. It is not known just when and how God created the universe. Those who do not believe in God say the universe, as we know it, could have started with a big bang. This creates more questions: who or what put the material there and the energy so that the big bang could happen, to form the countless heavenly bodies? Where did the intelligence come from to put them all in their orbits? Who devised our planet, Earth, to spin and tilt and all that's necessary to bring about and sustain life as we know it? Our reason looks for a prime mover, a power and intelligence greater than our own. There cannot be two infinite powers for they would cancel each other out, an inherent contradiction. When at grammar school we used to have a question: "What happens were an irresistible force to come up against an immovable object?" It sounds like we were looking for the big bang.

The mind is our highest faculty. It can perceive truth from what is self evident, and find further truths by the logical process of deduction. Still there are many unanswered questions about ourselves and the universe. "You knit me together in my mother's womb" "I am wonderfully and fearfully made" scripture says.

The study of philosophy had changed my way of thinking. Logic was very helpful. It gave me a new sense of the power of right reasoning. It alerted me to recognize when the conclusion was wider than the premise. This reminded me of one of my cousins we used to visit when growing up.

He claimed to have had a bad experience with a doctor. When telling the story he would conclude by saying he would not go to a doctor again because they were no good. We were warned against giving anyone a bad experience, because, such a one would be tempted to think and say all priests are like this one.

Philosophy gave me insights into the meaning of truth and freedom as they pertain to the human mind. It also helped me in my awareness of the presence of God by giving me a deeper understanding of Him. We transfer the way we think of people to the way we think of God. When I began to call God my Father in heaven, I unconsciously transferred my concept of my earthly father to God the Father. A greater understanding of the human person helps us in understanding God better and also helps us in understanding self better. All of this can greatly influence how we relate to others. My life is fulfilled to the extent I relate well to God and neighbor. St. Augustine wrote "our hearts were made for you and they shall not find rest until they rest in you".

We were made for God and our pursuit of truth, love and happiness all our lives is a pursuit of God. Those who do not believe in God do not think they are searching for God when they are searching for fulfillment in possessing truth and love. When we come to know the fullness of truth we will know God, for God is truth. Jesus said, "I am the way, the truth and the life." (Jn.14:6). "Everyone who belongs to the truth listens to My voice" Pilate said, "What is truth?" Jn.15:37,38. So, all truth and all love is a sharing in the divine. God is always drawing us, whom He made to His own image and likeness, into a loving relationship with Himself. As we search for truth, we are searching for God. To accomplish this He has given us the gift of revelation and for those who are open to it, the gift of faith. Thus, theology gives us more truth about God than philosophy alone can do.

Loving the neighbor brings us closer to God. St. John tells us, "God is love, and he who lives in love, lives in God and God in him." Jesus, when questioned about the greatest commandment, re-emphasized what was already revealed in the Bible. "You must love the Lord, your God, with all your heart, with all your soul, with all your strength and all your mind, and your neighbor as yourself."

After creation the second great action of God was revelation. He came through the great divide between the finite and the infinite. He broke through the veil that separates creatures from the creator; He crossed the chasm that we can only imagine and spoke to humans. He revealed himself. He spoke to Moses and the prophets for the benefit of His people saying who He was, giving commandments and guidance. God did not speak to everyone. He did not reveal Himself to everyone. Creation is explored by reason. Revelation is accepted by faith and explored by theology. Revelation is a gift from God and, the faith to believe what is revealed, is also a gift. One does not reject reason and what reason can teach us. Many reject revelation, not convinced God spoke to Moses and the prophets. They don't accept Christ as the fullness of revelation.

In France in the eighteenth century there was a movement, "The Cult of Reason", as a reaction against Christian teachings. The leaders were guillotined. In 1859 the first Vatican council solemnly declared that human knowledge is of two distinct orders: natural knowledge—reason—and supernatural knowledge—revelation. Even though human reason is able to obtain some knowledge of God by its natural light, God did reveal Himself and His teachings in a supernatural way. This enables man to cooperate with God in attaining the supernatural and all for which God has destined him.

It occurred to me many times to think about what was the most important doctrine revealed by God to help us on our way to salvation. While thinking of this I became keenly aware of the place of Jesus Christ in the history of revelation; he said, "He who sees Me, sees the Father." He was the fullness of God's revelation. Revelation through the prophets down the centuries foretold the coming of the Messiah. It was not known he would be the Son of God until he actually came. The angel said to Mary, His mother, "He will be called the Son of the most high." When He came He said, "I came from the Father. The father and I are one." To get back to the question of what was the most important doctrine revealed by God as it affects our human lives. The answer came. The mercy of God. The most distinctive mark of the teaching of Jesus was forgiveness. "I came to call sinners." This was a revelation from God the Father, the One who sent Him. He called his followers to a new birth. "You must be born again in the Spirit."

David, to whom most of the psalms are attributed, wrote: "Your mercy is above all Your works." Of all the great things God has done, where would we be without His mercy. He is the only one who can forgive sins. If He does not reach out to lift me up when I fall, then I can't get up. His mercy is an expression of His love. Jn.3:16. "God so loved the world, he gave His only son, so that everyone who believes in Him might not perish but might have eternal life." Love describes God best. His mercy is His greatest gift to us. If I am asked how I can tell God is working in my life. I say He enabled me to forgive others. "It is divine to forgive." We are forgiven and, called to forgive and be God-like. My ability to forgive is an experience of God in my life.

In the midst of trials, I remember how God called me. I know He will always call me. I will still have temptations. Temptations are not me. I am my decisions. God taught me discipline through which I learned self-control and the ability to recognize temptation for what it is and stand my ground. If I think every temptation is just me, I will drift with the temptation, instead of standing my ground. How many of us just drift with temptation, each time thinking this is me and I want to do this.

I believe You are calling all the time. I don't always hear You. What am I doing wrong? How do you want me to listen? Not with my physical ears, but with open mind, unglutted with other cares and daily distractions. A mind that consciously says: "Speak Lord, your servant is listening." At the beginning of each prayer I silently say: "Our Father, my mind is open to You and You alone, and I keep my mind open and keep all other distractions away for a short time, hoping You Who are always calling, will give me to understand what You want me to know. Several times during the day I ask Mary, the Blessed Mother, who listened so well to the Holy Spirit, to help me listen to the same Holy Spirit and understand what He would like me to know and to do. I find that the greatest respect you can show anyone is to listen attentively without speaking. It has to be the same in our relationship with God. We are happier talking to the neighbor or praying to God, than listening. To listen to God attentively is probably the greatest thing I do in our relationship. It is such a joy to know I am listening and God is listening too. Awareness that God is calling fulfills the soul's longing for God. I spend so much time allowing my mind to be filled with thoughts, ideas, plans and day-dreaming, before gradually becoming aware that God is trying to get through to me. Speak Lord, Your servant is listening as Samuel said, but I must make time to listen. As our psychology teacher told us, the perfect listener is the perfect counselor; so it must be in our relationship with God: the better we listen, the better the relationship. Dear Lord, teach me to listen to You.

As I approached ordination, and thought about the road I was on, and the unknown future that lay ahead, I found myself musing and communing with God:

DECISION TIME

You have known me from eternity,
You made me capable of loving You,
You called me to love You.
You sent me trials to prove my love.
Through suffering You purified me.
You rescued me from my doubts,
Then repeated Your call more earnestly.
I could have refused You instantly.
I could have said, "I don't hear You."
You knew my thoughts and my perplexity,
And still You called more insistently.
You did not take away my freedom,
You appealed to what was best in me.
What's lowest tried to drag me down.
Decision was to be mine,
I would be my decision.
When, again, I doubted Your call,
You did not give up,
You played "tug o' war" with me,
You let me think I was winning,
I thought I had snapped the rope.
From facing You in pulling,
I could now turn my back.
Then You called again but stronger,
The rope was as strong as Your love,
It was Your love.
Again I tried to run like a fish on a line,
Again You let me think I was winning,
Did I break the line?
Then, I felt You pull again,
It was a gentle pull, it must be You,
Saying, come to Me, I want you.
I found the strength to say:
Yes, You won.
So did I. I really wanted You.
I'll do Your work, but even more,
I will love You for evermore.
Rejoicing in Your love for me, eternally.

Love always wins.
Love is stronger than life or death.
Where do we go from here, lovers say,
One says, You lead the way,
The other says, no way, we're in this together,
I do not force you.
You cannot force me.
Whatever will be, will be two,
I'll never abandon you.
What I desired you freely chose to do.
You honored me in listening and responding,
I will honor You with myself.
As we move into the future unknown,
I know I'll never be alone.
Reaching Your people in pain and sorrow,
And those who think there's no tomorrow,
Where sometimes words of comfort fail,
And actions seem of no avail,
Your grace the hardened heart will melt,
And prayer bring hope now deeply felt.
Some who were alone and forlorn,
Are in your image again reborn,
For those who listen with sincerity,
You give hope for all eternity.

And remember: Love is not love 'til it's given away.

CHAPTER 17

Ordination and Coming Home

We had a week's retreat before ordination. The priest who conducted the retreat was in his sixties. He had preached missions and retreats for many years and had served as a superior in various capacities. We had three lectures a day. There was time for private consultation, for prayer, for solitary walks in the gardens and spiritual reading.

One of the students left. We were told he decided not to go ahead right now. It was not uncommon for some students to do this. Some did come back later, but most did not return. The retreat master emphasized to us that it would be better to leave now than wait until later, after we would become priests. We were going into the priesthood for life. The vows we were making permanent now would be for our whole lives. The call from God and the grace He was giving us now would continue for our whole lives.

Among other things he emphasized was service to God's people. We had spent many years in preparation, growing in union with God and living a life of study and prayer. Soon we would be launched into the great sea of the world, with all its opportunities to serve and all the pressures and temptations that go with it. You are coming to the third stage in your vocation, first you were called, then you were formed in preparation and now you are about to be sent. As we had been told many times, this is what Jesus did with his close followers. First, he called them, then he formed them, and finally, he sent them to teach and serve the people who were waiting for their ministry.

Speaking from his experience of many years, he told us to keep in mind and be faithful always, to the two dimensions of our lives: The call to union with God and the mission to serve God's people. It is very easy to become over engrossed in ministry to the point of neglecting prayer and union with God. There is a heresy out there telling you, you can neglect prayer because the demands of the people are so great. I have known some who fell into this trap, and it is very difficult to get out of it. It is like telling God, "I am too busy doing your work to have time to talk to you." The more you cultivate union with God, the more fruitful your ministry will be. Beware of the heresy of being too busy. There will be the personal and communal aspects of your lives: The personal will always be, knowing and serving God better; the communal will be faithful service to the community. They are not separate. They go together, hand in hand. When you are praying, you are growing in relationship with God and also in relationship with the community. The same is happening when you are serving the community with faith, you are growing in relationship with God and with his people.

As we approached the day of ordination to the priesthood, and I tried to understand fully the meaning and importance of the step I was taking, I sensed a great peace with the decision and a profound gratitude to God for calling me. The day of ordination dawned. I was up early. It was May 28th, the eve of Trinity Sunday. The ceremony was to start at eight in the morning and finish about eleven. I still have a very vivid memory of traveling through the city in a taxi from Mount Argus on one side to Holy Cross church on the other side. Arriving at the church I met Father Herbert, whom I had invited to assist me. It was a joy to see him, and he told me how happy he was that I had invited him. He said, "You are going to be a priest forever."

Our families were in the church, but we could not see them until after the ceremony. There were candidates to be ordained from the Diocese of Dublin, and from several religious orders, fifty-five in all. Each student was allowed five tickets for family members to attend. Present from my family were my father and mother, the two nuns in the family, Aunt Lilly and my sister, Marcella, and Uncle Mike.

The candidates, with an assistant priest beside each one, the ordaining bishop, John Charles McQuaid and his attendants processed into the sanctuary. A priest, acting as Master of Ceremonies, began by calling out the name of each candidate, and each answered in Latin, "Adsum", which means, "I am present." Then we lay prostrate on the floor, symbolizing we were dying to the world and giving our lives to God, to be spent in the service of his people, building the kingdom. After a few moments we got up and the ceremony continued. Most important was when the Bishop laid his hands on our heads, each in turn, ordaining us as priests in the tradition that has come down, unbroken from the Apostles, who were ordained by Christ himself. Our hands were anointed with holy oil, and bound in linen bands. Afterwards, these bands were given to the mothers. We were empowered to consecrate and absolve. We could say mass and hear confessions. The symbols used were a chalice and a bible as the Bishop commissioned us to serve God's people in the ministry of word and sacrament. We celebrated a mass with the Bishop, but the first mass on our own would be in our home parish with our families and the local people. We made a solemn promise of obedience to the Bishop, representing all of our superiors both now and for the future. Now I am "a priest forever."

I could see in the faces of others what I was feeling as the ceremony was coming to a close. This ceremony changed us. It also changed the direction of our lives. We would not live for ourselves any longer, but we would live for others for the rest of our lives. Like St. Paul we could say, "I live now, not I, but Christ lives in me."

After the ordination ceremony, each new priest joined his own family group, and gave each member his blessing. I was surrounded by my father and mother, Aunt Lilly, my sister Marcella, and Uncle Mike. We embraced and each one asked for my blessing. They were all excited and happy. I noticed my father was very quiet, and wondered if there was anything wrong with him. My mother saw me watching him, speaking to him and not getting much of a response. We agreed to meet for lunch in the hotel where they were staying.

I went back to Mount Argus, changed into street clothes and went to the hotel. We had a room all to ourselves. There was a table set for lunch with the best tableware and crystal. I greeted them all again. My mother took me aside and proceeded to tell me my father had begun to go senile, and someone had to be with him all the time. Uncle Mike had traveled with them on the train, because she thought it would be too much for her to take care of him on her own. She had him to a doctor. He said nothing could be done for him. She had not told me when writing, as she did not want to distract me from what I was doing.

Back in the dining room, I tried to talk to my father. He did not know me. On this day of great joy, there was now a great weight of sorrow pressing on my heart. He did not have the joy. He did not have the sorrow. He was out of it.

Coming home to Empor after seven years away, I had changed. I left at eighteen and now I am twenty-five. When leaving the people regarded me as still a boy. Now they look on me as a man. My family seemed to have changed, father is senile, mother thinner but as active as ever, Mary Jo is kept busy with four small children, Marcella got a week's vacation to come home with Aunt Lilly for the celebration. Brian and Frank are managing the farm. They are strong, young men and eager to buy more land. Vera, Celine and Mike are all teenagers and working on their future careers. Tony Lynn is very tall, happy and very attached to mother. He is the last now walking on his own to Empor school.

The local priests, Father Paul and Father Joe, had announced my ordination and the date of my first mass in Empor Church. My family was up in the front seats. Our cousins, the McGuires of the green were there. My uncles Johnny, Jimmy and Mike came as well as all the Fox cousins. The church was packed with people from the area and some were standing. I came into the sacristy to vest. There were about twelve altar boys in that small room. They all gave me their names, most of them familiar ones. Father Joe came in. He had arranged to be there in case I needed him. They rang the bell. We walked out to the sanctuary. The twelve altar boys went first. Sure enough, the biggest one led the way and positioned himself at the end of the steps, right in front of the big bell, and he sure rang it well.

With my back to the people, I started it in Latin and the boys answered in Latin. The whole mass was in Latin except for the preaching and announcements. After the gospel, Father Joe stood beside me facing the people and said, "I don't need to introduce this young man to you. Shane McGuire is one of you. He grew up here, went to your school, was an altar boy in this church and he has now come back among you as, (he hesitated and emphasized) Father Shane." One of the altar boys clapped then others joined in, then everyone clapped. The nuns stood up, then more people stood up, then everyone stood up continuing to clap. When they stopped and sat down, Father Joe said, "This is very unusual to clap in church. It is the first time I have experienced clapping in church, but I am not against it. If that is what you feel like doing, you should do it." Then I spoke. After telling Father Joe I appreciated his kind words, I went on to thank everyone for the warm welcome home and for the standing ovation they gave me. I thanked my father and mother for all they did for me, and for bringing me up in the faith by word and example. Without them I could not have heard and responded to God's call. I thanked my brothers and sisters for putting up with me, uncles and aunts and cousins and all in the extended family who had an influence in my life. I said a few words on the meaning of the scriptures of the day. Then I said that this was a mass of thanksgiving for the gift of priesthood. We were also offering this mass for all the parishioners. We extended our prayers for those suffering under atheistic communism and for everyone in the world. We remembered the dear ones in our families who had gone before us. That first mass was a time of keen awareness and concentration for all who were present.

At the end of the mass Father Joe announced that it was customary for everyone to receive the blessing of a new priest, so they all came up to the altar rails and knelt down. I moved along, placing my hands on each one's head and saying the words of blessing. I knew many of the older people, but many of the younger ones had grown up so much since I left seven years before that I could not recognize them now.

Mother and I talked a lot together. She was so happy to have me back home for a little while after being away for so many years. Dad spent most of the time sitting in his chair by the fire. He would get up and walk out into the yard. Mother would keep an eye on him, while busy with the housework and cooking for all of us. Sometimes Brian and Frank would have to go looking for him, as he would wander. He never was in any danger. We were far removed from any road or traffic.

I called in to see the local doctor. He was in the same house Dr. Byrne used to live in. The new doctor was young, just beginning his practice. He had examined my father and could not find anything physically wrong with him. He was sorry nothing could be done about the senility.

Father sat at the table and ate with us. He could not join in the conversation. I kept thinking of the old days when he talked so well and knew so much. I sat by the fireside in the evenings with him. He was responding to what I was saying by agreeing with me or repeating what I said. There were periods of silence. During those moments I found myself looking into his face and reliving in memory the long evenings when he told endless stories and had our full attention, when he spiced our conversation with wit and humor, and provoked so many hearty laughs.

I walked slowly out to the first field behind the house with him. We stood and talked on the same spot where he taught me gun safety, and gave me the gun to go out on my own for the first time. That confidence in me meant so much to me at the time. As I walked through the fields and along the riverbank, I felt his presence, even though he could not be with me now. I felt myself reliving the good times we had together when I was growing up. Riding the horse through the fields brought to my mind the stories he told on how he loved to ride on horseback and especially the time he rode fast at full gallop in the middle of the night to tell Dr. Byrne to come to the house because I was about to be born.

I cycled to Empor Church each morning and offered mass, asking God if he would work a miracle and give my father back his mind, always able to add, "thy will be done." One morning, on coming home, he was sitting down to breakfast, and looked up at me, dressed in priestly clothes. He said to my mother, "Give that young curate something to eat." He did not know me. She looked at me and I looked at her. There was an understanding of great pain.

Later my mother told me how badly she felt about the fact that he did not know me. She said he was careful not to put any pressure on me to become a priest, but he was very proud of me all through the years of study and preparation. She said he looked forward with great joy to seeing me ordained and now that it has been accomplished, he does not know you. "I looked forward to sharing this joy together with him", she said, "but now I am broken-hearted because of his condition, and feel I am already alone and the good life we had together is over and gone. I am left to live with memories."

It was a great joy living in the old house again if only for three weeks vacation. The two nuns, Aunt Lilly and my sister, Marcella were also staying with us for their vacation. No one had a car, so Brian took them around with the horse and trap. My uncles gave me a gift of a new bicycle. It was a man's bicycle, the first one I owned. Before leaving home there were two lady's bicycles. Mother rode a bicycle and so did my two older sisters. My father never rode a bicycle. He rode a horse in his younger married days and when he stopped riding a horse he used the horse and trap and would not learn to ride a bicycle. I went everywhere I wanted to go on that new bicycle. My sister Mary Joe, now Mrs. Ned Martin, was living on the farm about five miles away. I visited Mary Joe and Ned several times on my bicycle. They had four children now and I met them for the first time. Their names were Seamus, Bernard, Eddie and Celine. The last two were twins and were born just a couple of months before I came home. They were all delightful children, the first in the next generation, and I enjoyed them very much. Ned's father, who was also called Ned, was living with them and was there until he died in his nineties.

Mother had an interesting story to tell about Finn. He was always excited about shooting birds and hunting. He knew the gun and what the sound of a shot meant. We kept the shotgun in a cabinet in the parlor. Every time I would open the parlor door he would come behind me and watch me. If I took the gun in my hand he would jump with glee and dance a jig back out to the kitchen floor with an uncontrolled demonstration of delight. The sound of a shot meant to him there was game to be fetched. One day when everyone was out of the house and mother was alone with Finn, there was the sound of gunshot. Finn, who was lying peacefully by the hearth, jumped up, ran out the door and galloped down across two fields to the river. There were men there with guns and a duck floating on the river. Finn jumped in with his usual long leap, swam out and fetched the duck. They clapped and cheered, figuring this is a very obliging dog. When he got to the bank of the river he dodged around them and headed home holding on to the duck. Their mood and words changed, calling after Finn. When he did not heed them they were dumbfounded, thinking, would anyone ever believe this. Finn came into the house and in the middle of the kitchen floor presented the duck to my mother.

Mother told me many of the people in the area had asked to have me visit them when I would come home. So I visited many of the neighbors. They all had something to say about when I was a lad growing up, fishing, swimming and running.

Eliza Mac, on the next farm said, "You were a wild lad, always going through the fields, gathering mushrooms and running like a hare along the river bank. And look at you now. You had the trouble with your leg and you were away for a long time. We all thought you were going to be a cripple for life. And look at you now."

Every time I came into the front yard I could hear the blackbird singing from the top of the big sycamore tree. Listening to him brought back memories of my young days. I sat on a seat in the garden. This time Finn was beside me. The blackbird was singing joyfully. Memories of sitting there with Lab beside me and listening to the singing when I was ten years old and suffering the pain of osteomyelitis and waking up feeling Lab licking the sore leg, came back to me.

I roamed the fields of my youth and fished in the river that gave me so much joy in growing up. The river looked more beautiful than ever. It moved gracefully and whispered in the reeds as the wind blew gently. I felt it was saying to me, "Welcome back; where have you been? We missed you." The water hens called up and down the river, the curlew wheeled and circled above me with his distinctive sound of curl-u, the skygoat or jacksnipe dove from high heavens making the sound of a calling goat, the skylark ascended into the blue and sang from heaven filling my ears with joyful sounds and firing my imagination to wonder about the world beyond our senses and out of our human reach. It was all uplifting as I watched the cows grazing quietly, new cows as the ones I knew had been replaced. A gentle shower passed by keeping down the dust and making the grass glisten in the sunlight. This was creation as God made it. I belonged there and delayed, not wanting to leave. All creation was speaking without words, asking me to stay awhile.

I visited Empor School where I had gone as a boy and where I had suffered punishment for not answering the questions in Irish when I had a fever and great pain from disease of the bone before I knew it was called osteomyelitis. The children were in their seats. They all stood when I entered and said, "Good morning, Fr. Shane." The master came toward me with both hands outstretched. He shook my hands and said, "Congratulations, Fr. Shane. You'll be a fine priest." Then he fell on his knees before me and said, "Fr. Shane, please give me your blessing." Seeing him kneeling there before me brought back memories of how I feared him looking out the window every morning until I would see him coming on his bicycle. The times he stood over me with a cane in his hand and how he slapped me into dizziness with his right hand swinging at my face. I pressed my hands on his head and began the words of the blessing: "The peace and blessing of God . . ." I was choking up and a tear fell on the backs of my hands and splashed. I finished the blessing and gave him my hands to help him up. I was taller than him now. He was looking up at me. We talked about his family and my family and what I was likely to be doing in the future. I blessed the children. They told me their names. Some names were familiar, brothers and sisters of students who had been at the school with me. I felt very good being there in these circumstances. The children talked and asked questions. They were proud of me that I had gone through their school. I felt the gift of forgiveness and peace, healing all that went before.

And remember: Love is not love 'til it's given away.

CHAPTER 18

My Father Dies

The last six months before ordination and the first six months afterwards were spent studying and practicing what was called sacred eloquence. We were instructed and guided by our scripture professor and an experienced preacher. They gave us topics to write sermons on, based on scripture texts. They were submitted and evaluated. Then we had to preach them in front of the class in turns and each one had to comment, positive and negative, on what was just preached. At first, some of us did not want to be critical, but we soon got over that and became very honest and open with our criticisms. It was very helpful and progress was very noticeable as time went by and each one had several opportunities to improve.

We were also encouraged to listen to the preachers in the church on Sundays and when retreats or missions would take place. There was a large community of preachers who traveled to preach missions and retreats. When home, they took their turns in preaching in our church. We rated a few as very good and some not so good or very disappointing. Our teachers told us every class that came along was critical. Some always turned out to be very good and some not so great. They said it was easy to tell who was keeping up with studying scripture and writing their sermons. One of the teachers was Michael. He told us to watch out for signs of people being bored. When one of us would be preaching, if he felt bored, he would look at his watch. If that didn't help he would throw his head back and yawn. To one he said, "If you don't strike oil in five minutes, stop boring." To another, "The worst trait in a preacher is to be long winded." To another, "You don't know how to conclude, you've tried three times already, you have not thought the subject out clearly." To all of us he would say, "The first part you should write is the conclusion." Decide on the conclusion first.

My father's health was deteriorating. The doctor told the family he could go anytime. The only phone in the area was in the post office, four miles away. My mother cycled to the post office and called me in Dublin. She sounded very down and told me the doctor said I should come home as the end was near. When I got home he was in bed and could not speak, though his eyes were open and he seemed to be conscious as he would move his eyes toward me when I spoke to him. Mother, Brian and Frank were at home and they took good care of him. We prayed around his bed and we knew he was praying with us as he moved his lips a little trying to form the words. The doctor came and examined him. When he left the room he told us nothing more could be done for him, that we were taking proper care of him and that he could go any time, but probably had no more than a few days left at most.

Gradually, his breathing became more labored and he seemed to slip into a coma as there was no more reaction from his eyes when we spoke to him. We prayed a lot and read passages of scripture we knew he loved. Instead of gathering around the hearth to say the rosary, we gathered around his bed. We added the trimmings to the rosary that he was accustomed to, the prayer to St. Jude, patron of hopeless cases which they had added while I was in the hospital with osteomyelitis and never dropped, the prayer to St. Joseph for a happy death which he added in the month of March every year as March was St. Joseph's month, the litany of the Sacred Heart which he added in June every year as that was the month of the Sacred Heart and other prayers for the sick and the dying and our dear ones who had gone before us.

As he lay there dying, I was looking into his face. Those eyes that looked so kindly on us cannot see us anymore, that tongue taught us and encouraged us and told us so many stories is gone silent forever. Those ears that listened to all our problems cannot hear anymore. I felt saddened looking at my father dying, the father I loved so much and who gave me by his love and goodness my first concept of my heavenly father. It was sad to realize that heart that had loved my mother and all of us so faithfully and loved everyone in the world, would soon stop beating in death. I received a consoling awareness that he had fulfilled his mission from God on this earth, and fulfilled it exceedingly well, and was now ready to answer God's call to a better life with him forever.

On the third morning after I got home while I read the prayers and scripture passages to be used at a deathbed, and mother and Brian and Frank answered, father stopped breathing. His great spirit left his body and flew into the arms of God as we prayed, "Father, into your hands I commend my spirit." We observed a few moments of silence to absorb the meaning of this moment. Then we said the rosary for him, asking our Blessed Mother to welcome him into heaven.

Now funeral arrangements had to be made. We had no phone and no car. Who would we get to lay out my father's body? There were no funeral homes at this time. Traditionally, there was someone in the area who would prepare the body and the wake would be held at home. Brian said he knew of no one in the area who prepared bodies for the wake. Mary Burke, who did it for many years, has moved. The undertakers, in Mullingar only supplied the coffin and a hearse. Looking at my father, I got the feeling he would prefer not to have a stranger do it, so I said I would do it. I had no experience other than seeing the brother infirmarian in the monastery lay out the body of an elderly monk. He had asked me to help him as part of my "rounded training" though I was not of much help to him. He was experienced at what he did. Mother, Brian and Frank were amazed at my offer. They left the room. Brian and Frank kept coming in bringing me basins of water and whatever was needed. There was no running water in the house yet, just a hand pump in the yard. To me, my father was a saint.

St. Paul said, "Your bodies are temples of the Holy Spirit and will on the last day be honored in heaven." I lovingly shaved him, trimming his mustache the way he always did, cut his nails, washed him and did his hair. I dressed him in the Franciscan habit, which was his wish, laid him on his bed with his hands clasping a crucifix and his rosary beads over his chest. Mother, Brian and Frank joined me and we said a prayer now that we had him ready for the wake. Mother said to me, "You have a stronger nerve than Brian or Frank." She grasped my father's hand in hers and said words that have stayed with me. There was great sorrow in her voice as she said, "Will we ever see each other again?"

Paddy Ledwitch, a neighbor who was home on vacation, realizing we did not have a car, had told me he would be happy to drive me anywhere I wanted to go. I got on my bicycle and rode out the boreen to his house and told him my father had died. He sympathized with me and asked me where I would like him to take me. First, I had him take me to the parish house in Milltown where I made arrangements for my father's funeral. Next, we went to the post office and sent telegrams to relatives and friends, giving them the sad news and the details about the funeral arrangements. I also called the newspapers with all the information. Finally, we went to Dysart where my sister, Vera, was working.

We gave her the sad news and brought her home. Paddy was so patient and so helpful that even though I thanked him profusely, I still feel grateful to him. My brother, Mike, now a teenager, comes home from boarding school, Celine is in a convent school, Marcella is a nun and her order is very strict and she was not allowed home for her father's funeral. Mary Jo has a young family, four children. She came to the wake and the funeral mass. As was the custom, the wake lasted two full days with the burial on the third day.

The neighbors came to the wake. They would offer their condolences, go upstairs to the bedside, say a prayer, come down and sit around the fire in the kitchen or the fire in the parlor. They would share stories about the dead person's life and the important things he had done. People kept coming all through the evening. When the house would fill up, some would leave to make room for others. Tea and sandwiches were served, no alcoholic beverages, as that custom had died out having been condemned by the church because of abuses. All the visitors left by midnight. I felt for my mother who looked so tired and worn out. The family knelt by my father's bed and prayed the rosary, which he always did when we prayed it around the hearth. We pondered the words of scripture, "Blessed are the dead who die in the Lord." Then we all went to rest.

Next day people came off and on until it was time to take the body to the church. A crowd gathered at about six o'clock and we started walking the two miles to the church, four men leading the way, carrying the coffin, and all the others following behind. We prayed all the way saying several rosaries. When we arrived at the church, Father Willie was there waiting for us. We placed the coffin in front of the altar. Father Willie and I shared the reading of the appropriate prayers from the ritual. Then we said another rosary and we all left, leaving my father's body in his coffin alone in the church for the night.

The next morning we had his funeral mass at eleven o'clock. The church was packed with people and the sanctuary was full of priests. I was the main celebrant. As I looked at all the priests and people and my mother and family in the front seats, and my father's coffin before the altar, the full meaning of his death gripped me. We were praying to God whom we could not see, for my father whom we could not see now closed in his coffin ready to be buried out of sight in the dark earth, not to be seen again. Without faith this would be all emptiness. Thank God for the gift of faith.

It was the custom at that time and abolished since then, for the people leaving the church after a funeral mass to go up before the altar and place an offering on a table. The parish priest stood behind the table with the family of the deceased beside him as they watched to see how much each neighbor put on the table. The amount of the offering was a sign of the respect and esteem the donor had for the family and the deceased. The offerings did not go to the family but, to the parish priest. I had told my mother and the rest of the family they did not have to stand there. They said they did not want to and I said, "don't" and they did not.

We took my father to the parish graveyard in Miltown, five miles away. The family had a burial place there for generations. Neighbors had dug the grave. A high mound of fresh earth lay beside an open grave, which looked like an open mouth ready to receive the deceased. The coffin was lowered into the grave as we prayed "Eternal rest grant to him, O Lord." The gravediggers handed me a shovel, I looked at it. My father was the first to put a shovel into my hands and teach me how to move the earth, as his father had taught him. I took a shovel full of earth and threw it into the open grave and down onto my father's coffin. A hollow thud came back to my ears. The gravediggers filled the grave with the mound of earth they had dug out the day before. Earth had closed its mouth. It had swallowed him as it had swallowed his father and mother and other family members whose names were inscribed on the large tombstone that stood there, tall and silent, still unmoved by a new funeral, another grave swallowing another member of the family who had run his course in the everlasting evolution of the human race.

There was something keeping us from leaving the graveside, even though all the rest had left and gone their various ways. To walk away was the final separation and none of us in the family wanted to lead the way. I finally put my hand on my mother's shoulder and said to the whole family, "He is not here, his great spirit is with God and with us everywhere we go." So we walked away from the grave.

And remember: Love is not love 'til it's given away.

CHAPTER 19

Ministry in Scotland

In a conference with the Provincial Superior, I offered to go to Africa. He said, "Maybe at a later date." He was concerned for my health.

After the course in sacred eloquence was completed, the class was transferred to one of our houses in Scotland where we would get practice in preaching in surrounding parishes on weekends and in giving missions and retreats. The order at that time had two monasteries, two parishes and a retreat house in Scotland and they were part of the Irish Province. Members were moved from house to house and back and forth from Ireland to Scotland as the need arose. There was also an English Province with several houses and parishes.

This was my first time to leave Ireland. We crossed the Irish Sea by boat and sailed up the River Clyde into Glassgow, a large ship building port on the west side of Scotland, facing Ireland. Our destination was on the east side near the North Sea, on the Firth of Fourth outside the town of Musselborough. It was the monastery of Drum-Mohr, which had been an old mansion on high ground situated among trees on fifty acres looking out on the water.

It was a rather small community of about twelve priests and two brothers. We tried to observe the rule by chanting the psalms of the divine office at the various hours of the day. Sometimes it was difficult as so many members would be away helping in parishes or preaching missions and retreats. There was time for worship and prayer and walks in the extensive and beautiful gardens. On weekends we went to parishes near and far to help with masses, preaching, hearing confessions or in any way in which we were needed. A seasonal list of missions and retreats would be posted. We all looked forward to this ministry for which we had been specially trained. We were expected to write out all our talks and services and practice them before going on our assignments.

There was a parish attached to the monastery, which included the two mining villages of Prestonpans and Wallyford. There was a church attached to the monastery, which served the people of Wallyford, and the church of St. Gabriel in Prestonpans which served the people there. Most of the parishioners worked in the coalmines and they taught me a lot about what went on there.

I ran a youth group. Most of these young peoples' fathers were coal miners and many of them were waiting for the day when they could work there themselves. Many of the fathers told me how things in the mines had changed for the better. When they were young, they went "down the pit" at eleven or twelve years of age, and would come home black with coal dust from head to foot. Black men's faces did not look as black as they were. Now since the miners were unionized, the boys could not go down into the mines until they were over sixteen, and the mines had to have lockers and showers so that the miners could come home looking clean. They said there are many other improvements including better wages and more improvements planned, such as better ventilation of the mines.

My means of transportation around the area was the bicycle my uncles had given me as a gift. I used to cycle by a small park area and notice retired men sitting on benches. This day I recognized one of the men from seeing him in church. He was Pat Jennings. I stopped and said good morning Pat. He was happy to see me and introduced me to his two friends sitting with him. "Sit down here and talk to me," he said. "There is plenty of room." So I sat down and they all wanted to talk and tell me about their lives. Pat talked the most. I noticed he was having trouble breathing. He said, "I have to sit down and rest because I have silicosis of the lungs from coal dust." The other two said, "We are all the same, we have to sit and rest." They told me they started in the mines at eleven and worked 14 hours a day.

I was working in the parish for a while and living in the parish house with one other priest, Father George, who was my superior. I talked so long with the retired men at the park that I was late for lunch. When I came in, Father George was upset with me. He said, "I came by the park and saw you sitting and talking with those old cogers. You were wasting your time and keeping us late for lunch." I was feeling depressed, thinking of the retired men I had met in the park, the hard lives they had and now the misery of their last days suffering from silicosis. We ate lunch, but my thoughts were elsewhere.

As I stood at the church door the following Sunday, Pat spoke to me as he always did and told me Bart, one of the men on the seat at the park that day, had a bad turn and is now in bed. He feels he is going to die and would like to see you if you have the time to come to his house. Knowing none of them had a phone, I said to Pat, "I'll come and see him today. If you see him please let him know." Pat said, "I'll tell him and it will make him very happy."

That afternoon I got on my bicycle and went to see Bart, a retired miner, now dying of silicosis. I found the street and number. He was in a row of small, attached houses. The miners did not own these houses and could live in them as long as they paid the rent. I knocked on the door. The door opened and an elderly lady of short stature stood there. She seemed frightened and said, "Bart is expecting you" and walked inside as I followed her. She showed me into a room where Bart lay in bed. He thanked me for coming and said, "I don't know if you can do much for us." Then he said, "I'll call Nancy in. She is a better talker than I am." He added, "My voice is very weak, could you call her?" I said, "Nancy." The drapes opened and she came in. She was crying. When she wiped away her tears, she began to talk.

Nancy: "We were both baptized and brought up as Catholics. When we wanted to get married our families said we were too young, eighteen and nineteen. The priest sided with the parents. So we eloped and got married over the anvil in Gretna Green. Bart got a job in the mine here and this is where we stayed and raised a family. The neighbors tell us we are excommunicated and Bart will be denied a Christian burial. We never spoke to a priest because we were afraid of what he would say. Bart told me about meeting you at the park and you sitting on the bench with them and really listening with interest to everything they had to say. He told me we should talk to that man, meaning you."

I replied, "I'm here to help you." Bart said in a weak voice, "What can you do for us? I want to be at peace with God before I die." I said, "You will, because you have already accepted the grace to start working on it." He lived for one more week, during which time both unburdened their consciences and found peace. They renewed their wedding vows as we convalidated their marriage. The last words he said to me, which were barely audible, were, "I can die now at peace with God and everyone."

That was the parish church I started preaching in. My first retreat, a week long, was given there. When I would write a sermon, I would preach it in my room. Others did not like this, so I would go down to the water's edge and preach to the gulls hovering overhead. They did not pay any attention to me.

Some married couples and families came for counseling. I thought it was very important for people to have someone to listen to them and help them cope with their problems in life. This day a young man came in alone. He seemed very disturbed. He said he had problems with his wife and needed some help. I listened carefully as he talked. He said his wife had changed and was not the same person she was before marriage. "Before we married, I thought she was the nicest girl in the world. She pressured me to marry her and I felt the same. Now, she is so miserable and we are married only a couple of years. I feel I cannot take it any more. She is so moody, up and down, one minute laughing, the next minute cursing me: she complains all the time, she spends every penny I make. When I come home from work she complains about everything. She is jealous and does not want me to look at or speak to any other woman, she turned her mother against me and now she won't speak to me." He stopped for a breath and went on. "When we were dating I could not keep my eyes off her. She was everything to me: she made me feel so good, her words stirred my heart, her smile lit up my soul, I would just keep looking at her. She was so gorgeous and so sweet I could have eaten her. Now, I'm sorry I didn't."

   The Scott's and Irish were Celts. They had spoken the same Celtic language. It is still spoken on some of the Islands off the north of Scotland and in some parts of the Highlands. The Scott's were a tall people. However, some of the friends I made there told me that in some of the mining areas many people were short, due to the lack of sunlight in cases where they worked in the dark mines for generations. There were the Highlands and the Lowlands. There were no coalmines in the Highlands. Traveling through some of the areas where mining had gone on for a long time, there were high hills of coal dust and waste marking the landscape. As it was being explained to me, I was thinking that is the dust that did not get into the lungs of the miners. The coal dust gave the miners silicosis and marred the landscape. The old miners told me in their time they had to hack away at the coalface day and night in artificial light with tools in their hands. I found the miners to be good friendly people. They were humorous, warm-hearted and loved to take time to talk. They felt honored when you listened to them. Having grown up in the fresh air on a farm, I could not imagine myself living that life.

   In the area in which I worked, they were not all coal miners. Some worked in the cities, in businesses and professions. One Sunday afternoon, a group of men took me on a tour to see the areas where they fished in the streams and the beautiful scenery in the Lammermuirs which were heather covered hills rich in wild life.

After showing me around for a while, they pulled up in front of a roadhouse. One of them said, "We'll go in here and have a drink." I said, "I thought no drinking was allowed in Scotland on Sundays?" They told me that was true for the towns and cities. The pubs and bars are closed on Sundays, but the law caters for travelers. If you are a "bonafide" traveler and are so many miles from a town, you can have a drink and there are roadhouses outside every town, which are open on Sundays. There was a problem getting a space to park. Each one ordered a nip and a pint. They asked me what I would like. I said, "I am not used to nips and pints but I'll have a club soda." We sat and talked. They told me about their work, their families, their golfing and their fishing. In due time, one of them ordered another round of nips and pints. The nip was a shot of whiskey and the pint was beer. Each one threw the shot down in one cast and delayed a while with the beer. The driver said he was having only the one drink as he did not want to be weaving, leaving the roadhouse because the weaving would be what the police would notice as people drove away. When I got back, my superior said, "Where were you?" I said, "Some parishioners took me on a tour of the Lammermuirs". He said, "You are really getting around, aren't you?" I said, "I like to get to know people and for them to know I am easy to talk to when they need me." He knew about Bart's case because we gave him a Christian burial even though the old records indicated he was not worthy, which indicated he was not worthy to enter heaven either.

Growing up in Ireland, it seemed everyone was Catholic especially in the countryside where we lived. Across the river in Longford there were a few Quakers and Dippers. My father knew them all and respected them. Ireland was ninety percent Catholic and most non-catholics were in the towns and cities. Now I found, in Scotland, that we were a minority, Catholics being about one in twelve. Paul, a classmate of mine, and I were going through the city of Edinburgh and looking at all the churches. They were nearly all Presbyterian. He said to me, "Coming here makes me feel there was a reformation, with the vast majority of the people and houses of worship Presbyterian. This was a Catholic country before the reformation and John Knox, who started the Presbyterian Church, was a deacon in the Catholic Church." We knew about the reformation from studying history, but now we could experience the results of it by living with the descendents of the reformers. We knew the big problem had been the Pope. We knew there were abuses in the church. We knew some leaders of the reformation had pure intentions, but we grieved the division, feeling if only the reformers could have stayed in the church and we could have the unity for which

Christ prayed. "That they may be one." We visited the town of Haddington, only ten miles from us, where John Knox lived. We spoke to a Presbyterian minister, Reverend Andrew Anderson, told him who we were, and asked him if he could show us around and tell us about the beginnings of the Presbyterian Church. Everything we knew so far we had learned from the history taught us in our Catholic schools. He seemed impressed that we were so interested and so open. He gave us time, showed us around, and explained how they saw the origins of their church and what their practices were at the present time. When we were leaving he said, "I enjoyed the time with you and it makes me feel a little better about the Catholic clergy." We thanked him and said how much we appreciated his time and how well he explained everything to us. Paul said, "It motivates me to pray harder for unity". He said, "That seems impossible." I said, "All things are possible with God." He said, "I have to agree with you there." We parted amicably.

It seemed to me Presbyterians and Catholics did not always understand one another. Catholics were forbidden to go to a service in any Protestant church and the Protestants did not come near our worship. Some people were telling me what they were hearing from Protestant workers in the mines and at businesses. They talked about these things because they were not sure if they were true or because they did not want to believe them. Some of the things they were supposed to have said were, "Priests can't marry because they would have to tell the people's sins to their wives, as there should be no secrets between husband and wife." Another one, "Priests don't marry because the church does not want to support a wife and family." Another one, "There are tunnels between convents and priests' houses, so they can have fun and games every night."

I inherited a program of inquiry sessions to which non-Catholics could come and hear what the church really teaches and feel free to ask any questions. At the beginning of meetings I welcomed every one, told them I was there only to help and did not want to disturb anyone's conscience or criticize any other way of worship. I was not there to convert anyone. No one can convert you. It is a personal decision. We met once a month. There were about twenty to thirty who came each time. Some thanked me and said they were happy to have a correct understanding of what the Catholic Church teaches. Some told me they had already thought of becoming Catholic for various reasons, a Catholic spouse, raising children Catholic, example of friends and neighbors and so on. I formed a class of nine and prepared them to come into the church at Easter.

One summer's day a few friends invited me to go with them to a beach at Guillan, less than an hour's ride in a bus. The beach was beautiful, wide, with fine powdery sand, located where the Firth of Fourth enters the North Sea. When we went in I said, "This water is very cold." They said, "You know you are in the North Sea." It was surprising there were so many people there. It took a while to get used to it and it felt a bit warmer after we swam around for a bit. It was a really nice day and we sat there and talked. I had an evening appointment so I had to leave earlier than the rest.

On the bus on the way back a man in his fifties got in and sat beside me. We exchanged the time of day. Then he began a conversation. He told me he was a banker in Edinburgh. He was born in Aberdeen and now lived just where he boarded the bus. I told him who I was and what I was doing. He seemed very interested in the inquiry sessions I was running, gave me his phone number and asked for mine. The next day I received a call from him. He said he was interested in the inquiry sessions and would like to attend but first he would like to have lunch with me and get to know me better.

So we made a luncheon appointment. We met in the North British Hotel and sat for a while in the lounge. He had a martini and I had a soda. He said, "Before we go into lunch, I think we should visit the men's room." When we were finished and washed our hands he grabbed me by the cheeks with both hands and tried to kiss me and force his tongue into my mouth. I felt like leaving then. On second thoughts I decided to stay for the lunch and try to understand a bit better what this was all about. I wanted to help everyone but, I doubted if I could help here, but maybe.

I can learn something more about him. I am not against homosexuals: that's the way they feel, their orientation over which they have no control. We cannot control our orientation, but we are obliged to control our actions. I respect the homosexuals like I respect everyone else, but I hold them equally responsible with everyone else.

We ate lunch together. He told me when we first met, his name was Bruce. So now I said, "Bruce, you are a homosexual?" He said, "yes, and so were Christ and all the Apostles." I said, "What?" He said, "Christ said love one another as I have loved you." Bruce continued, "And all priests are homosexuals. That is why they don't marry." I said, "That is not true." He said, "Yes it is. Our bank is on St. Andrews Square where all the buses come in from all the towns in the country. Every Monday at eleven a priest gets off the bus from North Berick and another gets off a bus from Grangemouth. They meet, seem very happy to see each other and go off together. We see them from the windows of the bank and we know they are homosexual lovers." I tried to tell him he was mistaken, but he did not want to hear what I had to say.

He went on to tell me about his time of service in the armed forces as a young man. There was an army chaplain who befriended him and others. They had relations together regularly. This was the case with many of the young men there. Same sex relationships were quite common. Everyone knew and talked freely about it. Some of the young men told him they were exposed to this for the first time in the service and were delighted at how much they enjoyed it. Some had girlfriends back home and had to give them up. They were really homosexuals all the time but it took this opportunity to develop it and find out what they really wanted in life. Some of them said they could go either way, but he did not believe that. Union with a man was so much more exciting. He said most of the men despised him for what he was. They longed for women. He said he understood but had his own ideas and was happy the way he was.

After coming out of the service he was looking around. He felt the greatest attraction toward boys, especially those about twelve or thirteen years old. His sister and her husband took foster children and he visited the family often and brought gifts for the children. There was a boy, eleven years old, who had no parents and was there as a foster child. He felt very attracted to him and brought him anything he wanted as gifts. He would take the boy to his apartment where he lived alone. The first time he fondled the boy, the boy did not object. It grew into a frequent experience for both of them. Whatever he wanted, the boy went along with.

By this time I was beginning to boil under the collar and I was thinking of the millstone I was going to tell him about. I said, "I don't want to hear anymore." He said, "Please listen: I am telling you my life story." I said, "This is not a confession." He said, "No, but I want you to know all about me." He went on and told me he and the boy remained good partners as the boy grew up. He got him a job in the bank and they had a couple of good years together. Then I began to find he was losing interest in me and finally told me he was leaving. He was being unfaithful and I hated him and was happy to be finished with him. I said, "You actually seduced him when he was eleven years old? You know what scripture says about someone like you who does that?" He said, "What?" I said, "You should have a millstone tied around your neck." He interrupted me and said, "I never read that in scripture and you don't seem to know what is going on in the world. What I am telling you is going on all the time." I remembered Stan telling us in class about these things going on in the world. Now I am coming up against it in reality.

Bruce continued telling me how he had many more boyfriends and they all went the same way—unfaithful. He said he was now fifty and wanted a stable relationship. He said, "You are in your twenties." I said, "Yes." He said, "we could have a life long relationship. I have a home where I boarded the bus that day and would endow you with everything I have." I said, "You don't' understand me. I am not homosexual and I am horrified with what you told me about the boys."

"That was so sinful, leading young people astray. Scripture does say a person doing what you did deserves to have a millstone tied around his neck and be drowned in the depths of the sea." He said, "It is one thing not to agree with what I have done, but I don't want you preaching to me." I said, "You think I don't know what's going on in the world? You don't seem to know what a sin and crime it is to scandalize one of God's little ones." He said, "I don't agree with you: those boys went along with it willingly." I said, "But they were under age, as young as eleven. They were not consenting adults." He said, "That does not matter as long as they really liked it." I said, "What you told me about Christ and the Apostles is really blasphemous. Who ever started that story deserves a millstone." He said, "What was all this stuff about love one another as I have loved you?" I said, "It is time for my bus to leave. I'll have to go." I was torn in two directions, feeling horror at what he told me and wanting to be true in my mission to help everybody.

I made many friends while in Scotland and some of these friendships I treasure until this day.

The Gray family was always ready to help in any way. Mary, who was a secretary for a business in Edinburgh, a short bus ride away, typed my sermons. I preached retreats, usually a week long, in Scotland, England and Ireland. There were a lot of sermons to be typed and Mary did them all for me. She keeps in touch with me still.

I enjoyed preaching retreats, meeting new people and ministering to them in their need. Being new in the field, it was quite challenging. There was preaching every day, masses, time for confessions and visiting the sick and homebound, and being ready for the surprises.

On this particular retreat large numbers of people came and it was a very busy week. The local parish priests were very happy, saying it was a very successful retreat, a real renewal of faith for the whole parish. I was invited back to give a weekend retreat for the children of the parish. This was a very joyful experience. Coming home on a train I experienced pain in the leg where the surgery was done twice for the osteomyelitis. The pain persisted and I thought it would go away, but it did not. I could not sleep that night and the next day I saw a doctor. He had the leg x-rayed and there was the old demon back again, or rather, active after a dormant period of time.

I saw an orthopedic surgeon in Edinburgh, the city where Dr. Brodi had discovered osteomyelitis, which became known as Brodi's abscess. The surgeon was Dr. Lawson Dick. He said he would do more radical surgery than what was done before, chiseling out much more of the bone and giving me the maximum amount of penicillin. I spent four weeks in St. Raphael's Hospital, run by the Blue Nuns. The sisters took good care of all the patients, giving us comfort and peace of mind. Dr. Lawson Dick visited me regularly. He explained how he had done the surgery and how radical it was, saying there should be no recurrence of the disease. The osteomyelitis never came back again. He told me to use a walking stick for a couple of months as the bone was greatly weakened and a break would be very serious. I followed his advice and had no more trouble with the leg. I think of other boys in the Coole Hospital, so bad, they had to face spending their lives in a cripples home while I was pursuing a life's dream.

The Scottish people were very friendly and many families have kept in touch with me over the years. To mention just a few, there was the Fitzpatrick family: Margaret still writes to me every Christmas. The Dowds family were always ready to help: Mary and Anne write to me still. The Gun and Dolan families keep in touch with me. Tommy Dolan has visited me in the U.S. He was a member of the youth group I had in the parish. There was a small farm attached to the monastery. Andrew O'Brien lived in the gate lodge and milked the cows, also taking care of maintenance of the grounds. He and I had great conversations about the old days when he was a coal miner. His daughter Mary and granddaughter Rosemary were frequent visitors from Edinburgh, a half hour away by bus. I often gave them roses from the monastery rose garden to take home, which they greatly appreciated. Rosemary was training to be a nurse in a hospital in Edinburgh. She met and married a doctor Faird Shariff. They moved to Canada where he still practices as a surgeon. They have children and grandchildren, always keeping in touch with me over the years, which I greatly appreciate.

And remember: Love is not love 'til it's given away.

CHAPTER 20

Rome

The order elected a new Father General who was the top superior of all the members in the world. For the first time this superior was an American. One of the first decisions he announced was a visitation of all the houses and monasteries of the order. During the visitation, he would have a private conference with each individual member. He came to the Irish Province of the order and visited all the houses, having a private conference with each member. I remember the conference I had with him. He was very progressive in looking for information and insights to help him in solving problems and giving new impetus to the life and work of the members throughout the world.

Shortly afterwards, he called me to Rome. He wanted me to be the guestmaster at the international motherhouse and Basilica of Saints John and Paul. I read the letter while down at the home farm visiting my mother who was ill. My brother, Brian, commented to me, "You turned pale when you read that letter. Is it bad news?" I said, "No, but it is a shock. I have to go to Rome as soon as possible. The General wants me to be the guestmaster."

I had never traveled outside the British Isles. Now I am preparing to travel to Rome, by train, except for ferry boats across the Irish Sea and the English Channel. It will be interesting being in countries so close together and speaking different languages and having different currencies.

I stopped over for a day in Paris and took a guided tour of the city. The guide asked me where I was from. I told him I was from Ireland and was now on my way to Rome. He told me the road we were on then was the road that great Frenchman, St. Patrick took when he walked to Rome to become a missionary to evangelize the Irish. I did not tell him I had, within the past year, preached a retreat in the town of Old Kelpatrick in Scotland, where the people told me that's where St. Patrick was from, the great Scotsman who evangelized the Irish. On St. Patrick's Day in Rome, the dining room would be draped in green with a big sign on the end wall. "St Patrick, The Great Italian who evangelized the Irish." In Paris, we were shown all the highlights, and I headed for Rome the next day.

I took the Blue Train, that went from Paris to Scicily. There was a dining car and the meals were very good. I had a bench seat all to myself and, as night fell, settled in to sleep. In early morning, at first light, border guards wakened me as we were crossing the frontier into Switzerland. My head was close to the window and I looked up and saw the snowcapped Alps, pointing with stark grandeur into the blue morning sky. This sight remained with me.

All day long the train traveled at high speed down through Italy with changing scenery, Mountains, hills, rivers and plains. As I looked out the windows at farmhouses and flat farmland it was quite new and different to me. The houses were painted in bright colors. A woman would be standing in the midst of grazing goats, cows were yoked to ploughs tilling the ground. Another passenger who was Italian kept explaining everything to me. When I said I never saw cows pulling a plough before, he explained that they could not afford horses and that the cows were very economical. They would work during the day and be milked in the evening. You could not do that with horses. The vineyards and olive groves were also new to me and were a delight to look at.

In late afternoon we arrived in Rome, they called it Roma. I took a taxi to Saints John and Paul's. On the way we got into a traffic jam. I tried to engage the driver in conversation. He told me he was a communist. He never saw the Pope, he did not believe there was a god. He banged his hand against his head and said I was a fool being a priest. Suddenly he was shouting at another taxi driver who was very close to him. He jumped out of his taxi and the other driver jumped out of his. They faced each other, sparring with their fists clenched and shouting but did not make any physical contact. Traffic began to move. They jumped back into their taxis. That was my introduction to the eternal city.

I rang the monastery doorbell. A burly Italian brother opened the door. He was dressed in the black habit as all members were at all times, even on the streets of the city. He was very friendly and told me Father General was expecting me. He called him. He came to the parlor at the entrance and gave me a great welcome. Being American, he was the first non-Italian general in the order. We chatted for a while. He told me how happy he was to have me as guestmaster and tomorrow the retiring guestmaster, Father Mel, would fill me in on what I should do.

A brother, who introduced himself as Bernardo, took me to my room. The last room left. It was on the third floor, which was the top floor and beside the bell tower, which was called the campanile. There were two windows in the room, both on the side facing the bell tower. There was a walkway between my room and the bell tower. Those who walked by could say hello in my windows which were always open because of the heat and there were no screens and no air conditioning. The Bells in the bell tower rang every fifteen minutes and tolled the number of the hour on every hour. It was very difficult trying to get sleep and we had to rise and chant the psalms called matins from two to three in the morning and be up again at six. I suffered there and was told suffering would make me holy.

There was a wing for men making a retreat or visiting for a short time. Groups of priests and laymen came. Father Cajetan conducted retreats and was available to all who came. Father Mel was an Irishman who worked for many years in Australia. He was in Rome when the war started and remained there up until the time I came. He served as guestmaster for the English-speaking people. He was very gracious, loved people and was very highly regarded.

They took me all over the place and showed me everything. The city of Rome was originally established on seven hills. Saints John and Paul's is on one of those hills, the Coelian hill. Rome started as a city in pre-Christian time and became an empire. There were gardens of some thirty acres. While walking there we could look down on the coliseum. There were many fruit trees. I always remember the size of the purple figs hanging from the fig tree branches. Some cardinals from the Vatican came to walk in those gardens. That gave me the feeling of living in an age that is long gone.

The monastery was built over the original house of John and Paul, early Christian martyrs, who were killed there. This area was excavated and the various rooms in the house identified. The basilica dating from the fifth century built with very thin bricks and massive walls was very popular for weddings. In a basilica the celebrant faces the people. I experienced doing this before it was extended to all churches by the second Vatican council. There is a piazza in front of the church and monastery and it is paved with cobblestones as is the narrow, old road that runs down by the side of the basilica, which is popular as a lover's lane. One day an Italian priest and I were walking that lane to catch a tramcar when we passed a couple making out. The Italian priest said, "How do you expect to go to paradiso?" The boy answered, "We are going to paridiso right now."

Father Mel said he would work with me for a while and at the right time, gradually fade into the background, encouraging me to take over. Some visitors came to the monastery door. Those he took to his office and talked to them there. Most people wanted to see the underground excavations, revealing the house where John and Paul lived and were martyred and buried. Some groups of priests or laymen came to make retreats of a few days or a week. I conducted some retreats for English speaking groups, including an ordination retreat for students from the Beda seminary for late vocations. They were older than the students in other seminaries and had very interesting backgrounds.

Mel emphasized the importance of first impressions and expressing the joy of encountering people for the first time. We were always meeting new people and there were few repeat visits though there were some, as I will mention later. He repeatedly told me, even though we were trained to preach, we will be most helpful to people when we listen well with full and genuine attention. Some talked about their families back home, some talked about the trip they were on, some asked questions about the martyrs, John and Paul, and their excavated house we were showing them. Some wanted an audience with the Pope, Pius XII. We helped make arrangements and sometimes went with small groups. It was rather easy to get visitors into large audiences when the pope appeared on Sundays and Wednesdays at the balcony in St. Peter's Square or at Castelegandolfo in the summer. Getting people into private or semi-private audiences was more difficult. At the beginning of my time in Rome, I went with very small groups, where the Holy Father spoke to each individual and had pictures taken. In this way, I got to know him personally. From pictures I had seen, Pius XII looked tall, but when I stood beside him, he seemed small to me. I was looking down at him.

Father Mel was good not only at greeting people, but also listening to them and answering questions. He also considered it equally important when saying goodbye to do it the right way. He would say to me, "We don't just say goodbye and close the door or walk away." I observed what he did and did it with him. After saying goodbye and wishing them bon voyage, or God's blessing on their trip, we would not close the door but stand there as the people walked across the piazza to a car or bus. Invariably the visitors would turn and look back. We would wave to them and they would wave back to us.

As Mel faded into the background and let me take the leading role with visitors, he seemed to be quite pleased with how I was doing and told me so. I enjoyed meeting people and he knew it. At the beginning he was saying, "If you don't like sharing your life with people, don't stay in this job." Now, he was saying, "You really like people and you are the right man for this job."

As time went by I met people from all over the world, enjoyed greeting them and talking with them. On two days a week I took groups to the catacombs, galleries and historic sites. One day we had two buses filled with teenage girls from a convent school in England. There were two sisters, one on each bus. I greeted them all and began to show them around. We went down into the original house of John and Paul. In the midst of my explaining everything, the lights went out. We were in total darkness. First there were screams, then as I called for attention, they quieted down. I instructed them to form a human chain as I led the way out, hoping the lights would come back on.

I could not see anything and depended on feeling the walls and trying to remember just exactly where we were at each passing moment. We moved very slowly and they were all very quiet. Finally, I was on the stairway going up and began to see some light. When I told those close to me word went down the line fast. We emerged and they all ran into the piazza cheering. I found an electrician up on a ladder, working on the main electric box. I told him the lights were out in the underground area. He said he had to turn off the main switch in order to do his work. After that I invested in a flashlight and always brought it with me when taking people down into the underground. The two sisters and all the girls were in Rome for several days. I took them to other historical sites and helped arrange a group audience with the Pope. When leaving they were profuse in their expressions of gratitude, especially for leading them up out of the darkness.

It seems every cardinal had a titular basilica. Saints John and Paul's was the titular basilica of Cardinal Spellman of New York, and many U.S. visitors to Rome wanted to see it. At one point, Cardinal Spellman took a ship full of prominent people in his archdiocese across the Atlantic and came to Saints John and Paul's to a celebration in his titular basilica. There were several hundred of them and I greeted them all, including the cardinal as they entered. I figured the cardinal would not remember me as there were so many dignitaries greeting him. Later when I met him in New York, he remembered me.

One day two young men, dressed in long, black robes came. They said they were seminarians, studying to be priests in the Anglican Church in England.

They had made a pilgrimage to Rome on foot, wanted to learn more about the early Christian martyrs, and if possible, have an audience with the Holy Father. I welcomed them and told them I was very happy to help them. When I expressed surprise at their calling the Pope, the Holy Father, since their church was not in communion with Rome, they said emphatically they considered him their Holy Father and were very desirous of seeing him while in Rome. An audience with a small group was arranged which made them very happy. They impressed me as spiritual men with real strong faith.

The food was very different from what I had been accustomed to, vegetables and some other dishes seemed to be swimming in olive oil. There was a half bottle of wine put in front of each one at lunch and again at dinner, that was a full bottle of wine a day for each person. I tried to eat the meals but did not drink the wine. An Arab priest, a native of Jerusalem sat beside me. After drinking his own wine he swallowed mine also. This came to an end when the superior of the monastery had the house doctor speak to me on one of his visits, because he noticed I was loosing weight. The doctor talked to me. When I told him I could not stomach all that olive oil, he asked if I was drinking the wine. I said no because I was not used to it. He told me that was my problem, that the wine counteracted the olive oil. I followed the doctor's orders and felt a lot better. The Arab priest, Albert, lost out. I really enjoyed the fruit they served at every meal, especially the big juicy purple figs. During Lent we had meat only once a week, on Sundays. That was where I was introduced to baccala, dried codfish. It seemed we were getting it just about every day. I ate it because I was so hungry. That's when the wine helped a lot.

Italian was not one of my languages I had studied before going to Rome. So now I got down to learning it in earnest. I took some courses in Italian grammar and found it not too difficult. The spoken word was different. Father Gerardo, a college professor, graciously spent time with me nearly every day instructing me in speaking words, phrases and sentences. Those whom I could understand best and spoke the clearest were children. They played in the piazza. Sometimes I would join them, to their delight. I told them I was learning to speak Italian and they all wanted to be my teachers. They shouted and argued while they kicked a ball around. I was learning a lot of new words and repeating them, to their amusement. Sometimes they were telling me I was good, and at other times they were correcting me repeatedly. When they got angry with one another they used curse words or bad words and told me not to use them. So I avoided them in conversation. I found great satisfaction in learning new words and being understood when I spoke.

At Sunday masses I stood by the Basilica door and greeted people in my best Italian as they entered. Some became very friendly and a few asked me to hear their confessions. I told them I did not have faculties in the Diocese of Rome to hear confessions. Father Gerardo, who was very friendly with many of the local people, spoke to the monastic superior and recommended he petition the Roman Vicariate for faculties for me to hear confessions. The monastic superior spoke to me, commended me for the way I mixed with the people and said he would petition the Vicariate for faculties for me. He also said they are very strict and don't always grant the request. A few days later he showed me a document saying I was approved and granted faculties to be a confessor in the Diocese of Rome.

I was assigned for certain times. The brother sacristan put my name up on a confessional door. There were confession times every day, before and after morning masses and at other hours. It was very fulfilling for me to be able to help people from many countries find peace of mind and enable them to have properly informed consciences and not be burdened with fears and erroneous ideas. Most of those I dealt with were Italian speaking with a minority who spoke other languages.

Father Gregory Manly, from Dublin, was in Rome doing studies in scripture. On Sunday afternoons we went for walks. One of our favorite places was the Borgese Gardens, which we entered from the top of the Spanish steps. These were very extensive gardens with roads through them. We were always amazed at the numbers of young ladies in groups of twos, threes and fours, walking in the area. Most of them were very elegant. Their gait, posture and carriage were very impressive. We sometimes ended up in a German beer garden where most of the foreign students went to have a beer. In Italy all of the natives drank wine. In restaurants you would see children at tables drinking wine with their parents. Because of our garb, everyone knew we were clerics. In Rome, you do as the Roman's do. All clerics wore the black cassock or their religious habit. When you got off the train or plane and came to your residence, you took off your street clothes and donned your religious garb which you wore wherever you went while in Rome, on the streets, on busses and street cars, in restaurants and beer gardens.

The English, Scottish, Irish and Australian students sometimes met there on a Sunday afternoon. All of us were dressed in black habits or cassocks and all wore the large, black, broad-brimmed roman hats. It was an opportunity to relax together and share stories about the home countries. The German students wore red cassocks, which made them very conspicuous everywhere they went. Word went around among the other students that it was to keep them out of trouble.

Father Gerardo, who had helped me greatly with speaking Italian, asked me if I would help a teenage, local boy, who was learning to speak English, if I could find the time. I knew that would be difficult but said I would try and find a half hour each week. Sergio was dropped off by his older sister, Maria, to whom he introduced me. They were very friendly people and took me to see areas of ancient Rome, which they found most interesting. One day they took me to the Old Appian Way with the original paving stones, and explained everything to me. This was my first time to see it. The wealthy people of pre-Christian Rome had themselves entombed in mausoleums along the roadside, some with life size statues. When the barbarians came they found treasures hidden in some of the mausoleums and they raided all of them. They vandalized everything they came upon. Statues were standing there with heads and hands broken off. I tried to imagine all of this happening long ago as I looked at what was left to tell the stories. They took me with some of their young friends to the open-air opera in the area known as the Baths of Caracalla. As we entered, I was imagining the ancient Romans going there for their baths. We had a most enjoyable evening. One Sunday afternoon in October, they took me to the wine festival in Frascati. The fountain in the village piazza, instead of shooting water in the air, was shooting wine. As it came down into the large basin area, everyone could drink as much as they wanted.

This time when Maria came to pick up Sergio, she was coming from playing tennis, still dressed in her tennis outfit, all white, which contrasted with the color of her Mediterranean skin and her black hair. She looked like the perfect model any artist would love to portray. To me, she looked perfectly wholesome and beautiful. Something inside me was saying, don't get too friendly: she has such charm. The superior general who had brought me to Rome came in through the door as I was speaking with her. I introduced him to Maria. Later he commented on how beautiful she was and expressed amazement on how I had come to know the local people, warning me to watch out for these Roman girls because "you could get smitten."

There is a saying, "all roads lead to Rome." Walking the city streets one felt this was true. We brushed shoulders with people of so many different nationalities, so many languages could be heard spoken, like at the tower of Babel, and so many different physiques and features could be seen, that it truly felt like the crossroads of the world. Walking with Sergio and Maria one day we were noticing the numbers of young Germans, probably most of college age, very distinctive, with their long, bare legs and shorts, real short leather shorts and cameras strung over their shoulders or up to their eyes photographing monuments. Maria commented, "They are conquering Rome, again."

My commitment of giving myself in total dedication to God and to serving his people, living a celibate life, was indeed the sacrifice Father Herbert had warned me about when I first felt I was being called to God.

During the time I spent doing parish work in Scotland I met very attractive girls and found them to be less inhibited than the Irish girls. It was all I could do to stay on course all the time. Now I am meeting attractive Italian girls and find a new appeal in their delicate beauty and soft charm. They made me feel so good, especially being so patient with my broken Italian.

Father Albert, the Arab priest from Jerusalem, was very helpful to me. He was in Rome for many years, having been there during the German occupation of the city. He spoke many languages and was well received everywhere. He knew the Holy Father, Pius XII, the cardinals and officials in the Vatican and even the Swiss guards by name. He had many stories about the war years and his work in finding and hiding Jewish families with Italian families he knew well, and were willing to take risks to help others. He introduced me to Pius XII, explaining to him that I would be accompanying people coming for audiences. The Holy Father was very gracious and we talked in Italian. From the pictures I had seen, I expected him to be taller. He asked me about my family in Ireland and the work I was doing in Rome. He said it was very important to make the pilgrims in Rome feel really welcome, adding that many come only once in their lifetime and will remember their experience for the rest of their lives. I met him many times after, with small and large groups and he always remembered who I was, calling me by my name, Father David.

One evening, after dark, Albert took me up on the roof of the monastery from where we could see the papal residence. He pointed out the window of the Holy Father's study, lighted up, even after all the other lights were out. He explained that was where the Holy Father wrote all his encyclicals, working late into the night, sometimes into the wee hours of the morning. I often looked for the lighted window, late at night and imagined him sitting at his desk writing with the church and the world in his mind.

During my years in Rome, I met people, made many friends and have many interesting memories. Those who had the greatest influence on my life and who remained good friends to me all their lives were Arthur and Iphigene Sulzberger of the *New York Times*, and their friends George and Louise Woods. George was chairman of the World Bank and a Trustee of the *Times*. We met in my early days in Rome and became friends. They were frequent visitors to Rome and got in touch with me whenever they came. We had many good conversations about many things. I learned a lot about the history of the *Times* and its influence in the world. I also got some insights into the workings of the World Bank. They always impressed me with their thoughtfulness and the high esteem they had for me, calling me an idealist. Our friendship grew strong and we greatly enjoyed one another's company each time we met. On many occasions they took me to leading restaurants for dinner. This was always a welcome change from the monastic fare.

Riding on a streetcar in Rome one afternoon, we were all packed in like sardines in a tin. People boarded at the back and got off at the front. At each stop some people got off and more got on at the back, so everyone moved forward a bit. A man stopped moving forward when he came alongside me. We were standing, hanging onto the hand straps that hung down from the ceiling. This man started talking. He was Italian and spoke English to me. He said, "I knew by looking at you that you were not Italian." He was tall and handsome and seemed to be in his late forties or early fifties. He spoke English well with a distinctive English accent. He was telling me how he admired the way the cultured English people spoke. He said, "It sounds very smart, just like this" and he imitated them. He put out his hand and said, "I am Georgio, and what's your name?" I told him. He was very interested in where I lived and what I was doing in Rome. When I told him about showing people through the underground house of the early martyrs, he said he would come by some day and have me show him around. I got the feeling he was homosexual and interested in me. I am not quick to think that way about people, but I knew it was an intuition and it turned out to be true.

Some days later he came to the monastery door. I greeted him and he said he would like to have me take him through the underground. There were no other visitors there at the time so I asked Brother Stefano to come with us, saying to Georgio he has been here a long time and knows the underground much better than I do. We took the underground tour and came back up to the office. It seemed time for Georgio to leave but he wanted to remain talking. He said, "I'll give you my phone number," taking out a card and handing it to me. "Please call me and we will meet for lunch. I want to talk to you." I did not feel comfortable committing myself to a luncheon appointment so I said, We can go into a private office, right here, and we can talk." He said, "That's fine."

Inside the private office I offered him a chair and sat on another chair with a table between us. He said, "I go to a counselor and he won't have a table between us. He says it is a barrier to good counseling." I said, "This is the way the superiors here want us to interview people." He said, "If that is the way, then alright."

He proceeded to tell me how he was taken by me when he saw me on the streetcar. I reminded him of someone who had been very special in his life and is now gone to the next world. The story went like this. In his young days growing up in a small town there was a priest who became a very close friend of the family and visited them often. He paid a lot of attention to Georgio and brought him gifts. When he would come into the house he would embrace Georgio and press him to himself for several minutes. Then Georgio said, "One day when I was thirteen and there was no one else home, he had me lie on a couch with him. He touched me and was getting me excited." I said to him, "Isn't this a sin?" He said, "Don't worry about that. God gave you these feelings to enjoy them." I thought, "If a priest does it, it must be alright. So I enjoyed it and he had me do the same for him." I said to Georgio, "Do you want this to be a confession?" He said, "No, I don't go to confession."

"This priest invited me to his house and I went there often. He would take me to his bed and we would have a great time. Each time afterwards I would feel guilty and think it was a sin, but then, he was a priest and it did not seem to bother him. He used to say I would make a good priest and he wanted me to go to the minor seminary and he would pay any expenses. He used to say the priesthood was a great place to be if you liked boys or men. No one is suspicious of your male friendships like they are if you have a girlfriend."

"When the time came I applied for the seminary. I was cross-examined several times. My priest friend came to my rescue saying how suitable I was. They questioned me about my relationship with him over and over again. The outcome was they refused me and the bishop was told my priest friend was under suspicion. The bishop sent him to South America and I never head from him again. I found out he had another boyfriend here before he left. I had thought I was the only one. I was deeply hurt and did not want to hear from him anymore."

I asked him how he felt about how it all began when he was so young. He said he felt very guilty and blamed himself. While his priest friend was there he suppressed the guilt but after the priest left he could not suppress it anymore. "I felt I was a misfit with everyone, unhappy and moody. I was not sure whether I liked boys or girls or both. I really did not know what I was. The only experience I had was with a man, but I did find girls quite attractive." I asked, "How do you feel about that priest now?" He said, "I hate him. He harmed me by seducing me at such an early age and he did it all for his own pleasure, and had another boy and kept it secret from me." I said, "You know what scripture says about someone who does what he did to you?" He said, "What?" I said, "He deserves a millstone around his neck and be cast into the depths of the sea." He said, "That would be too good for him."

Now, he said, "I want to tell you the real reason why I am here. After I got a degree in business, I landed a very good job. My boss Carlo and I became very friendly and fell in love. He and I were about the same age. He was a lovely person and I adored him. After my experience with the priest, I had doubts of faith and did not go to church anymore. After many good years together Carlo died of a heart attack about a year ago and I am lost without him." I said, "Did you get back your faith?" He said, "No, that priest destroyed my faith."

He said, "When I saw you come on that streetcar, you reminded me of what Carlo looked like when we first met as young men. Now I am nearly fifty and alone and I really felt attracted to you and said to myself, I have to get to know this man." I said, "You know I am a priest." He said, "Of course I do. People in the circles I move in say many priests are in male, love relationships, and they are very clean cultured men." I said, "My orientation is heterosexual and I am committed to the life I am living as a priest." He said, "If you try my kind of life, I know you will come to like it." I said, "No, I am totally set against it and am happy living the life I'm in." He said, "I misread your friendly attitude."

He seemed to be a real nice cultured gentleman. I thanked him for sharing information about his life with me and told him I wished I could help him. At that moment, Brother Stephano knocked on the door, opened it and said, "Your appointment has been waiting for you." Georgio said, "My hopes are dashed again: what am I going to do? But thanks for your time." I said, "Pray that God will guide you."

And remember: Love is not love 'til it's given away.

Shane as Father David a passionist in Rome

The New York Times
Times Square

ARTHUR HAYS SULZBERGER
PUBLISHER

December 22, 1959

Dear David:

      I am so glad to get your letter of the fifteenth and learn that you're coming to this country. Be sure to get in touch with me at The New York Times. The telephone number is   and if you dial that, it is   . My son also works here and his name is Arthur also so you might ask for the Publisher's office and that will make it clear. And then, whether I'm in or not, there will be a secretary here who will know where I am and how to get in touch with me. Iphigene and I are both eagerly looking forward to seeing you.

      I am sending a duplicate of this letter to your mother's address. Please tell her for us that she has a very nice son and that we hope to look after him.

      Iphigene and I send our warmest wishes for a very Merry Christmas and a Happy New Year!

                              Faithfully yours,

Rev. David McGuire
Belvedere Hall
Bray, Co. Wicklow
Ireland

mh
cc: In care of Empor
    Ballynacargy
    Co. Westmeath

Letter from Arthur Hays Sulzberger, publisher of the *New York Times* to Shane as Father David in the Passionist Order

CHAPTER 21

Coming to the United States

After four years in Rome I was looking for a change in ministry, I did not want to return to Ireland, where there were an overabundance of clergy at that time. I wanted to come to the United States and find ministry where I would be needed. My problem was I did not know anyone in the church in the United States.

While still in Rome I shared my thinking with the Sulzbergers and the Woods. They showed a great interest in helping me. Arthur and Iphigene knew Cardinal Spellman and members of the clergy in New York. They said they would go to work on it. Shortly afterwards I received a letter from one of their good friends, Father George Barry Ford. The process started and was successful.

That friendship was a real blessing in my life and taught me a great deal about reaching out to others. I will be eternally grateful to these good people for what they did for me. The last time we met in Rome Arthur said to me, "You can use the New York Times as your address in New York." Iphigene said, "Your mother or others will want to get in touch with you." I was deeply touched by their thoughtfulness. They enabled me to bring to reality a new life decision I had made. Arthur advised me to take up writing, and said writing would develop the latent talents he could recognize in me. I did some writing but life got too busy. When I was deciding to write this memoir his words were an inspiration to me, and got me started. Getting ready to leave for America gave me mixed feelings, happiness that my hopes were about to be fulfilled, and sadness about leaving my family, especially my mother who was in failing health. She had been fighting diabetes for many years and it had taken its toll. Of course I would come home in an emergency, but I did not know who would pay the fare because I had nothing. My family was paying for my trip to the United States and I did not want to think of asking them to pay for a return trip.

I booked on the S.S. America and boarded that ship at Cobh, Cork. That is where so many Irish people left their home country for America at the time of the great famine. The ship was too big to come into the harbor, so we were taken out to deep open water in a smaller boat called a tender. There were about thirty of us and we were all helped aboard The SS America, which looked like a lighted building many stories high as we looked up from our small boat. It was the month of January and after dark in the evening.

We were to be on the big ship for five days and six nights while ploughing a long furrow of three thousand miles across the Atlantic Ocean, with calm sailing now, but it wont stay that way for long.

There was a social life aboard, bars, piano music, dancing and entertainment. I was up early every morning and took a brisk walk on the top deck. The ship management knew I was a priest. They asked me to say mass every day. This I did every morning and twenty to thirty people of many nationalities took part. Later, during the days some of them approached me in a friendly way for conversation and discussions. There was a group of college students from Germany. They instilled a lot of life into the passengers. Two of them had a big romance going and wanted to marry on the ship, but the captain told them to wait until they got to dry land, terra firma. Jim, an elderly man from Donegal spent time with me. His story saddened me. He had spent forty years in the United States and then returned home to Ireland, to the old home he grew up in. It was now abandoned and he wanted to restore it and spend his remaining years there. It was not working out the way he had planned and dreamed. There was a real problem getting tradesmen to come and work on his house. He got so disgusted that he decided to return to the United States, where he had many friends and spend his remaining years there. I felt bad for him as he explained how he did not want to leave home as a young man, and then how he dreamed for forty years of coming home and spending his retirement years there.

Alana, a middle aged nurse, who had spent twenty good years working as a nurse in the United States was returning from vacation bringing a nephew

Steve of twenty years and sponsoring him to enter the United States with a working visa. Alana became a good friend and kept in touch with me until her death. Steve got into a union as an electrician, did well, married and had a large family all of whom did very well and contributed to the building up of the country.

Two young ladies in their late teens were going to New York to be nannies for wealthy families. They seemed nervous and talked a lot about what they expected. Alana showed a great interest in them and was very helpful in answering their many questions. We got to know a great deal about one another during the six-day voyage.

When we were about half way across the Atlantic a storm came up. There were very strong winds and the ship rolled and pitched severely, causing some of the passengers to get sick. Some of us had been taking walks on the top deck looking at the horizon all around with only water in sight, but now that deck was closed. One moment the ship was so high on a big wave that it seemed to be ready to break in two. The next minute the bow went down at such a steep angle the whole ship seemed to be going under. Then the waves broke across the top deck and would have washed anyone, who dared go up there, overboard into the ocean. This lasted for one day and a night and then we were out of it and into moderate seas again.

We were due to arrive in New York Harbor at eight o'clock in the morning. The evening before we were all excited in anticipation of arrival. Those who had done the crossing before were telling the rest of us how we should be on deck early to see the New York skyline against the morning sky. Morning came and we were all standing looking. There it was, just like the postcard of the great city. It was dim at first, coming out of the darkness. Then getting clearer every minute with the brightening of the new day. The "old timers" in the group were busy explaining what we were looking at and pointing out the various buildings and naming them. This first sight of the Manhattan skyline is still impressed in my mind, even though I have seen it many times since then. We passed Ambrose Light House, sailed through the narrows between Brooklyn and Staten Island. There was no Varrazano Narrows bridge then. We finally docked. We had arrived in America. When we docked, those of us coming for the first time, the immigrants, were assembled in a large room for processing. Each of us was carrying a large brown envelope we got from the American Embassy in Dublin. We had to keep this envelope with us all the time. It was very big, measuring about two feet each way. Carrying the envelope marked us off from all the other passengers. The envelope contained x-ray films of the individual's chest and other documents pertaining to the bearer.

To us it seemed superfluous, having been approved by the American Embassy and now having to go through it all again. A group of four of five men, dressed in business suits were standing at one end of the room and we were interviewed one at a time. One official would hold up the x-rays to the light and examine them. Our line moved slowly. When my turn came and my x-rays were scrutinized, the radiologist I presumed, seemed dissatisfied, holding an x-ray up, commenting to another official and tapping the center of the film with his finger. One of the officials told me to take a seat on the other side of the room and wait. An attendant said to me, "That man is great at looking into ribcages." No one else said anything about what was going on.

I felt rejected and wondered if I would be quarantined. The two young ladies, who were going to be nannies, saw what was done to me. After approval they came over to me and said we are not going to leave you here alone. We will stay with you to see what they are going to do with you. It occurred to me, this is their first baby-sitting job in America. There we sat like we were in a vacuum while everyone was processed. It took a long time. No one else was asked to "sit over there." Louise Wood had told me in a letter she would meet me when the ship docked. I was thinking of her now waiting so long for me; it must be very wearisome, seeing all the other passengers disembark and wondering where I was. The ship docked at 8:00 a.m. and it was now near 11:00. All left the room and left us sitting 'over there'. I ran after them and asked one of them, "What are you doing with me?" He said, "You can leave now!" I was relieved. The two girls were relieved. I felt very grateful to them and told them how I felt. They said, "We would not have left you alone."

As I walked down to gangway off the ship, Louise Woods was standing among a group of people. She was waving to me. I waved over to her. My mood changed from feeling rejection to feeling welcomed. Louise gave me a warm handshake and hug. She said, "Welcome to New York, why did they delay you so long before letting you off the boat?" I explained to her what happened as I still held the large envelope with the x-rays in my hand. She said, "That was ridiculous. Come with me and we will hail a taxicab."

The first impression of New York City, that has remained clearly impressed on my mind, was the yellow taxicabs racing in all directions. European cities, like London, Paris and Rome did not have yellow taxis. This was unexpected. Louise said, "We will go up Fifth Avenue and let you see St. Patrick's Cathedral." After having been on the ship for almost a week, with nothing to be seen but the blue water, this city was throbbing with life and the tall buildings were very striking and impressive. We passed St. Patrick's Cathedral. I had seen it on postcards, but this was different, seeing this beautiful edifice close up. It was truly impressive. I loved gothic architecture with the pointed arches better than the Roman curved arches. We stopped at Wood's apartment on Fifth Avenue, looking out on Central Park. It was a beautiful place and I was very impressed. We went up the Empire State building then the tallest in the world. Looking down on the streets below people walking looked to be the size of flies. The view was different from anything I had ever seen. It was truly enchanting. We visited the Battery Park, the financial area, Wall Street and the New York stock exchange, China Town, the UN and more.

Arthur and Iphigene Sulzberger had invited me to dinner in their apartment further up on Fifth Avenue, looking out on Central Park. They gave me a very warm welcome and told me to feel at home. There were several pictures of royalty and famous people from many countries hanging on the walls. Among them was a picture of Sir Winston Churchill who was such a dynamic force in the two world wars. All of these were people who visited there. I felt honored and deeply grateful to be invited to such a distinguished home on my first day in New York, remembering my growing up as a farm boy on the banks of the river Inny very remote from the world I am now getting to know.

There were several other guests there, one who was born in Scotland in what he called a butt'n ben, which was one room that served all the needs of the family. He now wrote for the *Times* and was a really big name. His picture was on the cover of *Time Magazine* that month, February 1960. It was a most enjoyable evening, one to be remembered as my introduction and welcome to New York on my first day there. Arthur handed me a letter from my mother that she had mailed to the *New York Times*. She was praying that I would arrive safe on the other side of the ocean. She sent her sincere thanks to Arthur and Iphigene Sulzberger, and George and Louise Woods for befriending me. She felt greatly relieved that I had such good friends to welcome me to New York.

During the dinner conversation Arthur was telling us about some of the reporting he did during the time of war and how dangerous it was at times. Someone asked him why he took such risks. He said he felt patriotic and wanted to stay with our troops and go with them even when they were in danger. We were impressed. He was a good man and a brave man.

And remember: Love is not love 'til it's given away.

Shane arriving at SS Philip and James parish,
St. James, New York (1960)

CHAPTER 22

Ministry, Parish, Hospital and University

The Bishop assigned me as an associate pastor in the parish of Saints Philip and James on the north shore of Long Island, in the village of St. James in Suffolk County. The northern boundary of the parish was Long Island Sound. On my arrival I was greeted by Father Jack, the associate pastor, whom I was replacing as he had been assigned as pastor in another parish. Jack, as he liked to be called, told me the pastor, Otto was not in but was expected back shortly. Then he showed me around the place. The church of moderate size, surrounded by trees, was too small to accommodate the large numbers in this growing area. It was still used, but most of the Sunday masses were held in a new auditorium that seated larger numbers of people. There was a small, white, parish school, but most of the children attended public schools. There was a convent on the parish grounds where four sisters lived. They ran the school.

We came back into the rectory, a two-story tiled roof building, which housed, not only the priests but also the parish offices. Jack left me in my room and I began to unpack. The pastor arrived back and came into my room. He shook hands with me and told me I was welcome; then remained standing there, looking up at me. He was short of stature. The thought was occurring to me that he would be happier if I were shorter. We had a short conversation and he told me he would see me tomorrow. In a moment he was back and said, "Do the seven o'clock mass in the morning and I will see you afterwards."

Next morning there were about twenty people and the four sisters in church. I began by telling them who I was and then proceeded with the mass. After mass the sisters and all of the people came up to me and welcomed me. After breakfast the pastor came to my room and gave me some basic instructions. "Father Jack is leaving in a few days and it will be just you and me here. I will post a list of your duties for the week. Priests in this diocese get a day off when they need it, never on Saturdays or Sundays because these are very busy days in the parish. Your day off will be Monday or Wednesday, never an overnight. All calls for a priest will be your responsibility, sick calls, calls with problems and so forth." He is standing there looking up at me and I had that feeling again, that he would like me to be more of his own height: then he said, something that I could not accept: "and don't visit any family in the parish." I said nothing.

Later I asked Jack about the "no visiting." He said, "pass no remarks on that, he has no authority to stop you from visiting. If you are invited to someone's home, go." He added: "He is jealous of you, he hates being short and enjoys being called Napoleon. I also want to warn you he goes into depressions at times and won't want you to leave the house. The people here are great and they will love you. You should have a great ministry here." He was so right the people loved me and I loved them. There were a thousand families and I tried to get to know them all.

There was no tradition of Catholic priests greeting parishioners at the door as they entered and left the church. I did it and considered it very important. People milled in and out of the church every week and did not see a priest except at the altar or in the pulpit. The people were very happy to see me. Many shook hands and exchanged pleasantries. Some stopped to talk and a few shared their problems. As the weeks went by, I got to know some of the people and remember their names. Children, especially, loved to speak to me at the door.

Several families invited me to their homes for a visit or for dinner. One Sunday afternoon I went to the Ryan family. They had neighbors, the Hunt family present, who attended St. James Episcopal church, a short distance down the road from the Catholic church. They were all very friendly. Lisa Hunt said to me, "We are saying you must have stopped at the wrong church. You should have come a little further to the Episcopal Church where the priest always stands at the church door and greets the people." They all laughed and added their own humorous comments, approving of what I was doing.

DECISION TIME

Shortly afterwards I was in the local post office and noticed a clergyman there doing his business. As we were both dressed in clerical street clothes we exchanged greetings. Soon we were talking and telling each other who we were. He said he was Pastor Mills from St. James Episcopal Church. I told him who I was and that I had met some of his parishioners. "Yes," he said, "and our people are saying you are more like us, greeting the people as they enter and leave the church." He invited me round to see his church. I went with him in his car, for I was walking, not yet having bought a car. It was a beautiful white church with a tall white steeple. He said, it was a typical New England church, built over a hundred years ago. The village of St. James was named after it. He very graciously took me around and explained everything to me. I would be in that church many times in the future, taking part in weddings and funerals of people I had come to know and love.

When I got back to the rectory the pastor was waiting for me. He said: "Who was that that dropped you off outside?" I said, "The Reverend Mills from St. James Episcopal Church down the road." He put his hand up to his face and paused, then said, "Don't make friends with him or any Protestant minister. They are all against us."

A call came in from Nanette who worked in the Studebaker dealership saying she had a good second hand car that was turned in and could be had cheaply. The pastor had told her to look out for a cheap car for me because I had no money. He said there was a regulation in the diocese of Brooklyn that was still in effect for this new diocese of Rockville Centre, that priests had to write for permission to buy a car, and explain the reason for needing it. The pastor said, "Tell the Bishop we are out in the country and many of the sick calls are several miles away, with no public transportation." I wrote the letter. An answer came from Monsignor Baldwin, the chancellor, saying permission was granted me to buy a car. "It should be moderately priced and conservative in color."

She showed us the car. It was a black, seven year old Studebaker and had one owner, a local farmer. She said the price is three hundred dollars. I looked at the pastor and asked, "Is that moderately priced?" He chuckled and said, "Yeah, I'll loan you the money from the parish." He knew I had nothing. Then as we walked across the parking area, he said, "You can pay back fifty dollars a month." I said, "Alright, if I have it." He said, "You should have it out of the one hundred and ten dollars you get as salary at the end of each month." I was thinking of how I could have enough to go home if my mother should get very ill. Nanette would call when everything would be ready to pick up the car. On the way back in the pastor's used Cadillac, on which Jack had commented, that little guys like to drive big cars, he said, "Now, you will be all set to take all the calls that come in, and that car sure is moderately priced and conservative in color."

I picked up the car, the first one I owned. My family did not have a car. Everything was still done with horses. In the order I drove their car, in Ireland, Britain and Rome. This car had a lot of pep to it and rode very well. The altar boys loved to wash it and polish it. Apart from a few scars it had from being hit by tractors on the farm, it looked fairly good. They would pile into it and ask me to take them to the beach or go clamming, which they taught me to do.

One morning, when I had a day off, I told the pastor I was going to explore New York City and drive through the tunnels and over the bridges. I was fascinated by the Island of Manhattan and how it had developed to what it is today, with no way to get to it by car except to drive over bridges or through tunnels. When I got back that evening the pastor asked me, "How did you do?" I said, "I did the Midtown Tunnel, the George Washington Bridge, the Holland Tunnel and the Brooklyn Bridge." He seemed amazed and said, "Did you have any problems?" I said, "I stopped on the George Washington Bridge and took some pictures." He said, "You could not do that." I said, "Oh, yes, traffic was stopped and I took advantage of that to take the pictures all around." He said, "What stopped the traffic?" I said, "There were sheep running all over the place." He said, "There were sheep on the bridge? No sheep are allowed on the bridge." I said, "There was an accident and a truckload of sheep were spilled out onto the bridge." He said, "You are having an exciting life, you visit the local Protestant minister, you buy a new car for three hundred dollars and you see sheep on the George Washington Bridge. Nothing like that ever happens to me."

I had to teach the altar boys the Latin in the mass. Once a week, at lunchtime, when they were released I took them into the church for a practice. They worked hard at it in trying to remember the Latin. It was very difficult for them because they did not understand the meaning of the words. One boy, instead of saying "laetificat" was saying "lift the cat" to the amusement of the others. When new boys finished the training, the pastor examined them to see if they were ready to serve. They were afraid of him and he thought they were too casual with me. They played baseball in the local park on Saturday mornings and asked me to join them. The first time I went with them they were teaching me how to play the game because I had never played it before. I had played hurling and cricket but not baseball. When I went in to bat, I was swinging the same as if I had a hurling stick in my hands. When I connected with the ball, they shouted, "run, run." I ran and took the bat with me like I had done in playing cricket. As I ran with the bat, they were all shouting at the same time, so loudly, that I could not hear what they were telling me. I ran around all the bases touching each one with the bat. Now, they were all laughing and did not stop until I got back to home base. They started shouting again and I realized what they were saying, "You have to drop the bat." Then I began to laugh, realizing what I had done.

One day when I had time off some of them offered to take me fishing. One parent came with a car. The rest piled into my old Studebaker, filling it with fishing rods sticking out the windows. We went to Stony Brook Harbor, stopping on the way to buy a dozen sand worms. They cost sixty cents. I had no fishing rod and just told them to fish as I watched. A little guy named Peter, who seemed to be the youngest had a brand new fishing pole, as he called it. I never heard a fishing rod called a pole before. Little Peter was too young to be an altar boy, but came in his mother's car with his older brother. "You use my pole," he said, "because I never used it." Some flounder were caught and thrown on the ground until we would be ready to go home. I hooked a fish and said to Peter: "Just reel it in slowly." When he felt the fish chugging at the other end of the line, he began to shout, "I have one." It was good to see his face as he reeled in his first fish. When he pulled it out of the water, he sat down beside it and left the fishing to me. As time went on, more flounder were caught. Peter had his fish separated from the rest. I noticed when a bigger fish would be caught he would take the bigger one apart and put his fish with the others. He repeated this several times and the others took no notice of him. We ran out of worms and had to stop fishing. Peter's mother had come back in her car to pick up her boys. Peter took the biggest fish that he was sitting beside and holding it in both hands ran to the car and showed it to his mother saying: "Look mom, I caught the biggest fish." She thanked me for taking the boys fishing. I said, "They were all very good and now you have 'Peter the fisherman.'" Most of them were fish eaters, so we divided up the fish and went home.

Part of my duties was to be director of the C.C.D., that is the Confraternity of Christian Doctrine for all children at the elementary school level and at the high school level. All Long Island, Brooklyn, Queens, Nassau and Suffolk had been the diocese of Brooklyn. It had recently been divided in two. The new diocese comprised of Nassau and Suffolk Counties. That is where I was located. The new diocese was beginning to organize the Confraternity of Christian Doctrine under the leadership of Monsignor Joe Lawlor and Father Fred Schaefer. This was before I got a car, so priests from neighboring parishes, Tom Minogue and Ray Nugent picked me up and took me to a meeting at the diocesan level to learn all about running a C.C.D. program.

We were to appeal at all the weekend masses for teachers, who would take classes in their homes or in the parish facilities. We were to visit all classes during sessions, listen and answer questions. Fred referred to me as an import. Tom and Ray and I became good friends and frequently shared on how our programs were going. The people responded well in the appeal for teachers. The most difficult job was getting teachers at the high school level. Also, it was harder to get the high school students to attend as many of them worked after school. In as far as it was possible I visited the classes during sessions and found this to be very rewarding. Teachers claimed they too were learning a lot, and I too was growing by getting a better understanding of the challenges students were facing.

There were a number of homebound people in the parish. I visited each one once a month, but a couple of them wanted me to come once a week. I found it interesting that both of these were converts for many years. They both told me it was the rich, devotional lives of their spouses, who had been Catholic and are now deceased that influenced them to convert. On every visit to the housebound I first listened as each one always had something to say. Then we read scripture and prayed before they would receive communion.

When emergency sick calls came in it was different. The police and fire department would sometimes be there and sometimes a doctor, even an undertaker. In the first call where the person was dead, a policeman showed me into a room and said, "There is the person." I saw a bed with the shape of a body under the bedclothes and a sheet over the head. This was the first time I saw a sheet over the head of a dead person, and I felt it was so wrong. A new hospital, the Smithtown General, was opened in the neighboring parish. There was no chaplain assigned, so the priests in whose parish it was located had the responsibility to answer all calls. The hospital filled up rather quickly and calls were coming in to St. Patrick's Parish in Smithtown. Father Adam, the pastor there did not drive and his one assistant was frequently away because of health problems in his own family. I visited there often and Adam shared his concerns with me. During the day his maintenance man would drive him to the hospital, but the night calls presented a problem. I was very concerned for him and even more for the patients who needed the ministry of a priest, victims of sudden illnesses, road accidents and so forth. I told him he could direct the calls to me in the next parish when he did not have a driver, especially at night. It passed through my mind that my pastor would not like this, but I felt the good of the patients came first. I responded to several calls and said nothing to him about them. One evening he picked up the call. I heard him say, "You have the wrong number, call St. Patrick's in Smithtown," a pause and then, "you called there and can't get anyone to come, and this is a back up number?" He handed the phone to me and I said, "I am coming." He said, "I don't want this hospital to have our number as a back up number." I said, "I feel an obligation to the sick people if no one else is available." It was about four miles to the hospital and I went there often at night and no one else knew. The doctors and staff there were always very devoted, competent people and I made many friends.

There were many sad cases that came to the emergency room and many shocked and distraught families. Some patients were dead on arrival. Three teenagers were killed in a road accident and I got to the hospital before the parents. They were all fearing the worst and hoping for some glimmer of good news. I was in the emergency room and the attending doctor, whom I knew, had just told me the grim truth. The parents were in a waiting room just off the emergency room. The doctor was told they were waiting. He said to me, "Come with me." As we entered, the parents stood up, and stared at us, crying. No one said anything: they were staring and listening. One mother asked, "how are they?" Then they all started asking questions. The doctor and I were saying nothing. Then they were asking, "Will they be alright?" Then, "Are they dead?" The doctor nodded his head. They clung to one another in a group and cried and sobbed. After a short time the doctor was able to answer a lot of questions. They questioned me: "Did you see them?" "Yes." One father said, "Did you give the last rites?" I said, "Yes, let us pray together." We all joined hands and I led them in prayer. They all joined in, in the midst of tears and sobs. Presently, other family members arrived, and the place became crowded. The doctor had to go back into the emergency room. We talked for a few moments. "You did it as you should do it—doctor," I said. He added, "That was a very helpful session we had with the clergy and doctors. I follow now what was said. In the case of death let the relatives work their way through their questions and wait until they ask, is he dead, before you say, yes. I understand they go through a very fast process of adjusting of sorts on their own. I hate giving bad news. I guess, every one does, but it makes it worse if you are blunt and don't' exhibit any kind of compassion. They were all kind of expecting to hear the bad news when they asked the question. Are they dead?"

Two of the boys were from our parish. I knew the families. We had three days of mourning, the funeral parlors, the masses and the burials. The whole parish was in shock and grief, praying the like would never happen again, that young people would learn from this experience. I experienced the like happening again in every parish in which I served.

The case that embedded itself in my mind was that of a boy of seventeen, because I was with him every day for the last twenty-one days of his life. It was the month of June and numbers of young people were at the beach every day. Some of them were diving into an inlet near the harbor. Paul did not realize the tide was low this day. When he dove in his head hit the bottom. The others noticed he was in trouble. They pulled him out and realizing he was not able to move, called for an ambulance. I was called to the emergency room. A doctor told me he had broken his neck and was paralyzed from there down. I talked to him. He was able to respond but could not move his arms or legs. I prayed with him and tried to comfort him. He asked me to come back soon and see him. Dr. Fischler, whom I knew, told me they were going to try surgery and repair the spinal cord, but that they did not have much hope. I was there the day of the surgery. When it was over, Dr. Fischler told me they could not do anything for him. He said, "The spinal cord is like mashed potatoes." I asked this doctor if he could tell me the prognosis. He said the paralysis would gradually creep up to the brain and he would not last very long. I visited him twice a day until the end which was about twenty-one days. He asked me, during one visit, if he was going to die. I asked him what did the doctor tell him. He said the doctor told him nobody could say for sure, but if the paralysis moved up to the brain he would not be able to live. He cried a lot and was very fearful. My heart was breaking for him. I prayed with him on every visit, prayed and prayed with all my fervor. His family was in anguish. I prayed with them and tried to comfort them. On another visit he said, "I am going to die and I am afraid." I said, "You are at peace with God, and you should not fear," He said, "I am afraid," I said, "Talk to God, tell him you are afraid and tell him everything that is on your mind." I started in that form of a prayer asking God to give him his peace. He told

God everything he wanted to tell him, especially how he did not want to leave his family. We prayed together for Gods peace. I gave him the sacraments of the church. Before I left he said, "Thank you for all your help. I now feel at peace with God." I said, "Thank God, and I'll see you in the morning." The pastor was ready for dinner when I got back. He said, "Did you see that boy?" I said, I did and he seems to be sinking. He said, "You keep slugging up and down the road night and day in that old Studebaker. You really did your best for that boy."

Next day, when I visited Paul, he could speak only in a whisper and he was losing concentration but he was peaceful. I was listening carefully but he failed to communicate. I blessed him and felt I was choking up and tears were welling in my eyes. It was the end. He went to God in peace.

The parish was mostly middle class. The families owned their homes and were gainfully employed. There was a minority, not doing too well. I noticed from doing the baptisms, most of names were Italian, next largest group were Irish names then German and Polish and a mixture of others.

There were some poor, single parent homes, people renting and some on welfare. There was no organization in the parish to help the needy. When I first met needy people coming and looking for help I asked the pastor what to do. He replied that I should tell them to go to Catholic Charities. The nearest Catholic Charities office was a half-hour's drive in a car, and some of the needy did not have a car. One young woman came in with two small children, she said the welfare money was all used up and she needed help to tide her over and feed her children until the next welfare check would come in three days. She was a single parent, her husband having left her. I asked the pastor for some money for her. He said, "Send her to Catholic Charities." I went back to the office to tell her. She had no car and had walked from a low rental house half a mile away. The children looked famished. I gave her some of my own money, realizing this was not really the best way to help the needy. While she was still in the office I called one of the friends I had made in the parish, Harry Dwyer a policeman whom I had spoken to that morning as he had that day off from work. I explained the situation to him and asked him if he could check out the address she had given me. He said yes and I'll be right over. He said the address is okay and I'll take them to the store. Later he came back and told me he helped them in the store and also used a little of his own money. He said their welfare rented house was bare. There was no furniture. The husband burned it to heat the house and then took off.

Some priest friends I had made in the larger area invited me to their parishes regularly. I shared with them some of the difficulties I was encountering. They listened to me and tried to advise me. One would say, "Complain to the Bishop." I would say: "I am new here and don't want to start off as a complainer." Another would say, "Tell the pastor off. Tell him you are going to complain." I said I would eventually, but needed a little more time to get established. They were very concerned and very willing to help me.

Catholic Charities had started a program to have all the pastors work more closely with them and use some of the parish resources to help the needy. My pastor resisted and two priests from Catholic Charities came out to see him. One of them was a young man like myself, Father Emmet Fagan. After the discussion with the pastor, to which I was not invited, Emmet came into my room to talk with me. He was like a breath of fresh air. He showed concern for me, telling me I had a difficult assignment, and encouraging me to "hang in there, the people need you." It was the Christmas season, and when he went back he sent me a Christmas card with encouraging words. I was impressed for we had met just that one time.

Father Christopher Huntington who grew up in the area and became a convert from the Episcopal Church down the road, helped us out on weekends. He invited me to his family home where I heard again about the history of St. James' Episcopal Church where the Huntingtons always worshipped and where his brother Prescot was an elder.

Father Chris and I had many good conversations. He helped me a great deal in understanding the people of the parish and their history. He grew up in the area, graduated from Harvard and worked for the United States Intelligence when he converted. He was now teaching in our minor seminary and was loved and respected by everyone. He told me the new State University in Stony Brook was soon opening and the Bishop will be looking for a chaplain. I thought it was going to be a full-time job and said I would prefer to stay in parish work.

Bishop Kellenberg's secretary called and told me the Bishop wanted to speak to me. He told me he had been hearing very good things about me and all that I was doing in difficult circumstances. He said, "I want you to be chaplain to the State University at Stony Brook." I thanked him and said I would prefer to stay in parish work. He answered by saying he wanted me to remain on as an assistant in the parish and at the same time be chaplain to the University until such time as he could find a suitable, full-time chaplain. It turned out to be five years before he found a suitable full-time chaplain, and even then he gave me the option to be full-time chaplain if I agreed.

Baptizing Mary Dwyer

A few days later a letter came from Bishop Kellenberg assigning me chaplain to Stony Brook State University and also telling me to remain on as an assistant in the parish. The pastor came into my room with a copy of the letter in his hand "Did you ask for this assignment?" "No." "Don't neglect any of your parish duties." "I won't." The State University was not in our parish. It was about a half-hours drive away. When I reported there I was told I would have to meet with Dean Tilly and he would introduce me to the students. He was very helpful. He showed us space where we could hold meetings and a room we could use for private counseling. He told us we could not hold religious services in the buildings because of the separation of church and State.

The first thing we did was to form a Newman Club. We had a priest from St. John's University come to us and guide us in establishing the club. Cardinal Newman was a prominent Episcopal priest at Oxford University in England during what was known as the Oxford movement in the eighteen thirties. He became a convert to Catholicism and was present as a Cardinal at the first Vatican Council in the 1850s. His book on the Idea of a University is still widely studied at Universities and colleges. The Newman Club was for Catholic students, but others were welcome to join. We went through the process of electing officers and drawing up guidelines. The club was to assist members in their spiritual, social and cultural lives, and be willing to help all students in anyway possible.

There was a lady in our parish, Peg Freeman, who had impressed me with her outgoing spirit and social activity. I discussed with her the problem many of the students had in getting to church because they did not have cars. Peg knew everybody and in a short time she had about thirty volunteers who were happy to go with their cars and take the students to church. It worked out well. Peg and her group, also helped in arranging social events, sometimes using our parish hall, when our parish youth would host the evening. This was very well accepted by the students.

Some asked me if I would be hearing confessions at any time. I spoke to Dean Tilly and told him some of the students asked for the sacrament of reconciliation and could we have a room for a few hours once a week. He asked what reconciliation meant. I told him it is usually called confession. He said he did not think we should have a sign on the door for confessions and suggested a sign saying counseling and explain to the students at a meeting that confession would be available during the hours posted. I decided to be there on Friday afternoons for three hours and stated I would be available at other times by request. When I arrived for the first session, a few students were waiting. The first student to come in was a girl. She sat down and began to sob. After a little while she wiped her tears away and began to speak. She said she was Jewish and knew I was a Catholic priest. She asked if it was all right to talk to me. I said, "Yes, of course. I will listen to whatever you want to say, and will try to help you in any way I can." She went on to tell me, interrupted by occasional sobs, that she had a beautiful romance with a lovely boy and she felt he was losing interest in her: could I advise her what to do to win him back. I told her I felt for her and realized she was going through a very hard time and suffering a great deal. The best thing now was for her to talk and for me to listen. She talked quite a bit while I indicated I was hearing what she was saying. After a while she said, "I feel better because you listened to me, because I had no one to talk to but myself and it was driving me out of my mind." She said "I think I am holding up the others: can I come back and talk to you again?" "Yes, of course: I am here to help." "What should I do?" She said. I replied, "I cannot give you an answer, you have to find it yourself and own it, but you are smart to get help." The next one in, sat down and looked disgusted. He started off by saying, "Did you know that girl who was in with you just now is Jewish, and she wasted a lot of my time. You are here for the Catholic students, you belong to us." I just listened for a while and then said: "Is there anything else on your mind?" He said what he had to say. Before leaving I said to him, "You don't want me to turn anyone away who comes looking for help." He looked me in the eye and hesitated, then said, "you're right."

Many of the students were lonely and needed someone to talk to. At the beginning of the year some of the freshman, being away from home for the first time were dreadfully homesick and found it very difficult to adjust. I was available for as much time as I could manage. Orientation days were difficult. Some students who came to me said they were going home. After they talked it out for a while they changed their minds. I did not know anyone who went home at orientation time or afterwards. However, some did not come back for the second year because in some cases they did not have the self-discipline to study responsibly and were advised to try something else. Some were content to do that, but some were disappointed figuring they were letting their parents down.

Students were telling me drugs were coming into the University and they wanted this stopped. I listened well to what they had to say and asked if they felt able to go to the administration and make a complaint. They were reluctant to do so and asked me if I could do it. I told them it would be better for them to do it, because I was held to strict confidence, and did not want anyone to think I could not be trusted. They said they would go as a group and complain.

After I was appointed chaplain to the State University at Stony Brook Arthur and Iphigene commented that I was following in the steps of their friend Father George Barry Ford who was chaplain to Columbia University when their children went there.

In one of our discussions I said I would like to learn more about Judaism and how the Jewish scholars viewed Christianity. Iphigene gave me a book to read, written by a rabbi. The thrust of the book was, "The Christ was not in him." I read it carefully and learned more on how the Jewish scholars viewed Christ. It was helpful in understanding one another better.

I am always thinking and trying to put everything together. Harmonizing my God of philosophy with my God of revelation is sometimes challenging. Then I pray for grace like Augustin did.

The parish work was very fulfilling for me. I liked working with families at all stages of life, from the cradle to the grave, from baptisms through all the stages of life including funeral services. In the same day I had to rejoice with the happy people and grieve with the bereaved. The pastor had a hard time dealing with people who did not come to church and then the families would want to have him bury them from the church. One of his sayings was; "He never came except when he was carried in, carried in for baptism and carried in for his funeral." I used to tell him, "We have to take people as they are and serve them in their needs. We will never really help them by being harsh or critical." He told me I was too soft and that I would change through experience. I didn't. On the contrary I developed more feeling for the people as time went on.

It was also very rewarding serving the students at the State University, visiting the sick and housebound running to the hospital and taking whatever emergencies the day might bring. On some days it was hard to get everything done.

When I had a day off the pastor would prefer I would take off. I had no family here, but many families befriended me. I would visit priest friends in other parishes and we would go out for the day, maybe drive to the city, sixty miles away, visit historic sites, museums and art galleries and maybe see a show. The Sulzbergers and the Woods would invite me to dinner occasionally. This was always a real treat for me, and they were always happy to hear how I was doing. Most of my free time was spent with the students at the University. I fished and swam with friends or spent some time on local farms, sometimes drive a tractor and always interested in how different it was from back home. It was mostly potato farming with migrant workers from down south. I liked to talk with them and enjoy their accents. The farms I visited were Bottos, Hartmans and McGunnigles. Their backgrounds were Italian, German and Irish. I had constant invitations to stay for dinner. These farms are gone now, swallowed up by the urban sprawl. Because the parish boundary ran along Long Island Sound from the Nissequogure River to Westmeadow Beach, and included two marinas, one at Stony Brook and one at Smithtown, there was a lot of boating and fishing in the area. Two of the officers from the Stony Brook Yacht Club, Russ Micastro and Walter Hazlit spoke to me one Sunday as I was greeting people at the church door, and asked me if I would accept the position of chaplain at the yacht club. When they explained what it would entail I was happy to accept and thanked them for asking me. I did the blessing of the fleet every year and still do it. I attended functions such as the commodore's installation dinner, responded to calls of various kinds as the need would arise and officiated at funeral services on request. I enjoyed getting to know the members and accepted some of the many offers of boat rides and fishing trips.

One morning, after celebrating a funeral mass, the undertaker, Davis who was a member of the Stony Brook Yacht Club, told me the striped bass are being caught in Stony Brook channel. After my coming into the area I soon learned the striped bass was the most sought after fish by the fishermen around. This fish is shaped somewhat like a salmon and has distinctive black stripes from head to tail. Like the salmon, the striped bass also lives in salt water and fresh water, spawning in the upper reached on rivers.

After the funeral that day, I was off duty, and decided I would try for the striped bass. I borrowed a casting rod and reel from Harry Dwyer who was going to work that day. He and his wife Rosemary invited me to dinner that evening. I thanked them and said I would come. The man in the fishing tackle store when he realized it was my first time to try for striped bass, proceeded to educate me, telling me striped bass were very hard to catch, and fisherman are very careful not to give away their secrets about what they use and where they catch them.

I drove down to the Stony Brook channel parked the car and walked out on one of the stone jetties there. The tide was running out from full and that was good. I cast the lure up stream and let it sink while I counted three seconds, then started to retrieve. The rod was nearly yanked out of my hands and bent into a semi-hoop. Then the fish ran and pulled the line off the real with such strength I said to myself, this one is over twenty pounds. After a couple of runs he went to the bottom and did not want to move while I kept the pressure on him. After a while he tried to fight, making short runs. I was hoping the line would not break and was in no hurry to force him to the shore. After what seemed a long time, but probably no more then about twenty minutes, he came close enough to net. He was a beautiful, big striped bass, my first one and seemed to be well over twenty pounds. I stayed there fishing until it was near time to go back to Dwyer's for dinner. By that time I had five nice sized striped bass, but the first one was the biggest. At that time, striped bass over eighteen inches could be taken and there was no bag limit. Harry and Rosemary in unison asked: "Did you catch anything?" I said, "Yes, five striped bass," They laughed: "Who are you kidding." I said, "Come and see them." I opened the trunk of the car and there were the five of them lying side by side. They gasped and could hardly believe their eyes. Rosemary said, "Harry, I bought you that rod for your birthday two years ago and you never caught a fish with it." Harry said, "I never had the time." Harry weighed the fish. The biggest was thirty pounds and the rest were all over ten pounds each. Harry took them to the fire house, where he was chief that year and showed them to his buddies who were there playing cards. They were all fishermen and plied him with many questions, where did he get them? What did he use? And so on. Harry came back laughing. "I got them all going" he said, "And they had a million questions." They wanted some of these, but I said, "no."

Rosemary had cooked a very good dinner of bear meat while Harry was telling us all about how he shot the bear. It was excellent. If they had not told me what it was I would have thought it was a beef pot roast. Harry was an avid hunter and I savored venison, elk and moose in Dwyers house where I was invited for dinner many times, and always enjoyed their company and had an enjoyable and relaxing time. They also loved to eat fish and had other family members they wanted to give some to, so I left them four striped bass and brought the biggest one with me. The pastor was excited when he saw it and said, "I did not know there were any fish in the Sound, I thought they were all on the South Shore by the Atlantic."

Some of the good people who had volunteered to drive the students from the State University to church were having a barbecue in one of their backyards and had invited the students. I was also invited, so I asked our cook, Margaret, to cook the striped bass and I would take it to the barbecue. She did a beautiful job and gave it to me whole on a large platter. I placed it on a table in the barbecue area. Everyone had to take a good look at it and all had acclamations and questions, some doubting that I could have caught it where I told them. After much explanation of how it all happened they all believed I did really catch it. Everyone wanted to try it. One girl said "I never eat fish when mom cooks it, but this one looks so good." So, she tried a piece and when she ate it, she came back for more. In a short time there was nothing left but the skeleton.

And remember: Love is not love 'til it's given away.

CHAPTER 23

My Mother Dies

The phone lines had not come into our home area yet, so all our communication was by letters. Mother wrote to me regularly and kept me up to date with all that was going on in the families and the neighborhood. When I wrote I was always impressed by her quick response. I could see her there when the postman came and sitting at the kitchen table with dinner cooking on the open hearth and reading my letter. She would take her writing paper immediately and write back to me. It took three days for a letter from me to reach her and three days for her letter to reach me. I recall writing to her on a Monday and receiving a letter back from her on Saturday.

Her diabetes was getting worse and then she wrote from the hospital in Mullingar. My sister, Mary Jo wrote and told me she had a meeting with the doctor and he told her mother had sores on her feet and they were not healing. He thought of sending her to Dublin where she could receive more specialized treatment. Shortly after that mother wrote me a letter from the Mater Hospital in Dublin. She did not complain; just told me she was moved there for better treatment. Her letters came regularly and it became clear to me that not much could be done for her other than making her comfortable, and giving her the right medications.

I wanted to phone her in the hospital but the pastor had told me when I first came not to call Ireland, as it was too expensive. I tried the public call box but had difficulties getting through. The telephone system in Ireland was not good then like it is now. The O'Donnell family had become very good friends to me. Every time I met them they would ask about my mother.

There was Dr. Jack and his wife Peg and eleven children, seven boys and four girls. Four of the boys were altar boys. One evening when I was at their home for dinner and they were asking me if I spoke to my mother on the phone, Jack and Peg became aware of the difficulties and insisted I phone from their home.

While trying and waiting to go home and visit my sick mother I had asked the children in the school to pray for her. They did pray for her and some of them were asking me everyday how she was doing. One little girl, Susan Edgar then in the second grade, told me she was going to win a free trip to Ireland, which had been advertised in a local paper and to which she had her parents subscribe. I can still see Susan's beautiful smiling, freckled face, as she would run across the parking field to talk to me. She was sure she was going to win the free trip for me. No one knew the real reason why I was not going home to see my mother. One of the many families who welcomed me into their home was the Edgar's. Charlie and Peg and their eight children always made me feel very welcome. They took me clamming. Everyone had a clam rake and we would all wade out into St. James Harbor in low tide and dig the clams. The children were selling them and saving the money for college. When we would come back home, Charlie would bake trays of them with pieces of bacon and clam sauce. When they first introduced me to these morsels I was surprised at how good they tasted. The Edgar family, among others keep in touch with me still. The children are grown up and married and there are many beautiful grandchildren. I did call my mother in the hospital in Dublin from the phone in O'Donnell's home. For the first time she said she was not feeling well and was getting weaker. This gave me great concern and I wished to be close to her. I thanked Jack and Peg and offered to pay for the call. They refused and expressed shock that I would even suggest it.

I told the pastor my mother was getting worse and I wanted to visit her. He did not know of the phone call but knew I had received frequent letters from my mother. He said it has been the custom in the Dioceses of Brooklyn that a priest gets someone to take his place when he is going away. He gave me the national church directory and told me to write to religious orders in the greater New York area and ask for a priest to come and cover for me while I would be away. I wrote six letters long hand, as I did not type and had no typewriter anyway. There was a secretary who came one day a week and the pastor told me I could not give her anything to type or use the typewriter. Negative responses came back from all the six religious orders to whom I had written. When I told the pastor he shrugged his shoulders and said: "You cannot go unless you get someone to cover for you."

Monsignor Baldwin, Chancellor of the diocese was visiting the pastor who was a friend of his. He came into my room and told me they were getting very good reports about me from other priests and some lay people. He said, "Your boss says you do everything and you are very obedient." "We know a lot of that comes from your training in the order and the monastic life you led." I told him about my mother and how I was not able to get home to see her. He said, "Your boss tells me you are very involved in all the work of the parish and he could not do without you." He also said, "You are involved as chaplain to the University and visits to the hospital, but that has nothing to do with him." I asked Monsignor Baldwin if there was anyone in the whole diocese they could send out here to take my place while I would go home to see my sick mother. He said he knew of no one right now but would look into it.

The O'Donnells were going away on vacation. They gave me a key to their house, telling me I could use it on my times off and use their phone while they would be away. I called my mother's hospital in Dublin and she could not come to the phone as she was now confined to bed. They did not have a telephone that could be brought to her in bed, so I asked the sister who was speaking with me if I could speak to my mother's doctor. She answered, "I just saw him go through the ward. Hold on 'til I see if I can get him." Next thing the doctor was on the phone. He said, "This is Doctor McNamara speaking." I told him who I was and asked about my mother. He said, "You know she has had diabetes for many years and now there are some complications. She is going into heart failure. Come and see her because I don't think she will last long. Sorry I have to tell you this."

When I told the pastor, I was in touch with my mother's doctor and he told me to come and see my mother before it was too late. He said, "You can go." I said, "I am calling the hospital now and telling them I am flying over tonight and arriving tomorrow morning." He said, "Go ahead." First I called Aer Lingus. They said there were seats available on a plane leaving that evening. I booked a seat, called the hospital, told the sister I'd be there in the morning to please tell my mother and Dr. McNamara who was so helpful in advising me to take the necessary steps to come. She said she would be happy to do as I requested and knew my mother would be very happy. I called a good friend in the parish, John Miskell asking him if he were free to take me to the airport. He was delighted to help me in this way, and I boarded a plane for Dublin at eight o'clock that evening. The flights across the Atlantic Ocean were all at night. Flying eastwards, into the rising sun we cut five hours out of the clock. After praying for my mother I managed about one hour of sleep. Arriving in Dublin, I looked at my watch, it was two in the morning, that was New York time. In Dublin it was seven in the morning, with the new day on its way, people working, traffic moving and the sun shining brightly.

I went directly to the hospital. The sister in charge of the ward where my mother was welcomed me and said she had told my mother I was coming. She led me to my mother's bedside. A nurse was just then walking away from washing her. She looked thin and drawn. I said, "Mother." She reached out her two arms toward me and said, "I have my son." She placed her hands on both sides of my face, pressed gently and pulled me toward herself. She kissed me and kissed me repeatedly and said, "I've been waiting for you, I love you." This reunion was a moment of pure love between mother and son. I wanted to enjoy that moment and not speak. Words could not express or add to our joy in each other. My sister Marcella, who was working as a nun in England came and also my brother Mike, the youngest of the family. The three of us spent the rest of the day with mother. It turned out to be her last full day of life. The doctor came by and examined her. He called me aside and talked to me. He said, "She was waiting for you and she has not much time left. I've seen this happen before and I am so happy you are here."

Next morning mother went into total heart failure and could not speak. She died quickly. Looking at her lying there dead, I felt a great void: something inside me had died also. The three of us prayed and tried to console one another. There were no phones in the country areas yet. Mike had to drive sixty miles and race to tell all the families that mother had died. We brought her to the church in Empor where ten priests assisted us at the funeral mass. Looking down on her coffin from where I stood before the altar, the reality of death and eternity invaded my soul, how mother had gone alone into the great unknown. If only she could speak a word to us, but no, infinite silence has enveloped her soul. "Will we ever see each other again," she said at my father's death.

We took her to the family burial plot in Miltown graveyard where kindly neighbors had dug the grave, as was the custom there. The earth had its mouth open waiting to receive her into its bosom as her spirit had fled to God. The coffin was lowered to her last resting place beside my father, her husband with whom she brought eight children into this world and raised nine. With a prayer to God to grant her eternal life I threw the first shovel full of earth down on her wooden coffin. A hollow, deep thud filled my ears and I felt my heart sinking while I continued the prayer to God, "And may she rest in peace." All answered, "Amen." Something within me, some part of me was buried with my mother that day. My father was over forty and my mother was twenty-one when they married. He died at eighty-two and she at sixty-six.

And remember: Love is not love 'til it's given away.

CHAPTER 24

Variety in Ministries

After five years ministering in the parish of St. James and as chaplain to Stony Brook University the Bishop's secretary called me and said, "The University has grown so large it needs a full-time chaplain. The bishop wants you to consider giving up parish work and devoting yourself full-time as chaplain to the University. He wants you to think about this and if you have any hesitations you could come and speak with him." Much as I liked working for the students I did not want to give up parish ministry. I thought about it and spoke to the Bishop. When he realized how strongly I felt about parish work he did not pressure me. He said, "Everything I hear about your work in the parish and at the University is very good, but since parish work is your preference I will assign you to a larger parish. You need a different experience."

I did not know where this was going to be, but had to wait for a letter. Instead he told his secretary to call me. The secretary said the Bishop needed a chaplain for two summer camps for two months, and he thought I would be very suitable and also it would be a break for me after a difficult assignment. He said I would be going to a parish in September. A letter of transfer from the Bishop followed with a copy to my pastor. The morning the letters arrived the pastor came into my room with his letter in his hand. He was very upset. "What does this Bishop think he is doing moving you out of here?" He said. "I'm going to see about this." He got into his car and drove to the chancery to talk to his good friend, Monsignor Baldwin who was the chancellor. That afternoon he came back shaking his head. I said, "How did you do?" He said, "Not so well. I spoke to Monsignor Baldwin and he spoke to the Bishop. The Bishop told him he does not change anything after the letter is written." I said, "It reminds me of what Pilate said, 'What I have written, I have written.'"

When it was announced in the parish I was leaving the people expressed great disappointment as they said goodbye coming out of church. So many families opened their hearts and their homes to me that I felt I really belonged there. They all realized I had no family or a home of my own in this country. When I went through the school to say goodbye to the sisters and the children, some of them cried. One mother, whose family I scarcely knew and whose home I had never visited called me and said her eighth grade daughter was so upset would I please talk to her. Many families said they would come and visit me in the camp, which was only one hours' drive away, and they did. That was my first parish in the U.S. and many people there have remained good friends over the years and still come to see me in my present parish.

There were two camps, located in the Mattituck area in eastern Long Island. They were started by the Diocese of Brooklyn for city children to give them the opportunity of going out to the country and the beaches in the summer vacation time. The boys camp was on Laurel Lake and the girls camp was on the Peconic Bay. They were about a mile apart. Both camps took children from six to fourteen years of age. There was a director for each camp and counselors and helpers who were college or high school students. There was swimming and games and walks in the country. The counselors and helpers slept in the cabins with the children. There was a nice open air chapel with just a roof and no side walls. I was to work closely with the directors and help in any way possible including comforting kids who wanted to leave and go home. My only experiences in counseling kids came from growing as the fourth in a family of nine. I swam with them, played games with them, ate with them and worshiped with them, but I slept in a farmhouse on the property.

One day I was driving on the highway a short distance from the camp when I saw a boy on the side of the road, thumbing a lift. He seemed to be about ten years old. I pulled over and he jumped into the car. He was crying and said, "I want to go home." "Where is your home?", I said. He said, "In Brooklyn." I said, "You were in the camp." He said, "Yes, and I want to go home." We talked for a while. He had no money and Brooklyn was a hundred miles away. I tried to talk him into coming back to the camp and calling his parents to come and get him. He said his parents left him at the camp and went off on their vacation. "What's your name?" I asked. He replied, "Dan." I said, "Well, Dan, we will help you, but first we have to go back to the camp."

He did not object. I asked him what he would like to eat. He said, "chocolate." I stopped at a store, took him in, and he picked out his favorite chocolate. I brought Dan back to the Director's office. The Director said, "Oh, thanks be to God. We reported you missing to the police." The Director's name was Jim. He and I worked together on several runaway cases. He told me many parents leave their children in the camp and go on vacation. Dan stayed. I talked to him every day and he became attached to me. I helped him make friends with other boys in his cabin.

Many friends from the parish in St. James came out to visit me. I was always happy to see them. Some would take me to lunch or dinner in one of the good restaurants in the area. This was always a welcome change from camp fare. Harry Dwyer got me a used rowboat that was being given away. Charlie Edgar brought it out in his truck. I enjoyed using it on the Peconic Bays, so did others, including two sisters from the girls camp. It was a pleasant scene to see them sitting out there in the row boat a short distance off shore reading their books. Young Charlie Edgar, Kevin Barry, and Bob Gagliardi former altar boys with me and now teenagers would thumb lifts out and enjoy the row boat with me. They still keep in touch with me.

The counselors were frequently looking for a lift to the railroad station or wherever. None of them had cars. Two counselors were having a serious romance. The boy asked if he could borrow my car to take the girl out when they had an evening off. I gave him the keys. After that I was getting frequent requests from counselors. If I was not using the car I would let them have it.

One of the counselors had scuba diving equipment and was giving lessons to whomever wanted to learn. I was interested and he gave me lessons in Lake Laurel. I enjoyed going along the bottom and seeing the different fish dart out of their hiding places. Then he took us to Long Island Sound where the water was very deep and where there was a greater variety of fish. We always used the buddy system, which gave me a bit of confidence.

The nearest restaurant and bar was Cliff's Laurel Inn. The counselors frequented the place and often asked me to drive them there. Hamburgers were only thirty cents and that is what they all had, with a beer or soda. I got to know Cliff the owner who was also the chef. He would invite me into the kitchen to chat with me as he cooked fish for which he was renowned in the area. He was from the Island of Jamaica and was a chef all his life. When he saw I was interested in the way he cooked the fish he gave me some good tips. I always remembered the first thing he told me, "the biggest problem with most cooks when it comes to fish, is over cooking which dries out the fish very quickly and makes it taste terrible." He would emphasize "don't over cook." His place was small but very popular. On a Friday evening especially it was packed. A number of people who worked in the city had country homes in the area. Cliff's was their meeting place on a Friday evening while they had dinner before going home. I got to know some of his clients, business and professional people. There was a doctor who brought great life to the place. He was a surgeon in a city hospital and loved to stop at Cliffs. He was an interesting man to talk to and I regarded him very highly. One day I stopped by and Cliff told me he had bad news: the doctor committed suicide. "What happened?" I said. Cliff said, "He lost his life's savings in the stock market." I felt terrible and was sure I could have helped if only I had known in time. This sadness stayed with me to this day.

Cliff said to me one evening, "Can you get a day off?" I said, "Yes, I can." He said, "A group of us are having a days fishing on a charter boat next week and I would like to have you come along as my guest." I thanked him and told him I would let him know. I met Cliff and five other friends at the dock in Greenport early on Thursday morning. The boat was named "Seaboats" and the captain was Everett Smith. This was to be a day I would always remember. The captain took us to the end of Long Island to an area called the Plum Gut between Orient Point and Plum Island where the water rushed through from the ocean into Long Island Sound at flood tide and back again at the ebb tide. It was sometimes treacherous. It was also a good place to fish as the large fish would wait there for the smaller ones as they were swept through. It was drift fishing as the water was moving too fast to anchor. We were using diamond jigs and bouncing them off the bottom. I was astonished at the sudden action. Four rods bending over the side of the boat at once, the men trying to pump big bluefish up from the bottom and expending a lot of energy as the fish were very strong. In a few minutes there were fish coming over the gunwale and being thrown into a barrel with flailing of tails and spattering of blood. Cliff had pulled in a fish and immediately sat down and handed me his rod saying, "Need a rest, my heart is racing." He instructed me on all the fine points in fishing with a diamond jig. Quickly, I had a fish on and I knew it. I could barely turn the reel handle. Cliff said, "Pump him, lift the rod up as high as you can and bounce it reeling in hard and fast. I got him in and my heart was racing too, but I continued to fish.

When the tide slackened and the fish stopped biting Captain Smith said we will try the Race. That was the area of water between Gull Island and Fisher's Island where the water also raced through from the ocean into the

Sound. The tide was slack there also and the fish were not biting. Then he took us to the Pigeon Rip or The Boulders.

This was a deep area in the middle of the Sound between Plum Island and Connecticut. There was an area over two hundred feet deep with boulders coming up from the bottom leaving about seventy feet from there to the surface. One could find the area because of the rough waves on the surface caused by the tide rushing against the boulders below. Action started there on the first drift just as it had done in the gut. We caught some nice striped bass also in that spot. When the barrel was full, Captain Smith said, "Do you have enough fish?" All said, "Yes, let's go home." They divided up the fish. Cliff took some for his restaurant and so did two others who had restaurants. The rest took one or two. Cliff invited me to a fish dinner. It was delicious. He also taught me how to cook it and I've caught and eaten many of them since. From what I learned that day I would take a friend's boat into that area many times years later and catch fish using the same technique.

When the camps were ready to close down for the season, I received a phone call from the Bishop's secretary asking me to go as administrator of the parish in Medford as the pastor there had a heart attack and his doctor told him he could not return to his duties for several months. I left the camps with memories I always cherished, feeling sad I was parting with counselors and children I had grown to love. I had to move on.

I enjoyed working with the parishioners. They were very devout and charitable. There was a strong, active St. Vincent de Paul society which helped the needy families. Many of the older people were German, some of them born in Germany. A charming elderly couple, the Reinharts, who were German by birth, invited me to their home for dinner on New Year's Day. They had roast goose, stuffed with fruits, German style. I can still see and taste that goose. First we feasted our eyes on the goose, then we feasted our stomachs as we ate the goose. Many families in each parish kindly told me I was family.

And remember: Love is not love 'til it's given away.

CHAPTER 25

Bayshore Parish

After three months, the pastor in Medford was able to return and resume his duties. The bishop then assigned me as assistant pastor to St. Patrick's parish in Bayshore. The buildings took up two blocks on Main Street, which was the Montauk Highway. There was a beautiful brick church, hall and rectory, a school and a convent. Southside Hospital was located in the parish. There was no chaplain, so the priests in the parish had to cover it and take all the calls, day and night.

The pastor was Mike Purcell and the other assistants were Dick and Sam. There were four of us assigned there. It was a very busy place, with daily and weekend masses, a large number of baptisms, weddings, funerals, calls to the hospital, visiting the classrooms in the school, the CCD (Confraternity of Christian Doctrine for Children at public schools), visiting the sick at home, visiting three large nursing homes, reaching out to the needy, counseling and coping with whatever came our way each day. I tried to get an overall view of the whole picture and figure out how it all fitted together. I had to have my life organized, and still be ready for the unforeseen. Life had the planned and the unplanned and it was not easy to harmonize the two. One had to be pliable and calm at all times and never be too tired to serve the people, even after having been called to the hospital four times the night before.

I recall one night when I had several calls, I had gone back to bed and had just fallen asleep when the phone rang again. It was the hospital. An ambulance was coming in with a serious case, could I come? Once again I drove through the empty streets to the other side of town and entered the hospital. The ambulance had not come yet, so I stepped outside the emergency room and was looking up at the stars, praying for the patient whoever it might be and prepared to minister to him with the consolation of the sacraments. A man jumped out of the ambulance, took me by the arm and shoved me in through the door of the emergency room saying, "Don't let him see you, you'll frighten him. He is my father." The father said, "I want the priest."

The hospital really kept us busy. Each of the three assistants had two days each week and we rotated the Sundays. The hospital had a very large catchment area, and I admired the volunteer firemen in the surrounding towns who gave their time with great competence in rushing road victims and people with sudden illnesses to the hospital emergency room. Many people were saved, but there were some very tragic cases.

One day I was called to the emergency room. When I got there a nurse told me a ten year old girl was shot and was dying. When I saw her I was horrified. She was lying on a stretcher, unconscious as doctors worked on her. There were several small holes in her chest and stomach area. A doctor told me it was from a shotgun blast. As I ministered to her she died. The doctors said it was impossible to save her. The mother was in a waiting room and the father was at work. The mother already knew and told me what happened. She and her older brother and some neighbor's children were playing in the yard. The brother got his father's shotgun and was pointing it at the other kids. He did not know it was loaded and it went off. His sister fell to the ground. I felt very angry with the father, whom I had not yet met, for having a loaded shotgun in the house, especially with children. I thought of how my father trained us on gun safety and never having a loaded gun in the house. They were from another parish so we did not have the funeral. I found it very hard presiding and preaching at that kind of burial. Unfortunately, I had to do some terrible ones. Later the father came to see me. He said he was in depression and could not accept his daughter's death. I listened to him for as long as he wanted to speak. He was evidently, in such bad shape, I recommended he see a psychiatrist. When he told me he had decided to have the gun loaded to protect his family, my mind latched on to that word, decided, and thought "you are your decision". He agreed to see a psychiatrist.

On my days covering the hospital, I visited every room and talked with the patients who were able and willing to respond. I prayed with those who wanted me to pray with them and ministered to those who desired sacraments. Bringing some hope and comfort to suffering patients was very fulfilling for me. Sometimes non-Catholics would ask me to pray with them. One day I entered a room with two beds. One bed was empty and there was a young man, appearing to be in his late teenage years, in the other bed. The young man did not talk about himself but was very concerned about his roommate who was not in the other bed. He was in an operating room having serious surgery. The young man said he was Jewish and asked me to pray with him for his roommate. I said, "yes, of course." He took a yamika from the locker by his bed and put it on his head. He then knelt on his bed and bowed his head. I stood by his bed and bowed my head. We prayed for his friend, Gene, who was having surgery at that moment. We both said words from our hearts to God, and humbly asked God to give him a successful recovery. I was very impressed with this young man. He showed a love for his roommate, whom he had met for the first time just a couple of days before. Also, he harbored no barrier between himself and me. I said a silent prayer thanking God for him and asking God to make more of our young people loving and open like him to people of other religions.

It was the fall of the year and all the surfcasters were out every day on the beaches with their beach buggies racing up and down and casting into the breakers with their mighty long fishing poles. I loved to fish and was invited by some local fishermen to go with them. The best times were late evening and very early morning. It was a new venture for me as I had never fished the ocean from standing on the shore. It was very invigorating with the breeze and the crashing surf and freedom of it all.

One day, after an early morning trip to the beach and all of us catching striped bass, I got back in time to keep the office appointments. A lady came in who wanted to talk to me about a marriage problem. She sat down, and wiping away her tears said, "I think my husband does not find me attractive anymore." I said, "What makes you think that?" Then she went into a long story of how they dated and fell in love and married and had a great life together for several years and had two kids. She went on to explain how he has changed. "He does not show affection; he is always out; he works all day and goes surfcasting at night, coming home in the wee hours of the morning and no matter how I argue with him, it is no good." I was listening and thinking. When she asked what I thought she should do, I asked, "Does he catch any fish?" She answered me emphatically, "He tells me surfcasters never catch anything." I was thinking she did not want to face up to the fact that he must have caught something, but I wanted her to come up with the answer. So, I said, "When he comes home and tells you he caught nothing, and is so devoted to the fish and has no affection for you, do you really think he caught nothing?"

She said, "You are thinking what I'm thinking." I said, "What's that?" She said, "Another woman caught him?"

In most cases the wives and mothers seemed to be the leaders in faith and religious practices, both in the home and in the parish. I got to know and admire many women of faith, good wives and mothers and influential in the church and in the community. It was natural to feel attracted to some of them and feel some were attracted to me. Living the life of sacrifice was a daily matter.

A lady came into the office one day. She was quite troubled as she explained how her marriage was about to break up. At the end of the session she asked me if I would come to their home and speak to her husband. I said I did not go to homes for counseling. He would have to take the first step and come to me. This would show he was honestly looking for help. If I take the first step by even calling him, he will think I am siding with you. I cannot take sides. I must be objective. She called back and told me he refused to see me, and she had reached the point of no return and was leaving him with her two-year old child. Next day he came in to see me, crying, telling me his wife had left telling him, she had reached the point of no return. I expressed my regret that this had happened and advised him, if she should get in touch with him, to tell her he will go with her and speak to a counselor.

This was a frequent occurrence. One spouse would look for help; the other spouse would not come; then there would be the point of no return.

In our training we were told our relationship with the people we would serve in a parish would be like the covenant of marriage, being with the people and serving them in good times and in bad. This was borne out repeatedly through the weeks and months in parish life as we served the people and shared with them their joys and sorrows. We prayed with them and ministered to them in sickness, we grieved with them at funerals. I loved to work with our marriage preparation committee, helping young couples prepare for marriage. We had the engaged couples share in the discussions so that everyone was learning from one another. Every couple was different. With the large number of marriages ending in separation or divorce, we tried hard to help the couples be prepared for the pitfalls and concentrate on the positive dimensions of marriage. One could see great strength and promise in some couples. Then there was the occasional couple that made one wonder if they would make it in the long run. All were treated the same and we prayed together for all. It was always a great joy to see couples doing well especially when baptizing their babies. Of course it was a deep sadness for me when a couple broke up. Many couples went to live in other areas, and with some exceptions, I never heard from them anymore.

One young couple that remained in the parish had a baby boy and asked me to do the baptism. They called him John. It was a very happy occasion with the families and friends present. Before the baby was a year old the parents came to me and said a doctor had diagnosed their baby, John, as having brain cancer. They were devastated and so was I. There were many questions: How could a healthy baby get brain cancer? How could God allow this to happen to a beautiful, innocent child? Could there be any hope that medical science could cure him? I shared the parents' grief and anguish so much that I find it very difficult to write about it. I prayed over the baby, with the parents often. His head was enlarged and that was the first thing that alerted the doctor that something was wrong. The baby did not seem to suffer and he died peacefully, a child of God. I was impressed with the parents, how they were able to cope and go on in such crushing sorrow. That was such a sad funeral. Words could not describe it. I stood with the parents, the grandparents and extended family and many friends as baby John's little white casket was laid in the grave. The mourning was so deep and all shared in it while we prayed.

The couple went on to have four more children, all healthy. They are now grown up and their parents are happy grandparents.

We had a parish school, run very well by the Sisters of Mercy, which took about four hundred students from the first to the eighth grade. I visited the classrooms during sessions regularly, spoke with the children and answered their questions. When speaking with the older children, I would ask if anyone could remember what the homily (sermon) was about last Sunday. There was always a blank. After some time dealing with this I was looking for an answer. While greeting the people coming out of church I would ask some of the families I knew well, if they could help me in preparing my preaching. They would always ask, "What can we do?" I would then ask them if they could remember what the preacher said at this mass. The answers came something like these: "I don't know," or "I just can't remember," or "he did say a lot but I can't put my finger on anything right now," or "he said the bishop is coming for confirmation," or "he said be generous in the collection." It was rare to have anyone who remembered what the preacher said.

I figured if I picked one word from the scriptures of the day, start with that word, tell them it was a key to everything I was going to say, asking them to remember the key word to help them remember all I said. I tried this. It took a lot of preparation. I'd give them the word, repeat it many times and at the end ask them, "What is the word you take home today," cup my hand behind my ear and wait for an answer. The first time I tried it, the gospel had the Father speak from heaven saying: "This is my beloved son, listen to him." I picked the word "listen" as the key to remembering. At the end of the homily when I asked what is the key word you take home today, everyone shouted, "Listen." I have never been stuck to find a key word since then until this day. Leaving church many will tell me the word. Of course, I never ask at that point. Even children love to tell me the word. Some people coming into church will ask me, "What is the word today?" They look forward to hearing the word. Some will say, "I remembered your word all week."

The sisters in the school organized an in-home program for the children in the second grade who were going to public school. One or both parents, usually the mother, who had a child in the second grade, would take five or six other children in the area and run a class for one hour once a week. The sisters gave me a list of the places and times asking me to visit the classes while in session and if I could fit this into my schedule. The classes were all held after school when the children came home. It was a very rewarding experience going to the homes and joining the parents as they taught the children. Most parents were enthusiastic about the program and many said this made them revise their own understanding of the faith.

I did the rounds on my bicycle. The children in the streets were delighted to see me. They ran after me and all wanted to show me the houses I would be looking for. It was a great way to get to know the people and the area in which they lived. One day I was talking to a group of children in the driveway of a home. A seventh grade boy had to show me his pet skunk. I never saw a skunk before but heard they had a bad smell. I said to the boy, "A skunk is supposed to smell." He said, "Not this one, he is de-skunked." That day as I cycled home, a big dog came running after me and got me by the left leg. He was holding on to me and I could feel his teeth, but managed to get off the bicycle without falling. At that moment I saw a family come running from the nearest house. There was the father and mother and several children. They knew me and were very upset and apologetic. The father blamed his son of about twelve saying, "Mike, you were supposed to take the dog for a walk with a leash on him." They all wanted to help me. I could feel the blood running down my leg. The father took me to the emergency room. A doctor put fourteen stitches in my leg. He told me the biggest danger was rabies. The dog had to be watched for, I think, it was ten days. If he had rabies at the stage in which a victim could get it, he would die within ten days. If that happened, I would have to get injections in the stomach area, with a very big needle and it would be hard to take. The dog remained healthy and I did not have to take the injections.

I got a call from the police late on a Saturday night. The policeman on the phone said there was a shooting and would I respond. I said, "Yes, where is it?" He went on to explain and give me directions. I realized it was the tavern I had passed on the bicycle, and said, "I know where it is." He said, "I'll be out on the street and you'll see the emergency lights on the police car."

When I got there, I found him as he said I would. As he was taking me inside, he explained the situation. There was a fight. One man was dancing with another man's girlfriend. The first boyfriend drew a gun and shot the other one on the dance floor." He led me in, opening a way through the crowd. The picture, still clear in my mind, was a dance floor with a man lying there in a pool of blood, cordoned off by a rope all around, tied to the backs of chairs and a policeman standing guard. "There is the victim," the policeman said, "and we don't know what church he belongs to." I went on my knees beside him, said the prayers for the dying and anointed his forehead with holy oil. As I got on my feet I thought of the other man, now he is a murderer, he is his decision. I prayed for him too.

On one of my visits to one of the nursing homes, an elderly lady told me a sad story, the result of a decision she made. I had heard too many similar stories and continue to hear them. She was sitting on a chair in the bedroom and I sat on a chair beside her. She seemed to be in good health and could walk around. She spoke well and did not repeat herself as some elderly people do when losing their memory. She was a widow. After her husband died she was the sole owner of her home. She took in her son and his wife. After a while they told her it would be better for everybody if she would sign the house over to them. She did not want to do it. Then the daughter-in-law proceeded to make life very miserable for her. Her son said, "If you sign the house over to us, she will be nice to you." So she signed the house over to them. They were so grateful and nice to her she also agreed to sign over all her savings as well. She was fearful of making these decisions, but trusted her son that she would be protected and well taken care of for the rest of her life. She began to cry, then said, "Next thing I knew was, I was here in this nursing home. They told me it would be only for a short time while they were redoing the whole house and I would like it a lot more when I would come back." I asked her how long she had been there and she told me it was nearly a year now, and to make it worse, she said, "and they don't visit me anymore." I expressed my sorrow over what had happened and told her I really felt for her. She said, I made bad decisions and now I am living with them. Running through my mind was my favorite saying, "You are your decisions." She said, "I could still be in my own house if I had not listened to them and made the wrong decision." I said, "Is there anything I can do for you?" She said, "Yes, get me an attorney who can get my house back for me." I said, "When you signed the house over was there a provision made saying you could live there the rest of your life?" She said, "I don't know about that. Anyway, I would not live with them now. They would give me a miserable life and I would not feel safe with them." I said, "I'm sorry to say I don't think any attorney could get your house back to you alone since you legally signed it over." She said, "That's what everyone is telling me, and saying I have to live with my decision." I got a legal aid attorney to talk to her, but he could do nothing. When I would visit that nursing home I would spend time with her. Her daily needs were being taken care of but no one was coming to see her. She told me after a happy life with her husband, she was spending her last years living with regret and in loneliness. She would say, "Please tell the people in church not to sign over their homes." I know each case is different and each case stands on it's own, but I also knew from experience there are many bad decisions and regrets.

 The clergy of the area, including the local rabbi met periodically to get to know one another and share needs and challenges and address the community problems. Ours was the biggest religious community in the area. All the ministers and the rabbi worked very hard for their people and we helped one another in every way possible. The rabbi told me he had to have work done on their building where they ran a Hebrew school for their children. He asked if we would consider letting them use our school at the weekend when we would not be using it. All the priests were happy to agree to the request. We had the Jewish children coming into our school carrying their Hebrew books and sitting at the desks where the Christian children sat during the week. All of the parishioners were quite happy about this decision.

 One morning a man came into the office looking for a priest. I sat him down, told him he was welcome. He began to talk. "I am Episcopal," he said, "and I have a problem with my wife. Can you listen to me?" I said, "Of course I will listen to you, but did you try to speak to Pastor Frank, who is very kind and helpful?" He said, "The pastor's office is closed today, Saturday, and I cannot wait." He said, "I am very upset and I need help." I said, "I'll listen to you and if I can help you, I will." He said he lifted the phone extension and heard his wife speaking to a man. I asked what he heard that man say? He said, "I don't know. Hearing a man's voice just set me off." He said, "I can't make a decision to kick her out. Could you come over and talk to her?" I said, "I'll talk to her, but I will not go to the house. I never do that. The person has to take the first step and come to me." He called his wife and she came over. She said to him, "Mike, you were away for a week without telling me. Then you come back and hear me talking on the phone to my brother and you run out of the house again. He helped me while you were away." They agreed to see their own pastor.

A woman was killed in a road accident and we had a very sad funeral. There was a husband and four children, the youngest, a teenager. I had known them from greeting them at the church door. In the funeral home the husband was incoherent with grief, inconsolable. The only one who was getting anywhere with him was a brother-in-law. He kept on saying he wanted to die and be with his wife. He was so set on dying that I worried about him. He might take his life. I talked to the brother-in-law, who was very close to him and recommended he take him to a psychiatrist after the funeral. The brother-in-law said he was taking him away for a few days and that should help him. At the graveside, Joe was out of control and wanted to jump into the grave to be with his wife. After the burial I went back to the house and talked to Joe. He said he could not go on living without his loving wife. In between bouts of tears he repeated "I have to die. I have to die." I asked him what he thought his wife would want him to do? I was not getting through to him. I took his two hands between my hands and pressed them. He looked at me and I said firmly, "Joe, your wife wants you to go on living, that's what would please her most: she wants you to take care of the children: they are her children and your children." He went silent. I begged the brother-in-law to take him to the local hospital where a psychiatrist would see him and give him something to get him over this crisis. He said to me, "we are going away for three days and that should help him. Then he should start working again in his gas station."

A few mornings later there was a call for a priest to come to a service station, which I knew well. When I got there, there were police cars outside. A policeman told me a man was found dead inside, apparently having asphyxiated himself with the exhaust from a car. I went inside, got down on my knees beside the dead man. It was Joe.

Life in this parish was very busy and very rewarding. So many families befriended me and invited me to their homes that I don't want to mention names because I might overlook some. It has been a long time and I just want to say a big thank you to all.

One evening, I had been invited by a family to dinner. Jim prepared drinks and Ruth was cooking in the kitchen. Their ten year old daughter, Elizabeth, came over and sat on my knees. After a few minutes she said to her mother, "Mom, it is very nice sitting on Father's knees. You should try it." Her father and mother burst out laughing and Elizabeth did not understand why they laughed. She is married now and I receive a card from her every Christmas with a picture of her very beautiful children.

One day riding in my car through the parish, I saw a small boy pushing his father in a wheelchair. I recognized the boy from the school, so I stopped to talk to them. It was near where they lived so I walked to their house. There were other small children playing in a heap of sand in the front yard. The mother was in the kitchen. She said, "I am Kate and my husband is Joe. You're welcome to our home." I went inside and we talked for a while. As the result of an accident, the father was in a wheel chair and the family was on welfare. The house was very bare and it was evident they were struggling to make ends meet. I brought them vouchers to be used in the local grocery store, and spoke to a good neighbor who was willing to drive the mother and children to shop and to church, or wherever. I visited them once a month and gave the father the sacraments he needed. He and the whole family were most grateful for anything that was done for them.

Thanksgiving was coming and, knowing I had no family of my own here, they invited me to Thanksgiving dinner. I had not committed myself to any other family, so I thanked them and said, "Yes, I will come." I took the mother and the older children shopping and told them to pick out their choice of turkey and all the trimmings and the church would pay for it. I just wandered around and let them do their own selecting. They had a great time. I had been to dinner in many homes with great families, but I looked forward to this one as having its own special appeal. They were poor: they were on welfare and they had such a little house for a large family.

Thanksgiving came and they welcomed me to their humble home. We were all in the kitchen. They had borrowed tables from neighbors so that we could all sit together. They asked me to say grace. I said, "The father of the house should say grace." The father said to his eight-year old daughter, "Mary, you know how to say grace." Mary said, "God is great, God is good, help us to enjoy our food," and all answered "Amen." The mother said, "It is an honor for us to have you for Thanksgiving dinner." I said, "It is an honor for me to be here." The father said, "This is the first time for us to have a priest join us for a meal." I said, "It looks like you have prepared a great one." There was plenty on the table, a very big turkey and all the trimmings. Joe sat at the head of the table in his wheel chair and managed to carve the turkey. He was smiling as he sank the knife into the juicy breast and the kids were rubbing their hands together with delightful anticipation. Kate was very attentive to the little ones as we all chatted and ate the delicious food to our heart's content. Sharing the meal made me feel I was one of them. It was a truly charismatic experience. It meant a lot to the family and it did a lot for me.

I stood in front of the church every weekend greeting the people. None of the other priests did it. Father Sam tried it and was uncomfortable, so he did not continue. I got to know many people and what was even more important, they go to know me and feel they could approach me with any problem they might have. Many of them invited me to their homes, or out on their boats. I worked with teenagers and found out some of them sold clams to get money for college. I was invited to go clam digging with them and went when I could. I liked it so well I bought my own clam rake with an eighteen-foot handle to be used from standing in a boat. Mike and his three friends had a clam boat. The first time I went out with them we drifted in the Great South Bay with the rake heads dragging along the bottom and the long handles on our shoulders as the wind pushed the boat across the flats. We got a lot of clams as we drifted for hours.

At one point we came close to a seagull flapping its wings and trying to lift its head out of the water. The area had sand flats that would be uncovered at low tide and get covered again when the tide came in. On coming close to the gull, we saw that a big clam had a hold on her beak and would not let go. Apparently, in low water, the gull tried to pick the clam out of his shell, which was partly open. The clam closed on the gull's beak. A clam is very strong and when he closes the shell, or "clams up" one has to use a clam knife to open him up. So were we having a clam from the mud killing a gull from the sky? Mike set the gull free.

At the end of the day, they divided up the clams. I took only a few to have on the half shell at dinner. They were very grateful and said I pulled a lot of clams into the boat. Laughing one said, "Can you come again tomorrow?"

One of my friends persuaded me to join him in taking classes on boating in the local power squadron. They were given in a local school one evening a week. I found the classes very interesting and received certificates in seamanship, piloting and celestian navigation. I learned about the lighthouses in the sky.

There were a large number of poor and displaced persons on the streets in Bayshore. A big mental health institution which housed some eight thousand inmates had a new policy of putting patients back into the community. Bayshore was close by. The state was paying people to take inmates into their homes or into houses they owned. I had many calls to those places and it seemed to me many of those people were not capable of being on their own very much. There were many of them walking the streets, sitting on benches, standing at church doors, and wandering around. We had many poor and displaced people come to us every day, and we felt very deeply for them. We had an active St. Vincent DePaul Society. All the members were volunteers. They were very committed and did wonderful work.

We had a Legal Aid Society in town. The attorney in charge asked me to come on the Board of Directors, which I willingly did. We gave free legal services to those who needed it. So many don't know what is available to them. I steered people to the Legal Aid Society and they received very valuable help.

A needy man or a woman with a child would come to the door. They would declare an emergency, no food, starving, welfare money used up, needed money now. We had a policy not to give money, knowing it would likely be used for drugs. Instead, we would give vouchers they could use in a local grocery store and the church would pay the bill. That seemed to work well for some but others insisted on getting money. We found out that some were selling the vouchers for less than they were worth to get money for drugs. It was so difficult to always do what was best for the needy.

A young priest was assigned and we instructed him on how we helped the needy, and not to give money. One day he met a man in the office who said he was from the Veteran's Hospital in Northport and needed a taxi to go back. The young priest called a taxi and gave the money to the driver. The taxi driver came back soon after and said "That man demanded the money and did not want to return to the Veteran's Hospital. I threw him out of the car. Here is the money. Tell that young priest to wise up."

There were ferries going from Bayshore across the Great South Bay to the small communities on Fire Island. Numbers of people went every day in the summer to bathe at the ocean beaches. There were churches in some of those communities. Priests who taught in the seminaries would be assigned to serve in those churches in the summer months. One of those communities, Ocean Beach, had residents there year round. On my trips to the ocean, I got to know many of them. When the church there would close in the fall, those people would come over by ferry to the church in Bayshore. They were always talking of having their own priest, resident year round.

A group of them came to me and told me they were going to write to the bishop and ask him to assign me there and how would I feel about that. I told them I felt honored they asked me and said I would think about it, the pros and cons. My biggest concern was the numbers there in the winter; would the situation justify having a priest there full time? After several more visits it seemed to me there would be enough people and work to justify having a priest there, so I said, "Write to the bishop and see what he says."

The bishop's secretary called a few days later. He told me the bishop's office had looked into the matter and concluded there would not be enough income there to support a priest full time. It crossed my mind that I could subsidize the income with clams and not go hungry. The people were very disappointed.

Many of the parishioners had summer homes on Fire Island. One day, while I was on a ferry, which was crowded, a girl from the dock shouted, laughingly to her friends as the boat pulled away, "Cindy, did you remember your pills?" There was a lot of romancing on the beaches, friendships made and friendships broken, rejoicing and regrets.

One family got in touch with me as their daughter was expecting after a summer romance on the beach. The girl, very charming and delightful, was now suffering greatly from pressure and blame from her immediate and extended family. One wanted her to have the baby as a member of the family; another advised going away to a home for unwed mothers and after the birth, put the baby up for adoption, some suggested having an abortion as the sure way of putting an end to her problem.

I had been counseling families in this situation for years and seen all kinds of solutions attempted. In my early years, most girls expecting a baby out of wedlock went to a home for unwed mothers and put the baby up for adoption. Most of these homes are closed now for a variety of reasons. There has been a change in thinking. Many families are not that much influenced now by what neighbors think. Then there are the increased number of abortions. I always felt the girl should be helped in making a decision. Parents sometimes thought the girl to be too immature to make a decision. It is a life decision, the life of the unborn and the life of the expecting mother. I have seen a great deal of heart wrenching trying to make the best decision. I visited the hospital when the baby was born, a healthy, beautiful baby boy. The young mother said to me, "I can look my baby in the face and say, "You are my decision."

In my experience, looking back over the years, those who decided to keep the baby as a member of the family proved to be the happiest. I have seen those children grow up and bring great joy and happiness to the family. What suffering was endured in the old days and still in some cases today. In this case they made the decision to keep the baby in the family. As the child grows they continue to live their decision—they are their decision.

The boating community had a tuna club. They asked me to be their chaplain. I was happy to accept. At the beginning of the summer season they had a mako shark tournament of three days, Friday, Saturday and Sunday. I went out with them on the lead boat on one day. They fired a cannon in the marina at six o'clock in the morning and the fleet of boats headed out across the Great South Bay, out the Fire Island Inlet and got lost from sight of one another in the vast ocean.

The captain asked me to sit with him in the tuna tower. As we glided along on the surface of the calm sea, we saw sharks basking in the morning sun. The captain said, "Watch and see how they don't even try to get out of your way until the last moment." We were heading straight for a big one. It looked like the boat was going to hit him, but he moved at the last moment. As he seemed to slip along the side of the boat, he looked up at us and rolled his eyes. It was all intriguing to me.

We were the communication boat. Every catch of the day would be radioed to us with the approximate length and weight and the variety of shark. Soon the radio started humming with garbled information, so many trying to speak at once. As we were the radio information boat, we did not fish, we just kept receiving and recording information all day. There was a lot of action going on and coming in to us. Many sharks caught were being reported, mostly blue sharks, a few makos, one or two hammerheads and duskies. Everyone wanted to catch makos. They were man-eating sharks and the tournament was meant to help the bathers on the beaches by catching those makos. They were also good to eat, just like swordfish. Some people said they were better than swordfish. A boat came close to us. The crew was fighting a shark. He was rolling on the top of the water and did not want to come near the boat. I said to the captain of our boat, "That shark does not want to go aboard." He said, "They don't want him aboard. The only ones that come aboard are the ones that jump into the boat. This has happened and the shark chops everything in sight." I said, "How do they bring him home?" He said, "they tie him on the outside of the boat." Now the shark was close up to the boat. There were three men working on him. One man got a rope around his tail and lifted it, thrashing furiously, out of the water. When the tail is out of the water he has lost his power. They did not take him aboard, but tied him alongside the boat. They estimated him to be about seven feet long and weighing about two hundred pounds. He was a mako.

All the boats had to be back at the docks by four o'clock. As we came in through the Fire Island Inlet, the boat traffic reminded me of rush hour on a highway, every one was heading home. Most of the boats had sharks tied to the outside. When we got to the dock, the sharks were measured and weighed. Most were blue sharks, with a few makos, hammerheads and duskies. Afterwards they were cut up into pieces that people could take home, I watched the procedure. I saw this man with a very large knife, cut a shark into sections like you would cut a tree trunk into round logs, about a foot long, and there were rings on the shark sections like rings on a tree log. Anyone who wanted could take sections. There were plenty of takers. One man told me it was very good eating. He came there all three days, gave some to his friends and froze some. A truck was waiting there to take the cleanings to a factory. As there were no Saturday evening masses in those days, the Catholic members asked me to say mass at four o'clock on Sunday morning so that they could go out on the tournament. I obliged them but could not go with them as I had Sunday obligations. That evening one member brought me some mako shark steaks so that we could share in the fruits of the tournament by eating part of a man-eating shark.

There was a shooting at a school in the next town. The victim was brought to Southside Hospital and I was called. He was lying there being prepared to be operated on. I attended to him and he told me what happened. A teenage boy came down a corridor with a shotgun, looking for another boy to shoot him. He said, "I met him and decided to stop him. I stood in front of him. He opened fire and hit me in the stomach area. I am sorry I decided to stop him." The doctors were not able to save him. By his decision he lost his life and probably saved others. He became his decision.

There were two things going on at this time, and the altar was used at times for both. These were demonstrations against the Vietnam war, and the changes made by Vatican II were coming in, including turning the altar around and facing the people, also the change from Latin to English in the mass.

Young men who were deacons for the last six months before becoming priests, spent those six months in parishes to gain experience in the life and ministry they were preparing for. We had a deacon and he was given his turn in preaching. On the first Sunday morning, he got going on the war in Vietnam. He was vehemently condemning it. Several people got up and started walking out. One man shouted back to the deacon, "I have a son in Vietnam." Another shouted, "Don't use the church for your political views. We are a captive audience." The pastor never listened to what was being preached in church. This time he got some calls and letters complaining. I told the young deacon it was one thing for us to demonstrate peacefully, but the people who come to church to worship are a captive audience of families of all ages and must be respected.

Instructions were coming from Rome on the renewal brought about by the Vatican II council. We turned the altar around so that the priest would face the people. Also we were to use the vernacular, for us, English.

The first time I faced the people and said the mass in English, I got a wonderful feeling of being more united with the people and giving them a more intelligent sense of participating in the worship. People responded very well. For some it was emotional. There were a few wet eyes and sobs. Only one man came to me and said he did not like it. I asked why, he said, "You took away the Latin and I don't like it." I said, "So you understand Latin?" He said, "No, but I liked the feeling of mystery it gave me." I felt the teachings of the council were bringing the people and the priests closer together. This reminded me of what Cardinal Newman said in words such as these: "To find thee my God I could climb the highest steeple." Then he felt God was saying to him: "Go down my son, you will find me among the people."

And remember: Love is not love 'til it's given away.

CHAPTER 26

Called to be a Pastor

I received a call from the Personnel Director, Monsignor Daly, later to become Bishop Daly, asking me to come to his office. When I got there he asked me if I would like to be a pastor, and added, "Don't answer until you know where it is going to be, and take time to make a mature decision." He went on to explain that this would be a new parish and if I accepted I would be the founding pastor. The place is Sound Beach. It was established as a mission from the parish in Port Jefferson many years ago, and there is a little white mission church there, but no resident priest. There is no other building or place to meet and no residence. The people in the area have been asking to become a parish for a long time. The bishop has a stack of letters, shoulder high, from people asking that their mission church become a parish church with their own resident pastor. Decision. Take a few days to think it over and get back to me. Now I am saying to myself, I'm going to become my decision. If I accept I am a pastor; if I refuse my decision will be a disappointment for all concerned.

I went to see Father Carpenter, pastor of Infant Jesus Parish in Port Jefferson to which the mission belonged. He told me his order was losing members and finding it very difficult to take proper care of the mission. He gave me the name of a layman, Tom Hennessy, who attended the mission church and who would be willing to take me around and show me everything. I made an appointment with Tom, and taking a few priest friends with me, met him at his home on a Sunday afternoon. He welcomed us with open arms and graciously answered our questions.

We visited the church. There was no one around. It stood there on a hill with a steep driveway, white, alone and dignified looking perched on a horseshoe shaped area that had been cut into a high cliff of sand and gravel, with an unpaved, limited parking area around it. It had one level with no basement and folding, steel chairs to sit on. There were speakers mounted on the walls outside. Tom explained how the people would sit in their cars and listen as everything that was said inside was piped out through the speakers. At the same time the space inside the little church could be crowded.

Bill said, "If you become pastor here, you know you will have a big job ahead of you." Jim said, "Where would you live?" Joe said, "I would not come here as a pastor. This is a wilderness. When I become a pastor I'll have to have a good, adequate church, a residence and all the necessary buildings." Joe died without ever becoming a pastor. I said, "The people are the most important. If I can get them to work with me we can accomplish everything." They all agreed. Joe added, "I still would be afraid to undertake this task." We knelt in the little church to pray. I prayed for the people of this mission and asked the Holy Spirit to enable me to make the right decision. I was thinking of how these good people were waiting for a pastor, a shepherd to lead them. I felt an inner peace and an awareness the people were praying for me to come. There in the church I made a firm decision. I will tell the bishop I would love to come to the people of this mission and be their pastor.

I told the bishop my decision was yes, and I became their pastor. I was my decision.

In conversation with one of my priest friends, Father Alex Manley, I was sharing my excitement about becoming a pastor. I said, "A new parish which never was a parish before, and a new pastor who never was a pastor before." Alex said, "It's a new beginning all around." I said, "I have a concern: I may not be able to continue the course of studies of the new theology that has emerged from the Second Vatican Council. I go to St. John's University and am working on a Masters Degree in the new theology. It is going to be a much longer drive now and there may not be time for the study." What Alex said then stayed with me as it helped me make an important decision. He said, "You don't want to start a new parish with old theology." I decided to continue no matter what. I learned a great deal which enabled me to lead the new parish with clear vision and completed the course with the degree in the new theology.

Preparing to come to Sound Beach as pastor, I was well aware the universal church was in transition since Vatican II council ended just a short time before. There was also some division in the church. There were those who did not want some or all of the changes, and those who welcomed some or all of the changes with enthusiasm. Some parishes with more than one priest were divided.

The parish I was in before becoming pastor, formed a parish council, which all parishes were told to do by the bishop, as this was one of the changes coming out of the council. The day the parish council first met, Father Sam said to me, "This is the end of the clergy dominance." The pastor, Monsignor Mike, a much older man, discussed the changes with me that evening. Among other things, he said, "There is no need for parish councils. The church has done very well without them for a long time." He added, "All a good parishioner needs to do is pray, pay and obey. If every parishioner did these three things we would have a great parish." I said to Mike, "In the past when the word church was mentioned, it brought to people's minds an image of the hierarchy, Pope, Bishops and priests. The laity, of course, were included. Now Vatican II council defines the church as 'the people of God.' We are also members of 'the people of God,' called to serve." He said, "some of those you call the people of God are no good to the church. They don't pray, pay and obey. Some of them enter the church only three times in a lifetime, that is when they are hatched, matched and dispatched. Then some come when they are getting something free, ashes on Ash Wednesday and palms on Palm Sunday. We call them A&P Catholics." I said, "The Vatican II council tells pastors to call forth the talents of the laity to serve the whole community." Mike said, "What if they want to take over? If they stop obeying, it won't be long until they stop paying and maybe praying." I said, "I'm not afraid of the laity. I believe in them and trust them. Otherwise how can I lead them?" Mike said, "You are about to start a new parish as a pastor for the first time. Make sure you don't lose control of the laity." I said, "We are members of the people of God as well as the laity, but we are servants. We would not exist without the laity. We came from the laity. After us it will be children of the laity that will take our place. It won't be our children because we won't have any children. We must trust the laity and encourage them to use their talents for the common good." Mike said, "If things were good enough for so long, why change them now?" I said, "Now is the time things have to change. The world is changing, becoming more and more secularized, if not paganized. The people of God are the leven, as Christ said, to change the whole world." Mike said, "You seem to have your mind made up." I said, "I do, and when I go as pastor to the new parish I intend to do my best to empower the laity." Mike said, "More power to you, and I emphasize, YOU."

 The appointed day came when I would be installed as pastor. It was to be on a Wednesday at seven o'clock in the evening. I drove to the mission church knowing I had no place to lay my head. Monsignor Flynn was delegated by the bishop to install me. A group of my priest friends have come also. While vesting, a lady with her arms full of beautiful flowers came in to decorate the altar and get water in the sacristy. John Daly was at the little organ at the back of the church, surrounded by his small group of choir members, playing and singing. The little church was full, standing room only, as we walked out into the sanctuary, all vested the same. I could hear whispering among the congregation "Which one is it?" Very soon they knew as Monsignor Flynn called my name and directed me to stand in front of the people while he went through the ritual of installation. Among the prayers and questions, he said to me, "Father John McGuire, do you accept the position as pastor of these people of St. Louis de Montfort parish?" I answered, "I do." Then he said to the people, "Parishioners, of St. Louis de Montfort parish, do you accept Father John McGuire as your pastor?" They all answered, "We do." It was like a marriage, I do, I do, and everyone clapped.

I preached a few words telling them how happy I was to be among them as their pastor and looked forward to working together with them as in a good marriage. I explained how fortunate we were in becoming a new parish after Vatican II, being in the position of implementing all the teachings of the council that referred to parish life, reminding them they all had gifts and talents to be used in building up our family of faith. I said I would be calling forth these talents, empowering all to use them to the best of their ability, emphasizing that the Eucharist we were then celebrating, and would be celebrating together every Sunday is the summit and source of our spiritual lives, giving perfect worship to God. A great pastor is not one who just does great things for the people, but one who enables the people to do great things. We can become a great parish only if we work together as in a good marriage.

After the installation ceremony, I greeted the people at the door as they were leaving. They emphasized how welcome I was and how they looked forward to working with me. There was a small group of ladies waiting to talk to me. They introduced themselves. Kay Ress seemed to be the spokesperson for the group. She said they had been discussing before I came what they could do for me since there was no residence. Then she said, "Lilly Chapman here wants to talk to you." Lilly had keys in her hand. She said, "These are the keys of my little house. I'm a widow and I live alone. I have arranged to live with my married daughter, Mary and her husband, Joe. You use my house until you find a suitable place." She handed me the keys. It was a moment to remember. She reminded me of my own mother. I was moved and told her how much I appreciated her thoughtfulness and generosity. I said, "Your house will be the first rectory in this new parish." It was a lovely little house. I was there for a month before I found a suitable house in a suitable location to rent as a rectory. What a beautiful memory for me.

Next morning my first visitor was Frank Vogelle. He told me he was retired as a lieutenant in the New York City Fire Department and he had plenty of free time to help me in any way I wanted. From our conversation it turned out we had a mutual friend, Father George Barry Ford in New York City. He admired him very much and I told him Father Ford was instrumental in my coming to the diocese of Rockville Center. Frank was a talented parishioner, always willing to help. Later I asked him to be the chairman of the building drive to build a new church. He graciously accepted and saw the project through to completion.

The next person that came to help me that first morning was Terry Curtin. When she came in I remembered she was the lady who brought the flowers to the little church the night before. She told me she was a typist and would volunteer to do any typing I might need. It was now Thursday morning and I said, "I would like to have a simple bulletin to hand to the people at the masses on the coming weekend." She said, "That should be easy." So we composed a bulletin, Terry typed it and took it to the parish in Port Jefferson, where they let her use their machines to run off enough copies.

The third person who came to me on that first day in the parish was Jack Kelly. He and his wife Ginny and family lived in my first parish and I had baptized two of their five children. Jack welcomed me. He was now working for the diocese in parish development. He was very good at his job and always had new ideas. I used his services many times as we went through organizing and building the new parish. It was a delight to work with Jack. He was always so willing and capable and gave me the feeling he liked working with me.

The first weekend came. There were two masses and both of them were so packed I asked the children to sit on the rug in the sanctuary to relieve the congestion in the seats. There they sat at my feet. The parents were happy to see them around the altar and hearing them answer my questions while I was preaching. We gave everyone a bulletin as they left and called for an open meeting for all who could come. This was the first of many meetings. They were always well attended. I asked the people for input in developing the new parish. They shared many ideas.

For the second weekend I added a third mass. The attendance had grown so much I felt we had to look for another place for masses. Some members led me to the Dolphin Inn within the parish, which was owned and run by the

Lavin brothers. They had a large restaurant, which they did not use on a Sunday morning. They very graciously told us we could use it. We decided to double up with the two masses in the church in mid-morning on Sundays. I had a problem. I could not be in two places at the same time. I needed another priest.

I managed to get an Indian priest, who worked part-time in Brooklyn. Within a month from starting the parish we had gone from two to five weekend masses, and we were becoming more crowded. I received a call from the Bishop's secretary telling me they had a complaint from the pastor in the adjoining parish of Rocky Point saying I was stealing his parishioners. I said I did not know where the people were coming from. Nobody told me they belonged to another parish. People were going where they wanted and not asking or telling anyone. The bishop wrote to the pastors saying people should be told where the parish boundaries were but if some wanted to go to another parish, their freedom should be respected. The numbers kept coming and increasing.

The religious education program for children in the mission area of Sound Beach, Miller Place and part of Mt. Sinai had been well organized. Father Canon from Port Jefferson was the moderator. Many talented volunteers came forward to run the program. Leaders, among them, were Carol Paul, Mary Larsen, Pat Curtin, Margie Battillo, Lucy Kempinger, Teresa Malecki, Ginnie Osborne and Anna Mae Mann. Sister Elizabeth Mary from Port Jefferson worked diligently with the group. They took courses at the Cenacle Retreat House and became very competent and updated in the recent teachings that had come out of the second Vatican Council. Religious education for children took place in people's houses. Parents who had children in the program would take a number of children in the neighborhood and teach them in a session once a week with their own children. We owe a real debt of gratitude to those and all the good people who worked so hard in the mission and prepared it to become a parish.

Being on my own, I was very busy as there was help only on the weekends. There was morning mass and daily prayer, office hours, baptisms, marriages, and funerals, meeting with groups, visiting the sick at home and in hospitals and dealing with surprises.

A couple came to the office with three children from three to eight years old. They said they wanted to baptize the oldest, Jamie, again. I said, "You want to baptize him again?" The father said, "Yes. We want to have a new godfather. His godfather is no good; we don't like him and have nothing to do with him anymore. He never comes to see his godson and never gives him a gift." The mother said, "That godfather is a real louse and does not deserve to be a godfather. We have a very good friend who would be a wonderful godfather." I said, "I can see you are very upset and suffering because of this. I feel for you and would like to help." The mother said, "Please do help us, we are very upset." I said, "I have to tell you, baptism is a rebirth in water and the Holy Spirit. One cannot be reborn a second time. I would like to help but I cannot baptize Jamie a second time. You have to live with your first decision." I prayed with them and blessed them. As I waved to them leaving I said, "See you in church." On the following Sunday I was happily surprised to see them come in and welcomed them at the church door. Before leaving they told me they had gone to another church asking to have Jamie baptized again, before coming to me, and they had a bad experience.

I did my own cooking, as I did not want to be tied down to hard and fast times for eating. Some families very thoughtfully invited me to their homes for dinner. I was happy to accept when possible. Knowing my position of not having a cook, several families told me I had a standing invitation. Among the first I had dinner with were the Curtin's, Dan and Terry, who had four children, the Ross's, Dave and Kathleen, who had seven children, and the Osbornes, Dick and Ginny, who had five children. They all filled me in with stories from the days of the mission. They and many others had written letters to the Bishop for years asking for their own pastor. It was the repeated requests from all these good people that finally moved the bishop to appoint me a pastor.

As I got to know people, I invited them to take positions in different ministries in the area of liturgical worship, religious education, outreach, the parish council and the hospitality ministry. Some were eager to take positions and some were reluctant. I realized they needed training and introduced the program of parish renewal. It was quite successful. It was also challenging with a lot of sharing. Later we took advantage of the pastoral formation courses given in the diocese. We had more people in the pastoral formation of the laity than any other parish in the diocese. It was and still is a wonderful training for lay people to be involved in parish life. Also, later we went in a small group to Hartford, Connecticut and to Florida to receive training and learned from the experience of other parishes in forming small Christian communities. Leaders emerged and all our programs were successful.

We made a conscious effort to be aware of how much we needed one another and made sure we welcomed one another and especially those we did not know to Sunday worship. We called ourselves a family of faith. I kept reminding them, "You are the parish."

The people kept asking for a new church, so I asked the bishop for approval. He sent three members of his board of consulters out to Sound Beach to evaluate the area. They got lost on the way and called me for directions. I welcomed them to the little rented house, showed them the church and took them through the area of the parish. They were not impressed with what they saw. I told them not to underestimate the people who waited so long to become a parish and are now cooperating so well in building up their family of faith.

After their return to the bishop, I received a call from the chancellor. He said, "The commission that evaluated the parish reported that the area did not have the resources to build a church or pay back a debt that would have to be incurred." The chancellor then outlined what the bishop had in mind for the parish.

We were to build a hall and pay it off with Bingo. I called an open meeting of the parishioners and explained what happened. Then I explained what it would be like if we had a hall instead of a church and trying to pay it off with Bingo. We would come to church in a hall, with a tiled floor and folding steel chairs, and the smell of soap and smoke clinging to everything. Smoking was permitted in those days. The people were disappointed and distressed with what they were hearing. They did not want to go along with what the bishop had in mind. I told them the bishop also would require us to raise half the cost of a church before he would approve of our building one. They asked me if there was anything else we could possibly do to have the church of our dreams?

I said I would meet with the parish advisory group, recently formed, and get back to them. In meeting with the advisory group, I emphasized that we must have sufficient worship space for the people if we are going to wait to raise half the cost before building a church. If we do not provide adequate worship space, some people will go elsewhere and we will lose them.

Parishioners kept telling me the numbers coming to church would increase dramatically when the schools would close for the summer and families would come out from the City to their summer homes in the area. After much discussion we decided on a tent. We would get a large tent for the summer. First we would have to level the ground, remove the cliff of sand and gravel behind the little church and fill the gully behind it. We got in touch with three companies that dealt in sand and gravel. The first two said it was not what they needed. However, one of them, Marino's Sand and Gravel kindly offered to use their machinery to level the area if we got someone to take what we did not need. The third company, Gotham Sand and Gravel, agreed to take the cliff of sand and gravel. I wanted them to fill the gully behind the cliff. They said it would take about half of the material to fill the gully and they would take the rest for a project they were working on. There would be no charge to the parish. There were some trees in the gully that had to be cut first. I got a volunteer, Joe Morin, to come with a chain saw and I borrowed a chain saw from Gene Geoghan Well Drillers and we went to work. We went down into the gully. It was the month of June and one hundred degrees down there. The perspiration was falling from my forehead and splashing on the chain saw as I cut. On the last day as we finished the job, Joe cut his hand on the chain saw. I rushed him to Mather Hospital Emergency Room for stitches. It was not serious. Gotham Sand and Gravel trucked some of the materials away and put the rest of it in the gully. The Marino's came in with their machinery and leveled it. We had it covered with crushed stone, had it rolled in and we were ready for the tent and the parking for the summer. We were landlocked at the back. There was one lot not built on between us and Syosset Drive. We bought it and opened a driveway at the back of the property onto Syosset Drive. Cars in great numbers started using it right away. It was a very good decision, facilitating parishioners coming and going to church. By decision we were strongly committed to save money for the building of the new church. I had no cook and I did not employ a maintenance man. I did the maintenance myself with the help of volunteers.

All were looking forward to the tent. We announced the need for volunteers to help erect the tent on a designated day. A large crowd of people, men and women, came. Some had days off, policeman, firemen, and people from other employment. Also many seniors came and were very helpful. One man Ray Reardon announced he had worked for Ringling Brothers and had experience in putting up tents. We asked him to show us how. He was very good. In minutes we were driving spikes in the ground, setting poles and tying ropes. The tent was coming together and went up quickly. We all stood back and looked at it, a beautiful tent with blue and white stripes, our Blessed Mother's colors. We were ready now for the increased numbers we were expecting at the end of June when schools would come out.

The tent was for the summer. What are we to do about the winter? We asked the local town officials if we could use a town recreation center for seniors to hold masses on Sunday mornings. They graciously agreed. So now we are set for Sunday masses in the tent in the summer and in the mod recreation center in the winter. There were volunteers to set up everything necessary and put them back where they belonged. We were going to be doing this for the next six years.

Masses in the tent were very popular. We were able to accommodate the extra people who came. The side flaps, six feet high, were rolled up except when there was high winds and heavy rain. It was a very open and free atmosphere. Children parked their bicycles and their dogs outside the tent. Some handicapped people sat in their cars and followed the mass. It was easy for people to talk and make friends. The tent was a real community builder. It was a good decision to live with while waiting for our own dream church to be built.

The tent was a big success. It was always crowded to capacity for masses. Volunteers responded to every call for help. The response of the people was my greatest comfort. We grew close together as we shared everything needed to be done in building up the community and donating for all the programs we developed with special emphasis on outreach for the needy, including children of single parent households. We started a building fund for the new church and it received a generous response all around. We took up a census. There were approximately one thousand families year round, increasing to fifteen hundred families in the summer.

Our religious education program for our children was a big priority for us, but we had no building from which to operate. A local farmer donated a little shed used as a farm stand which he had stopped using. A friend I had in another parish who moved houses moved the shed, free of charge. Parish volunteers converted it into an office, installing a telephone, heat and air conditioning. We took on a wonderful Josephite Sister, Veronica Murtagh, as coordinator of religious education. Sister was very successful in getting teachers and volunteers, always appreciative of the good people already involved. Later on, as the numbers increased, we took on another sister who was very enthusiastic about the new parish. She was Sister Betty Calfapietra, a Mercy Sister who brought her own competence and zeal to the program. The sisters, from their experience in dealing with children, taught me some valuable tips in dealing with the young members of our parish. I learned a great deal from these good sisters. They were very effective in religious education of children and motivating parents. We met every week. First we read the scriptures for the coming weekend and discussed them. The sisters gave their thoughts, which would be helpful at the Sunday homily. Then we had reports on what was going on and planned for the near and distant future. We enjoyed the meetings, sharing and encouraging one another.

Everyone accepted the tent as a wonderful idea, and a great solution to our need for space. We used it for confirmations, weddings, funerals and all large gatherings. It had its own peculiar attraction of openness and airiness. We ran operas, parish socials and barbeques there. There was a ham operator next door, Big Harry, and sometimes what he was saying came clearly through our public address system. One day, during a wedding, when I said, "Do you, Tom, take Judy here present for your lawful wife?" A man's voice came through the loudspeaker saying, "I cannot do that?" I ran out of the tent and through a gate in the fence to Big Harry next door who was not a parishioner but a friend, and told him what was happening. He broadcasted what I said and then cooperated and terminated his conversation. Back in the tent, I told the people what happened. They were greatly relieved for they thought it was the groom, Tom, who had spoken saying, "I cannot do that" and I ran away. They had a friend taking a video of the wedding. He was very excited and said afterwards, "I think this would be good to show on public television."

Most of the time the weather was good while we used the tent, but we had some stormy weather. One Sunday morning there was thunder and lightening, wind and rain. People were coming to mass, running from their cars with umbrellas and finding the water scurrying under their feet as the tent swayed and danced in the wind with the poles stumping the ground in nature's rhythm. While I was standing there worried that the tent would take off, a lovely young lady came running in laughing. She shouted to me, "Isn't this exciting?" as she waved her arms. She repeated. "Isn't this exciting?" She was so lovely and vivacious she made me feel better and I agreed with her, "It sure is exciting." As I started mass with the storm still blowing I used her words "isn't this exciting". Some laughed, the children clapped and we went through the mass safely and the tent was still dancing.

We were always afraid of a hurricane coming. Some people would say, if a hurricane comes, it will take the tent out to Long Island Sound. Right enough in August, a hurricane was forecast as coming our way in mid-week. We were relieved it was not coming on a weekend. On the Monday before the hurricane was to strike, I asked the secretary, Terry Curtin, now working full time for the parish, to call everyone who had volunteered to help with the tent. On Tuesday we took the tent down, laid it flat on the ground and put the poles lying on top of it. The hurricane hit us on Wednesday. It was a wild one. The tent would not have had a chance of staying up. There were very strong winds and torrential rain. It went its way in one day. We called the tent crew again and re-erected the tent on Friday. At mass in the tent on Sunday, I asked as I always do before preaching, "What's the good news?" People usually share, birthdays and anniversaries. We welcome visitors from far and near. We rejoice and we pray. One lady shouted out, "The tent stood up in the hurricane!"

People organized social events, Irish nights, Italian nights, Halloween parties, barbeques and even opera nights. Every morning I walked the two miles from the temporary rectory in Miller Place to the church. I would check out the tent, loosen ropes, push out water forming in pockets, then tighten the ropes again, all before saying morning mass. There would be about twenty people at mass, some on their way to work, some retired people and the seniors who used to be my altar boys. There was usually a gentle breeze blowing through the tent, bringing soothing sounds of birds singing in the trees. On Sunday mornings there was no time to go back to the rectory for breakfast. There was a little German lady who lived on the other side of the fence beside Big Harry, the ham radio operator. She, very kindly, asked me to come into her house for breakfast, so every Sunday morning, between masses I went through the gate in the fence and into Hedwing's house for breakfast. After a while a lady in the tent said to me "Curiosity has got the better of me. Why do you go through that fence every Sunday morning?" I said, "There is a nice little German widow living there and I go to see her."

When the end of September came we had to take down the tent and store it for the winter. We started masses in the town recreation center called the Mod. Joe Morin got a group of volunteers who went there early to set everything up. They brought books, bread and wine, a portable address system and whatever was needed and the music was provided by Ken Swinson, accompanied by his wife, Betsy, and their four children. Ken was always there and always willing to use his talents in getting everyone to sing. He was an excellent guitarist and the people responded to him very well. The Mod provided ample space at two over flow masses every Sunday for the people at that end of the parish. It became popular with people who knew the little church could not hold everyone.

On the first anniversary, we had a parish dinner dance in the local Moose Lodge. It was very well attended and everyone was having a great time. In the course of the evening, I visited the men's room. While in a stall there, two men came in and began to talk about me. One said, "What do you think of this new guy?" The second one said, "Someone in the chancery must have known he was just what we needed." Number one said, "I always thought they were a bunch of nut heads down there. They waited so long to send us anyone, I was sure they would send us a loser." They both continued to talk about me in very flattering statements. I felt too embarrassed to come out of the stall and waited until they left. A couple of times I wanted to laugh out loud at what they were saying, but managed to keep quiet.

Everything was going very well but the bishop and those in the chancery had been talking for some time about the heavy load being carried by one man. My answer was that the people were empowered to carry the load with me. I did not complain. So, one day I got a call from the chancellor saying they were assigning an assistant priest to me. His name was Father James. He was young and had been in two parishes in a short time. Those pastors and he did not get along. Would I take him? I said, yes. James was dedicated to his work. He loved to counsel people with problems.

James was very energetic and took a lot of pressure off me. I was now able to have some free time to myself which I could not have while I was alone. We were renting a small house with two bedrooms. We set up an office in the basement and used the dining room for interviewing people. We needed more space but we managed.

In the winter while taking a walk, through the area with a covering of snow on the ground, two boys playing in the driveway of their house recognized me and I knew them as they sat at my feet at the altar on Sunday mornings. They greeted me and we got talking. Their mother came out and invited me in. She told me they were moving as her husband got a position out west. She said they were renting and the house would be for rent again after they would leave. I said I was interested as the house we were renting was too small for a rectory. She showed me through the house. I said this would suit us well. She gave me the owner's name and phone number. I called him and after talking a while I asked him if he would consider selling it. After a couple more conversations we agreed on fifty thousand. He asked for a binder. I gave a check from my personal checkbook.

Now I had to get the bishops approval. The first answer was no. I told him it would be a good investment as we would have to be there for several years until the church would be built and paid for. Then we could put the money from the sale into a new rectory by the church. The idea of an investment interested him. He said, "This is the first time I have permitted a house, outside of the church grounds, to be bought as a rectory, but you really seem to know what you are doing. You can go ahead and buy the house." I was so happy that day. The house made a very good rectory and it was located in the geographic center of the parish area. We were there for many years while we built the church and paid for it. We sold the house for two hundred and fifty thousand and built a new rectory by the church.

The parish was growing. We now had two resident priests and the workload was greatly increased. We needed a cook-housekeeper. I spoke to Lilly Chapman, who had given me the keys to her nice little house when I first came, and asked her if she would accept the position. She agreed. Now we had Terry Curtin as secretary and Lilly Chapman as cook-housekeeper. They were so good; we could concentrate on parish work, serving the people. Sometimes we did not know what they were scheming up, but they always made us happy. One day I came back from a sick call and the two of them were trying to cut a large, frozen striped bass in two, because I did not cut it before freezing it. Terry was sitting on the frozen striped bass on a table and Lilly was cutting it with a hacksaw. They were sliding all over the table and laughing. They did not want me to see the performance and they did not want my help-just leave.

One Sunday outside the tent, Frank Zimmerman, who was then chairman of the Board of Directors of St. Charles Hospital and Rehabilitation Center, asked me to come on the Board. Among other things, I would represent the people from our area who went to the hospital as patients. Being active in the parish I would have my fingers on the pulse of what was going on and how the patients were satisfied or dissatisfied. I accepted the offer and attended a meeting every month. After several years, I was voted to be chairman of the Board for a term. It was a serving and learning experience. The members, all volunteers, were very devoted and used their time and expertise in serving the hospital. I was on the Board for twenty-five years and was always happy to serve in any way possible. It was a very rewarding experience. I saw big changes in my time on the Board.

Our outreach program for the needy had grown and Terry was running it as well as being secretary. So we did two things: we asked Helen MacClean to take a position as another secretary and she graciously accepted. Helen was very experienced and talented. Among her talents was stenography, which helped me a great deal. She took all of my dictation and was not only competent but always cheerful and positive. We also had Terry take courses given by Fordham University, in social work, dealing with the needy. She got a diploma in the subject and continued to work with renewed enthusiasm.

The outreach program was very important to us. We had a food pantry and people brought food when coming to church. We paid mortgages when families were in arrears, so that parishioners would not lose their homes. We helped with back rent so that people would not be evicted. There were several homes with single parents and many of those parents came to us regularly for help. Their children were not experiencing normal family life. Terry asked for approval to start a day school program for pre-schoolers to give these children and their mothers a break from the monotonous and deprived life they had.

The day school would be for all families who wanted to send their preschoolers, but the children of single parents, who were needy, would be free.

This was a striking success. Single parents made friends with couples who had a normal home life, because all parents had to donate so much time to the program. The children of single parents made friends with children from two parent homes. Single parents were encouraged by the other parents not to let men who came and went or came around promising everything, to take advantage of them. Many single parents got jobs, went off welfare and learned to live with more self-esteem. At least one single mother started her own house cleaning business. The hope was to break the cycle of children being like parents, for that was happening all the time, even being victims.

My assistant James came to me one day and said he had something important to tell me. He was in love with a girl and he now felt he should leave and marry her. He thanked me for how I treated him while he was my assistant. It was not a total surprise as I had seen the girl several times when she came to visit him. I told him I respected his decision and wished both of them a happy future.

I asked the chancellor for another priest to be assigned. He told me there was a Father Noel, a priest from Ireland, who had asked to come to the diocese for the summer, and he would send him to me. Noel came to replace James. We all welcomed him to the parish. Noel was full of enthusiasm and worked well with everyone, especially the children and the youths. He asked to remain permanent in the parish, he liked it so well. His request was granted. He loved to play the guitar and lead groups in singing. I can still see him standing in the sanctuary at Christmas midnight mass, playing the guitar and leading the congregation in song.

Marriage encounter was the big thing at the time and our parish was very supportive of the movement. Noel got quite involved. The husband in one family died suddenly. Noel did a lot for the couples in the marriage encounter movement. He joined groups in homes and they were always very happy to have him. More than a year later, Noel told me he had been with a group of couples who were helping console the widow of the man who died suddenly. She was a school teacher and had several children. She was now getting back to normal. A short time later Noel told me he and the widow had fallen in love and he was going to leave and marry her. He said he hoped the good people would not be disappointed in him. He said, "I am sure they understand the sacrifice it is for us to live alone all our lives." I was not judgmental. I wished them both well and if I could help, get in touch with me.

I understood very well how these priests suffered, the burden of the sacrifices involved in living a celibate life and how they fell in love and left the religious life to get married. The decision these people made in entering the religious life was a life decision. At a certain point in there lives or gradually, they changed the life decision and made new decisions. They were not their old decisions anymore. They would become their new decisions. I prayed for them and was always ready to help in anyway I could.

Of those I knew who left the priesthood and got married, most did very well and had happy lives. Those who married single spouses and had their own children or adopted children seem to have been very successful as were those who married spouses with small children. In cases where the other spouse had older children or teenagers, it did not always work out well. I knew one priest very well who married a woman with teenage children. They resented a new daddy and made life so difficult in the home that the couple's marriage ended in divorce. He continued to come to our church. We were good friends.

I am grateful to the many good priests who served in our parish over the years.

The parish was progressing very well. We had a good parish staff and good willing volunteers serving in all the many ministries we had developed. The building drive was doing exceedingly well. After five years in the tent and the mod recreation center, we had nearly enough funds to build a church according to an architect friend we had consulted with.

When the annual report went into the chancery, I wrote a letter to the bishop stating what we had and what the architect had told us, and asked for his approval to build a new church. He wrote back and gave his approval. I gave the good news to the parishioners at all the weekend masses. They were so happy, they clapped and clapped. At the same time I asked for volunteers with experience in dealing with architects and builders to form a building committee. I said it would be good to have a mixed group of men and women, if possible. Nine people came to the meeting to join a building committee. They were all men, engineers, and builders with one woman, Kathleen Ross, a teacher in Suffolk Community College. They were an amazingly competent group. It became very clear that we had tapped more talent than what they had in the diocesan building office, or the architect's office.

The diocese wanted to give us an architect, but we said we would pick one ourselves and they approved. We found six architects who were interested. We had an architect friend, Don Donaudy, who was not interested himself but helped the committee with the interviewing. We selected Larry Smith

Associates. Larry and his assistant architect Jim Campbell, worked closely with us in drawing up the plans. They presented three different designs and we selected one. It was for a church that would seat eight hundred, with a lower level the same size, housing a hall, kitchen, four classrooms and restrooms.

The tenders were sent to six builders for bids. O'Healy Brothers came in the lowest, just under a million and two hundred thousand lower than the next lowest. The others were much higher. Roger Healy told us they made that low bid because of their friendship with me from the time I was in their parish in Bayshore and baptized some of their children. We appreciated this very much. The O'Healy's did a superb job in building the church.

For the interior we engaged a liturgical artist called Herbert Gunther who was Austrian by birth and had his business in New York City. He was an interesting and humorous person, who thought it was all right to smack a lady on the bottom as he passed by. How did we get him? He and his wife and two children had a summer home in the next Town of Rocky Point, near the beach. He was in Harry's Bar bragging about all the work he had done in churches across the country, including St. Patrick's Cathedral in New York. The owner of the bar was Oliver Whelehan, a parishioner of ours. He told Herbert about our new church and that he should go there and speak to the pastor. Herbert came to see me. He was short, wore a goatee and looked very dapper.

The church under construction

We were able to pay for the church. The diocese loaned us the funds for the interior. Herbert Gunther designed everything, the seating, the flooring, the sanctuary with the altar and pulpit. A big item was the reredos wall behind the altar. This wall would be the center of focus for everyone who walked into the church. He showed us pictures of walls he had done. Some of them were out of state. A good parishioner Bernie Duffy took me to see them. We were impressed. We had him make us two sketches of what the wall would look like. One was a still wall with the dead Christ, the other was a living wall with the risen Christ. We showed them at all the masses in the tent one weekend. About ninety-eight percent of the people wanted the living wall. That is what we have today, a curved, embracing wall with wheat and grapes, symbolizing the Eucharist being swept up to Christ as if by a tidal wave while rays of the morning sun shine out from him, symbolizing the grace he is offering to all of us.

After six years in the tent in the summer and in the mod recreation center in the winter, we were able to set a date to enter our new church. It would be the last Sunday in September. So this was goodbye to the tent and the mod as places of worship.

On that Sunday morning, waiting to say the first mass in the new church, I stood in the large vestibule between the outer doors and the inner glass doors, greeting the people as they entered. When the first family came in the father was a couple of steps ahead of his wife and children. As he got a glimpse of the interior with the white reredos wall illuminated, he turned around threw out his arms and said, "It is so beautiful." As people walked in they expressed their wonder and delight. They pointed and commented on the soaring arches that spanned the entire width of the church without any pillars to support the roof, the wood decked ceiling, the solid oak pews and the red carpet that ran from the entrance doors all the way to the reredos wall. The church was crowded for all the masses. Everyone was so happy. The music director, Jim Sheridan, and choir had been preparing for a long time. They gave a joyous expression in sacred music and song to the worship in everyone's heart and on everyone's lips. The church was designed to bring the parishioners together and feel they were a family. The design was basically the shape of a scallop shell, with the reredos wall at the straight end and the seating in the fan shaped area with the maximum number of people at nearest proximity to the altar. We had low backs on the pews and low ends. When people looked across the church they could see others' faces, and it gave the feeling of a family circle. John, the retired priest, helping at one of the masses, stood in the middle of the church, threw out his arms and shouted, "This is beautiful space." He got a big clap. Then he turned to me, as if surprised at himself and said, "I never said anything like that in church before!"

New Church, 1978, St. Louis DeMontfort, Sound Beach, New York

Bishop McGann came to dedicate the church. He said he was very impressed. The chancery people started telling pastors who wanted to build to go out to Sound Beach and see what John McGuire built. This was after they had tried for so long to prevent us from having our dream church. Monsignor Joe Colligan in Centerport was going to build. He came and looked at our church and was impressed. He built but said he could not build as big as we did. Father Bill Karvelis was going to build in Bohemia and came to see our church. He liked it and said he would try to build one like it. He said he could not afford a lower level. I convinced him to build it and not to underestimate the people. They would pay for it when they had it. He made the right decision and the parish is still living with that decision.

We moved our religious education headquarters from the shed to the lower level of the church where we had designed offices and folding door classrooms. The staff was very happy and the program could function much better now.

Having open space as a hall, and a kitchen we could now run socials and all kinds of meetings. At dinner dances, there was good space for dancing, thanks to the engineers on our parish building committee. They had made the architect change his original design of steel columns to holdup the floor of the church above. We had engineers who were experts in steel working for the State of New York. They said there was a new steel on the market which would carry the weight from above requiring fewer columns and giving greater clear space for dancing. The architect had changed the design and we now had the larger space between the columns at no greater expense.

The architects in Larry Smith Associates gave us such a beautiful, practical design, and the O'Healy's built the church so perfectly that we received the architects' award for an outstanding contribution to the architecture of Long Island.

I got in touch with the pastor of the local community church, the pastor of the congregational church and the Episcopalian Franciscans in a local monastery and asked them if we could form an ecumenical group and have interfaith services. They all agreed. We would meet and have discussions. Each year in January we held an interfaith service in one of our churches and exchanged pulpits in rotation. We encouraged our congregations to take part and the attendance was very satisfying. I preached in the other churches when my turn came around, and the other pastors did the same.

After doing this for four years, the pastor of the community church told me his people did not want to continue this faith sharing because his little flock knew they were all saved. So, they were out of it. The same year, a new pastor came to the congregational church and he was too busy to get involved. That put an end to our efforts to build ecumenical groups in our area.

The sisters, Veronica and Betty, told me they spend no more than "X" number of years in any parish and then they must move on. I was sorry to see them go, but they had their own rules and ideas and also must have been regulated by their orders. We would miss them greatly.

We looked for a new coordinator for religious education and were very fortunate to find Pat Ennis. Pat was an ex-sister who had taught in Catholic schools, and held administrative positions for many years. She came for an interview. I was very impressed with her outgoing personality and her resume. She kindly told me some time afterwards, she was favorably impressed with the way I handled someone who came to me in the church while Pat and I were talking, and insisted I help him with some problem. Pat and I had never met before, so we were both looking for some insights into each other's personality and character qualities. We offered Pat the position and she accepted.

Pat was married to an ex-priest, Joe Ennis, who had an excellent background in education and was at the time employed in a school district on the Island. They were exceptionally good people. When they failed to have children of their own, they adopted four teenage children from one family as they had lost their parents.

Pat was very successful as coordinator of the religious education program and picked up where sisters Veronica and Betty left off in a job they did so well. All the staff and volunteers were enthusiastic and worked hard and willingly. Joe Ennis got a position as superintendent of schools in the Rochester district of New York State. They moved up there and we lost Pat.

Now we were without a religious education coordinator and we were looking for someone suitable. When we were ready to call someone recommended by the chancery, a man got in touch with me, John McNamara. I had known John from the time I was in Valley Stream for a short term. John had been teaching religion in Maria Regina High School and had experience in youth ministry. I had him help me develop a program for youths in that parish. John came for an interview. He told me he and his wife, Cathy, and young family had bought a home and moved into our area. Maria Regina High School was too long a commute, so he was looking for a position near his home. When he told me the salary he was receiving, I said we will offer you more. We put him in charge of the whole religious education program, including youth ministry and adult education.

As associate coordinator we took on Sister Margaret Judge who had taught in Catholic schools in Brooklyn for many years, specializing in preparing children for first communion. She has a charm in roping parents in.

Cathy Sweeney came aboard as associate coordinator with great talents and many years of experience in teaching in Catholic schools. Cathy had special training and experience in family dynamics, and teaching parent child relationships. She is good at everything.

Margie Batillo has been with us from the beginning. Margie knows everyone and can do everything. Mary Lou Pinto is secretary to the program and fulfills her position with eagerness, competence and a smile. We have over two thousand children from seventeen hundred families in the program, plus a large youth ministry.

Claudette Kosciuk developed a boy's choir, a girl's choir and a youth choir. They are magnificent when they lead us with music and song in worship.

Jonathan Wright is the music director. He trains and conducts an adult choir, whose members are very talented and devoted. We all love to hear them sing and lead us in joyful worship. Tom Wilkinson, a competent and genial organist served the parish well for many years.

We have well-trained and committed ushers, lectors and lay ministers who also take communion to the sick and home bound. There are over eight hundred volunteers who do more than just go to church on Sundays.

The church was serving us very well. It was very popular. We had many visitors from neighboring parishes and relatives and friends of parishioners from far and near. We were constantly being told what a welcoming community of faith we were and how beautiful the church was. The lower level was not adequate for all our needs. The religious education program had grown, so had the music and outreach departments. We had always planned a second building phase. Now was the time. We had paid what we owed on the church in ten years, and we had saved for the second building phase. The extra we might need, we could borrow from the diocese.

Having learned from what some other parishes did not do, we called the heads of the departments together, religious education, liturgy, outreach and maintenance and asked for input as to what should be incorporated in the center we were going to build. It would be primarily a religious education center with classrooms, library and offices. We got good input from those who would work there. The head of liturgy wanted music rooms, one for choir practices, one for instrumentalists and one for books and robes. The head of outreach wanted a waiting and greeting space, offices for a director and counselor and storage space for non-perishable foods. It all worked out very well. The music rooms ended up being a music chapel with an organ and piano, capable of seating one hundred fifty. It is very popular, not only with music groups, but with other groups who love to meet there, and for small weddings.

We designed and built a new rectory on the church grounds with space for three resident priests and two visitor rooms. There is a wing for adequate offices and a large meeting room in the basement. We put the funds from the sale of the temporary rectory in Miller Place into the building of the new rectory. Bishop McGann came to bless the new buildings. He was very impressed. He said it was the first time he had blessed a music chapel. He also said the offices at the rectory were better and accommodated more workers and visitors than the offices in the diocesan rectory by the cathedral.

At a clergy conference the bishop came over to me and said, "I'm happy you came to this meeting because I have something to tell you. I have just received a communication from the Holy Father in Rome. He has conferred Papal Honors on you and you will now be called Monsignor. I will send you the letter he sent." As he waited for a response I was thinking I really don't want this, so I said, "I am grateful for the honor but I really don't deserve it." He said, "it is an honor not only for you but for all the parishioners who worked so well with you. I will come out to your parish for your investiture in the monsignor's robes." The following letter came from the Holy Father.

PRELATE OF HONOR

HIS HOLINESS JOHN PAUL II

TO THE BELOVED BROTHERS:

GREETINGS AND APOSTOLIC BLESSING

In an offering kind prayers and supplications, since we have discovered that you have shown particular characteristics of spirit and talent by which you have succeeded in Catholic cares and concerns by devotion and labor, so that by our good will we now publicly designate you,

N. John A. McGuire
Diocese of Rockville Center on Long Island

PRELATE OF HONOR

This we chose, this we create, this we announce.

We concede to you those privileges, honors, and prerogatives that belong to this position that are declared and truly mandated which are found in the instruction, ut sive," of the Papal Secretariat of State.

Given at Rome, at the See of Saint Peter, February 8, 1985.

When it was announced in the parish at the weekend masses, the people clapped and were very happy. I let my family know and they were all happy to hear the news. My sister, Marcella, a nun in England flew over for the ceremony of investiture. She was thrilled. During the mass, the bishop explained to the people the meaning of what was taking place. He told them this was an honor for all of them in recognition of the great teamwork and all that was being accomplished in our parish. I had to go into the vesting room and come out wearing the purple. I really felt embarrassed but the people gave me a standing ovation. There was a reception afterwards in the lower level hall. My sister, Marcella, was very proud of me and said I looked very good in the purple. I was finding it hard to get used to it. The bishop told me I did not have to wear the purple every Sunday, but only on special occasions. That was fine with me.

The town was revising their ethics committee, which had stopped meeting some time before. The supervisor asked me and four others to form a new ethics committee. I accepted and at the first meeting they elected me as chairman. We met once a month. The town attorney gave us an agenda of cases to look into and determine if we considered anything unethical, or having the appearance of a conflict of interest. The people on the board were very good, knowledgeable and fair minded. It was very interesting and a good learning experience. The members were all lay people except for me. I worked on the board for five years and then resigned because my life had become so busy, I could not do it justice. I recommended another member of the clergy to take my place. He was well suited. The supervisor asked him and he accepted.

The Suffolk County Police Department needed a chaplain as the one they had for many years had recently retired. The bishop asked me to take the position, part-time, and continue being pastor of the parish. I accepted and was sworn in as chaplain. I was to be on call at all times, if needed. They gave me a police telephone in my car and I could hear the communications from headquarters day and night. I visited sick members in the hospital, officiated at wakes and funerals, and attended official ceremonies. A dimension of the work I found very rewarding was counseling officers and their families. They could come to the chaplain with any problem and whatever they said was kept in the strictest confidence. I visited the academy and gave talks to recruits on ethics and attended graduations. I grew in my admiration of the members of the department and appreciation of their dedication, skill and competence. I am also a chaplain to the Police Association of Suffolk County and enjoy attending their meetings. The members are great people, do a lot of good work, and have a very supportive fellowship.

And remember: Love is not love 'til it's given away.

CHAPTER 27

The Church In Transition

There was a great transition that took place in my lifetime and the lifetime of my counterparts. What happened would have been unthinkable in our early days. From one perspective, put briefly, we grew up and became priests as children of the council of Trent. Then, after many years in the priesthood and ministry we found ourselves to be children of another council, Vatican II. I am a child of both and have lived the teachings of both. They were not contradictory so much as they presented a change in emphasis.

Vatican II developed the theology of marriage very well, while doing little with the theology of religious life and priestly ministry including celibacy.

In my student days there were clerics everywhere, very visible because they all wore the clerical clothes, black suits and Roman collars. We dressed that way as did the clerical students from the many seminaries in the country at the time, even getting onto buses and going to the beaches. I used to be amazed at the numbers and wondered if they had all gone through the difficult process of making the decision and if they now felt the sacrifice as much as I did. There was no way of knowing, for those things were never discussed and anything to do with sex was taboo.

Catholic people held the clerical and religious states to be on the highest level. They showed great respect to all clerics and religious. Any family who had a member in the religious life felt very highly honored and blessed.

The theology of marriage, coming from Vatican II continued to develop and movements came into being that promoted the good understanding of marriage and the improvements of marriage relationships, such as Marriage

Encounter and Serendipity. The theology of religious life and the priesthood in relationship to celibacy was not developed in the same way.

Father Chuck Gallagher, a Jesuit, was a talented promoter of Marriage Encounter. He conducted weekend retreats in many centers and they were very well attended by married couples of all ages. These weekends were not intended for problem marriages, but for good marriages to make them better.

I attended some of those weekends as a learning experience. He had trained couples to give presentations. They and Father Chuck would answer questions. After each presentation they would break up and go into quiet places separately and write to their partner for ten minutes. Then come together, exchange what they had written and discuss it. Couples got insights into each other that, in many cases, they had not expected. Many couples benefited greatly and their marriages grew stronger because of it. We were told the priest was married to the church. While the couples wrote notes and shared, Chuck and I wrote notes to each other and shared. It was some help but I found it to be in a different vein.

These movements to help marriages became very popular and spread to many countries. Priests, like myself, who were involved in helping, were very happy to experience couples grow in their marriages while experiencing a tremendous challenge ourselves to live happily the life of sacrifice to which we were committed for the building up of the kingdom.

For generations, and indeed hundreds of years, the state of the priesthood and religious life were very stable. A few left and returned to the secular state. These were generally considered failures and looked down on. Now the door had opened a bit and it had become easier to get dispensed and leave. Some of the best were leaving and returning to the secular state.

Many were highly qualified and able to get good positions in the world of education and counseling and other professions. There were those who found it hard to adjust but in general, they did well. Our parish did benefit greatly from those who became members and served the community with competence and dedication.

The laity were changing their views on the stability and permanence of the religious state and that of the priesthood. It was not the same safe haven anymore. Parents were not as eager to encourage their children to become priests or religious. There was a progressive secularizing taking place in society and young people did not have the same incentives that generations before had. They were being drawn into the mainstream of materialism and consumerism. Vocations fell off dramatically. Dioceses and religious orders began feeling the effects of both losing members and not getting many candidates to join. There had to be a cutting back of services and the closing of churches and religious houses. The trend continues. Looking into the future: who knows where we are headed. Everyone can have an opinion. Experts can have an educated guess. The church believes the Holy Spirit is very active and will bring us into a new era.

Priests and religious made serious life decisions as they live out their lives. These are their decisions. Deciding to leave and entering new states of life, they again are their decisions. A decision can be for better or for worse.

My youngest brother Mike also entered the priesthood. After graduating from Garbally Park College and Maynooth College he was ordained for the diocese of Clonfert. He spent a few years serving there before coming to Long Island. He served in a couple of parishes and was highly regarded. For a long time now Mike was saying priests should be allowed to marry, that celibacy should be voluntary. He used to frequently say, "It is not good for man to be alone," quoting the Book of Genesis where God said before creating Eve, "it is not good for the man to be alone." I knew he was suffering, but so was I and the other normal priests.

He and I got together about once a week and spent time relaxing. We fished, visited friends and had long discussions together. During one of these discussions, Mike told me he wanted to leave. I said, "You mean to leave the priesthood for good?" He said, "Not right away. First I would take a leave of absence. That would give me time to think things out better." I knew that was what most of those leaving did. First they would take a leave of absence for two years, which could be easily obtained. At the end of the two years, they could return and some returned but most did not.

When I asked Mike if he could tell me why he was leaving, he said he did not want to spend the rest of his life in the priesthood. There did not seem to be any specific reason, so I spent some time telling him what a good job he was doing and how much he was needed by the people, especially with the declining number of priests. After spending more time telling him how much he was needed and the amount of good he could do, I realized I was not getting anywhere. Finally, I said to him, "Mike, are you in love with a young lady?" Without hesitation he said, "yes." He said he did not know how to tell me and he was relieved I asked. "May I ask what is her name?" "Alana", he said. I said, "I wish you both well and will pray to God to guide you."

Fishing with my brother, Mike

Mike took me to see Alana and her family. She was very pretty and charming. Her mother and sisters were very nice. Her father was deceased. Mike and Alana married and moved to Ireland, where Mike got a position as a counselor in a High school and Alana got a position teaching. They built a home and had two daughters. They are both delightful young ladies and I love them very much. Mike, the youngest, was the first of eight children to die. His family and all of us miss him greatly.

The dying of the great vocation movement that had gone on, and kept increasing for generations, and the exodus from the priesthood and religious life created a heavy burden of worry and concern for the church, worry about continuing all the essential services and concern about the unknown future. Was this burden too great for the church to bear? Recent popes had granted dispensations to leave the priesthood, get married and live in good standing in the church. The present Holy Father, John Paul II, must have thought the burden was too great for the church, too many were leaving and tried to stop the exodus from the priesthood by closing the door, not granting any more dispensations, except in extraordinary cases. This meant that priests who decided to leave and get married could not do so honorably and if they did go ahead without the necessary dispensation, the marriage would not be recognized by the church.

Now, those priests who had decided to leave honorably and get married validly were stopped from doing so. There was much disappointment and anguish of conscience, anger and confusion for those who could not understand the church doing this while their lives were in midstream. This decision by the Holy father did succeed in keeping some in the priesthood who would otherwise have left.

A priest, Dan, who had been waiting for his mother to pass on before leaving the priesthood, because he did not want to break her heart, came to me after his mother's death and discussed his plans with me. By now the door was closed and no more dispensations were being given, except in special cases. This bothered him very much as he wanted to be in good standing in the church and if he married, would want it to be recognized. He said, "If I had asked for the dispensation earlier, when they were giving them out, I could have had it. Now that I have waited for my dear mother to go, I cannot have it. I am angry and confused. It seems to me to be acting like God, being in complete control, only I believe God does not change his mind."

Some Episcopalian clergymen had converted to the Catholic Church and requested to minister as Catholic priests. Permission was granted by Rome and also approval to remain married and live with their wives and families. Dan said, "I was happy to see this happen, but wondered where it was leading to. It did not lead anywhere. The lay people welcomed those priests and had no problem accepting them in all the ministries of a priest. Their wives are very involved in supporting their husbands and helping to build up the community. This looked like it might be a step toward voluntary celibacy; but so far it has not."

Dan and I met several times and discussed this matter at length. He had served the people of God very well for many years in several parishes. He loved to talk about the ministry he was involved in and how he helped so many people overcome crises in their lives and find peace. I sensed he was torn between leaving and staying. He felt he was at the stage in his life when he could marry and have children. If he was going to leave, he did not want to wait any longer. I said to him, "You don't have a lady friend that you are in love with and want to marry?" He said, "No, but I could find one." After further discussion, I said, "You don't seem to have your mind firmly made up." He said, "No, I am all confused about making the final decision." I said, "The Holy Father has to make decisions for the good of the church and would you refuse to let the Episcopalian converts keep their wives?" He paused for awhile and said, "I am happy for them." "I think the Holy Father and my mother are enabling me to reconsider what I had in mind to do." After a long struggle, Dan veered away from his plan of leaving and getting married to a yet unknown person. He recommitted himself to his work in his parish with renewed enthusiasm. He told me later the crisis he went through made him a better servant of God's people. After Father Noel left, Father George Michell was assigned to our parish. He served during the final years in the tent and the first years in the new church. Father George was devoted especially to the young people.

When Father George was transferred we were assigned two assistant priests, Father Bob O'Connell and Father Tom Murray. They both worked very hard. They loved the parish and the people loved them. Father Tom first came as a deacon and after six months was ordained a priest. He remained with us for several years and was involved in all the ministries in our parish.

Father Bob was very committed to serving the people and was greatly loved. When he was with us for six years, he was due for a transfer. He asked for an extension and was left with us for another three years, at which time he became a pastor.

After Fathers Bob and Tom were transferred, we had several assistant priests assigned to us for limited periods of time. The good word they did was greatly appreciated.

We were then reduced to one assistant because of the shortage of priests. It was now Father Donald Hayden and me. Father Donald was very energetic, was loved by the people and served them very well. Father Frank Pizzarelli, a Montfort missionary, has helped us for many years and is a real asset to our parish.

And remember: Love is not love 'til it's given away.

CHAPTER 28

The Church in Turmoil

Since the Second Vatican Council, the church has been in transition and has made headlines in the news media about changes in the church. Now there are alarming news headlines, and they are not about changes in the Catholic Church. These headlines are about abuses in the church, priests molesting children. The church was exposed, people were horrified and the world gasped. The image of a priest dedicated in the long and glorious tradition of service to God's people now being revealed as a wolf in sheep's clothing, devouring the spiritual and psychological life of a child for his own erotic pleasure, made good people everywhere react with unbelievable horror, disappointment, disgust and anger. The faithful reeled with the anguish of scandal, shock and suffering.

I thought of my own case. I was molested by a layman. A priest gave me healing and counseling. Now I am a priest myself and I know the vast majority of priests are good ones. They bring healing and good counseling to countless numbers of disturbed children and grownups all through their lives. I feel deeply concerned for the welfare of those who have been molested by our brother priests, who were ordained to bring healing and comfort to God's children, and turned out to be wolves in sheep's clothing, harming instead of healing, devouring instead of saving, bringing distress instead of comfort, and leaving them with troubled consciences instead of peaceful minds.

What am I aware of? I am well aware that good people suffer in the same way that we, their priests whom they know, suffer. Parents who know good priests trust their children with them and feel for them that they have been cast under a shadow of suspicion that has descended in many people's minds, on all priests. A few bad apples make some people think they are all bad. All good priests have compassion in their hearts for the victims, and at the same time, are conscious of a shadow over their own heads, placed there by the priests who are wolves in sheep's clothing. The church is conscious of the importance of the clothing when she uses the word "defrocked" for the process of throwing out a bad priest. Even though the wolves may be defrocked of their sheep's clothing, the shadow still remains over the heads of priests who are good to the very core of their beings.

I am so grateful the priest who helped me in distress was a good one. He brought me healing and steered me right. I wonder what would have happened to me if he had been a wolf in sheep's clothing? Where would I be today? I cannot imagine myself being other than what I am, a priest who loves everyone in the world and who is always ready and willing to bring healing and peace to all who come to me.

The bad news of priests molesting children shifted in main focus to the bishops who reassigned those priests to other parishes after having been found guilty. A bishop who had a guilty pedophile priest in his jurisdiction and reassigned him to another parish was now considered guilty of making it possible for the molester to strike again. So many cases were surfacing in the news that we and all good people found it hard to believe this could have happened on such a large scale. Now the bishops are being attacked as guiltier than the pedophiles, because they could have saved so many children from being abused by not reassigning guilty priests.

So many were coming forward, some after twenty or thirty years from the time they claimed they were abused, accusing priests of having molested them, that the picture was getting bigger and worse by the week. As these cases continue to make headlines in the news, I always think the same thoughts: why did this person not deal with the problem at the time it happened instead of waiting all this time? The victim should receive help and experience healing without delay. Waiting all those years with a damaged conscience or personality must be a lot of suffering, and, maybe, despair of ever getting true healing. In my case, I just could not wait. Of course, every case is different. Are those who are coming forward now doing so because of all the publicity? If there was not all this publicity, would they ever have surfaced? Maybe there are other reasons for victims accusing predators, all apparently at the same time, after so many years. There are many unanswered questions. The numbers may have given them courage. Whatever the reasons for delay, they should all receive healing and peace in their lives.

With the zero tolerance that bishops are now following, a priest who is reported by anyone of having molested a minor must be removed immediately before any guilt is proved. He is now not innocent until proven guilty, which everyone is entitled to, but he is treated as guilty until proven innocent. There have been some cases where the accusations were withdrawn and cases where no proof could he had. If such a priest is declared innocent; even if he is reinstated in ministry, there are people who will always look on him with suspicion, and he will suffer from this suspicion, probably for the rest of his life. Is full reparation possible? While the guilty priests should be removed from ministry and punished, the ones accused and proven innocent should be treated with appropriate justice. Cardinal Bernadin suffered greatly. Then the accusations against him were withdrawn as untrue.

The main focus is now on the bishops. Those involved are on center stage in this whole pedophile matter. They have to appear before district attorneys for questioning, open up the files on all priests against whom there were complaints of molesting children. There are more than anyone would have thought there were. Constant publicity has put those bishops in a bad light. Many people are blaming them more than the perpetrators. The bishops say they are striving hard to bring about healing for the victims and at the same time making sure these crimes by their priests will not happen again.

Some bishops are saying they did what they thought was the best thing to do at the time. When they were informed about a priest molesting children they had the priest see a psychiatrist who would recommend the priest go to a treatment center for rehabilitation. Thereafter, getting a report that this patient is now all right to go back into ministry, the bishop would reassign him to another parish. The problem would reoccur.

The publicity has brought about a very painful learning experience. These predators could not be rehabilitated. Bishops and psychiatrists were often mistaken in judgment and made bad decisions. The constant bad news has been more than a wake up call, it has been more than a painful education, it has degraded the church in the eyes of the world and left some bishops striving hard to survive in their exalted positions as shepherds of their flocks.

When we were students, we were told we should be striving for perfection. We were also told a bishop should be in the state of perfection. That does not mean he should have perfect knowledge and know that a pedophile cannot be rehabilitated. In this and in other matters he has to consult with experts in their fields. Then why is the bishop blamed for it all, and why are so many saying such a bishop should resign? People I speak to who condemn a bishop for reassigning a pedophile priest say he should have more concern for the victims than for the perpetrator, and this has not always been the case. If our people want to talk about the clerical abuse of children, I think it is important to listen to them. They are suffering. They are trying to comprehend how the situation got so bad, and want to see healing take place. What is commonly heard are statements like; that bishop did not put the children first, he was more concerned for the priests, the bishop's motivation was fear of bad publicity; the bishop wanted to protect his good name and his reputation among the people. All the bishops I have known are good, holy men, dedicated to serving their flocks at all times. Those who reassigned predator priests are paying the price. All bishops have been enlightened in this matter, and it does not seem this chapter of abuse in the church's history could ever be repeated.

All bishops are now committed to protecting children: clergy, staff and volunteers have to sign documents giving permission to have their backgrounds checked to see if they have clean records. There is also zero tolerance. If there is a single complaint against any of these people, that person is to be removed immediately and the case reported to the civil authorities.

Are we being buried now under an avalanche? The bad news has been growing in volume and coming at us with increasing momentum, threatening to bury us alive. There are so many predators, thousands of victims and millions of mourners, grieving over death to innocence, irreparable damage and often loss of faith.

Every time I hear of a case of sexual molestation, I think of what Father Murphy had told me, quoting the gospel of St. Matthew, Chapter 18, Verse 6. "Whoever scandalizes one of those little ones who believes in me, it would be better for him to have a great millstone hung around his neck and to be drowned in the depths of the sea." This is a very strong, condemnatory statement from Christ who said he came to call sinners and preached the mercy of God. It shows how strongly he felt for the spiritual welfare of the little ones. His statement seems to demonstrate very strongly, what we might call a "holy anger" against anyone who would hurt any of his little ones by leading them into sin or causing them to lose faith.

A millstone was known to everyone in those days. It was used in a mill to grind grains and as far as I know, was used for this purpose in many parts of the world up to modern time. It was well known in olden times in drowning an animal or a human, a weight would be tied to the neck to make sure the victim would not survive. We have heard, in our time, of a person being drowned with their feet in a bucket of cement.

As I think of these things, it strikes me to be very much out of character for Christ to use this kind of language and this kind of imagery. It shows how strongly he felt for the good of his little ones and also how strongly he wanted to impress his listeners about the gravity of this horrible crime. The molester is the first to put a heavy weight, a millstone around the victim's neck. I felt it and it was heavy, and had to be gotten rid of. Indeed the weight of the millstone is felt by everyone who hears of the crime, parents, family, members of the church, the priests, the bishops and the Holy Father. We all feel the weight and it won't go away.

As I ponder the saying of Christ and his condemnation of pedophiles, I like the words he used, "little ones." These words touch a loving chord in all our hearts,

"Little ones" they bring to mind,

> The lambs of the flock,
> The innocent ones,
> The most lovable ones;
> The most cherished ones,
> The most treasured ones,
> The most trusting ones,
> The most vulnerable ones;
>
> The ones most attractive to the wolves;
> The ones the predators fear least,
> The ones in greatest need of our protection,
> The ones in greatest need of our love,

"The kingdom of heaven belongs to these."

We all know the "little ones" of today will lead the world of tomorrow. We all have the obligation and privilege to teach the "little ones" by word and example, to love all people on this earth.

So many "little ones" are taught what is wrong by the words and examples of some adults around the world: bias, prejudice, racism, deception, revenge and more.

The worst damage is done by harming the "little one" in himself. If he cannot live happily with himself, because of what has been done to him, how can he live happily with others as he goes through life? This is where the abuse does so much damage.

When Christ said anyone who scandalizes one of these "little ones" he deserves a millstone around his neck, he was referring to harming a "little one" and also leading him away from faith in God. How many millstones does a predator deserve? Some bishops are weighted down by many millstones. Still, the "little ones" carry the greatest weight.

The weight of the millstone is felt by all members of the church from the pope down to the humblest of the laity. As every member shares in the joy of the church, so do all share in its suffering. Parishioners tell me the pope in Rome and also all the bishops who gathered together in Dallas should have focused as strongly as Christ did, on the unthinkable evil done to children and the fate that the perpetrators deserve. They said many good things and made some good decisions, yet those parishioners did not feel they were as strong as Christ in empathizing with the "little ones" and in condemning the perpetrators.

The Holy Father feels the weight of the millstone and when he speaks to the world he must be conscious of it. His listeners share the weight of that millstone, suffer and pray and wonder how it was allowed to get this heavy. When will it go away? Will it ever?

In the view of some the millstone is so heavy it threatens to sink the barque of Peter, but we must always remember Christ said no evil would prevail against the church and that it would endure to the end of time.

While speaking with one bishop about this matter, I said I was writing a chapter in my memoir on "The Church in Turmoil." He asked, "When do you think the church will come out of this turmoil?" At that moment, someone else got his attention. I am convinced we will come through the turmoil by our unity, all listening to one another, working and praying together. We have to go beyond the stage of blaming this one, or that one because this always foments division. The bishops and the faithful must listen well to one another. The spirit works through everyone, but the bishops must lead. Theirs is the hardest task as they must show the way, shepherding their flocks. The confidence and trust, eroded during the turmoil, must be restored. Bishops cannot do this alone. All members of the church must work together, the bishops, priests, deacons, religious and the faithful. There is so much faith, love and good will that listening, sharing, working and praying together we can, as church, come through the turmoil to a better and more fruitful future.

The priestly state has suffered a severe blow. Lay people are divided, some confused that all of this could have happened, some rallying to the support of good priests and some suspicious of all priests. Some parishioners came to me saying they could not cope with it and did not want to lose their faith. A neighboring priest was driving through his parish in full clerical attire. At a traffic light a car pulled alongside him. The driver rolled down the car window and said, "Father, I want you to know we support you and are happy to see you wearing the priestly clothes." A layman friend of mine told me, with fury in his eyes, of witnessing a scene where people were standing in line, two deep, waiting to get on a plane when a priest in clerical garb joined the line. A man noticed him, pulled his young son close to himself and said, "Stay away from that black bastard." Priests in black suits and Roman collars were a very common site on the streets. There are very few, if any, today. What happened to the respect for "a man of the cloth?"

The priestly state, revered by so many, inside and outside the church for so long, has been dragged through the gutter by those who deserve to have a millstone hanging around their necks and be cast into the depths of the sea. Instead, innocent priests are bearing the weight of the millstone and striving to keep the faithful from the depths of despair. Christ told Peter, "You are rock and on this rock I will build my church and the powers of evil shall not prevail against it." I see the church as a beautiful woman, a mother to so many, standing firmly on a rock with a millstone around her neck. The harm done to her children and the weight of suspicion is heavy and hard to bear. Who will take it away or will it remain forever?

For those who do not like the church and do not want to see her prosper, this is grist to their mill. They will not let the church forget the millstone of sexual abuse of children that hangs around her neck. It is part of the history of the church now. Can it ever go away? Has this abuse ceased for good or will it surface again? Is there healing for the victims and for the church? It baffles me to know how these predators got through into the priesthood. I suppose all in sheep's clothing look the same. There is psychological screening and long years of supervision and testing. There is the voluntary and wholehearted commitment of the candidate to a life of service and sacrifices, and yet there is something not revealed.

Where does the church go from here? First of all it must be dedicated to the healing of the victims. Secondly, it must take real steps not only to eliminate those predators now in the church, but to make as certain as possible that unsuitable candidates are never again admitted into the priesthood.

Standing back and taking a broad view of the whole matter, there are certain aspects of it that come to mind. There has been a loss of the sense of sin in some people and to some extent, in the whole world that we live in. To sexually abuse a little one is a grievous sin against the child, humanity, and against God and deserving of the severest punishment. Christ, in his words of condemnation, branded it as a most sinful crime and showed anger against the predator. Every true disciple should have the same mind. "Let that mind be in you which was also in Christ Jesus." For so many priests to have abused so many little ones is a sign of the loss of the sense of sin. It is putting sexual gratification before everything even the welfare of little ones who should be cherished so highly. To these people, what is the crime of sin anymore?

How could these predators preach to decent people and tell them how to live their lives? How could they sit in confessionals waiting for honest sinners to come in and ask for forgiveness? No wonder some people told me their faith was shaken. In this way these priest predators are abusing everyone in the whole church and beyond. My conviction is that any candidate who does not have the mind of Christ in this matter and have a deep and burning detestation for anyone who would think it all right to scandalize a little one, should be barred from entering the priesthood. Would we be better off with married men with the mind of Christ serving in the priesthood, working with the good priests in voluntary celibacy?

With the growing crisis of the shortage of priests, bishops may be hard pressed to accept candidates who may not have all the qualities to the degree the bishops would like to see. There is danger here, danger of some slipping in who may be trouble later on. Better with fewer good ones, than to have any doubtful ones.

Many of those victims who had been abused as "little ones" are now adults, some advancing in maturity and in their professions. There is a valuable resource here for members on a bishop's committee to help in the process of admitting and training candidates for the priesthood. Many of those have remained faithful to the church and have grown as stallwart members over the years. They each have unique qualifications to bring to the service of the church. They are such good people they could have a significant healing role in the church and greatly lighten the weight of the millstone. Healing will take place and I would like to see the leaders in the healing process to be the wounded healers to whom we owe so much and who have so much to give which everyone cannot give. Many victims with deep love for the church are doing this heroic work and many more will follow. This is truly being like Christ who is our number one wounded healer, the one from whom we all receive healing.

One friend, Father George said, "I'm not wearing the priestly garb in public anymore. It used to remind people of service and dedication. Now it brings to people's mind the scandal and shock some priests have caused by molesting children. I don't want to be a reminder of that horror."

> When father X wears his priestly dress,
> He feels some measure of distress,
> Like walking through roses and thorns,
> Who looks for a halo and who for horns?

While writing this memoir I am driving by a church on Ash Wednesday. Because of the numbers trying to get into the church we were passing, traffic was very slow, stopping and starting. A man in a pick-up truck behind me started shouting loudly. My first reaction was to think he was shouting at me, but there was a car close in front of me. As he continued to shout I made out some of what he was saying, "Why are you going to church? The priests are queers. The priests molest children? They are homosexuals. Don't listen to priests." At first I thought he knew I was a priest as I was concentrating on the driving, but he was behind me and could only see the back of my head. I realized also that I was not wearing a roman collar at the time. His shouting and his words bothered me, but I took comfort in two factors, in the number of faithful going into church and knowing the pastor of that church to be a holy, very dedicated servant of God and of God's people. Still the ugly experience of the man shouting and his offensive words stayed with me. I prayed for him.

In the eyes of some, we have gone from halos to horns

I experienced the church in transition brought about by the second Vatican Council, and now the church in turmoil brought about by the scandal and shock of priests molesting children. As one priest friend put it to me, "Many Catholics regarded good, dedicated priests as saints, now many critical Catholics are suspicious of all priests. Most still regard priests highly, as dedicated men, and reassure us of their support, realizing we are living in very difficult times."

We priests, like all good people, are deeply shocked at the molestation of children by some priests. Our first concern is for the victims: we hope and pray that they will be rehabilitated and that there will be no more victims. We hope the church will strictly enforce all the new regulations to protect children. We are also deeply concerned for the members of the faithful whose faith is shaken by the scandal. We remind them that God, the giver of faith, will strengthen our faith in this time of trial.

Most parents are not encouraging their children to enter religious life or the priesthood. There has been a significant falling off in vocations since Vatican II. Now, with the pedophile scandal the situation on vocations has become much worse. The strength of the faith of the faithful is the foundation of the good that is done by the church in the world. The state of the priesthood, in the past, was looked upon as stable and secure. Now, with the number of priests leaving the priesthood and the pedophile scandal, people see the state of priesthood not to be as stable and respected as it was in the past. People's faith is constantly being challenged from within the church and from the larger world outside. Questions do cross their minds, and they need to have answers. The secular world continually presents ideas and doctrines that challenge the faith. To cope with all of this our people must be enlightened in their faith. From the beginning of our parish we endeavored to train our people to live the teachings of Vatican Council II. We ran Parish Renewal weekends. We brought in experts to spend days with staff and those in ministry. Father Joe Lynch, a priest psychologist came to us, on invitation many times. We all found him very effective. Monsignor Charlie Swigar had an office in the chancery for parish development. From the very beginning he helped us greatly in long time planning for the future of our parish. The diocese very wisely had introduced a program on pastoral formation of the laity. We strongly encouraged our people to take the courses offered. So many people responded that the diocesan director of the program, Pat Megale, with whom we worked closely, told us our parish had the most members in the program.

Those parishioners who took the courses, were and are very committed and effective in all the ministries of our parish. Some continued their studies and became permanent deacons. They have their own special calling, and serve the parish very well. We have Deacons, Joseph Bartolotto, Peter Schultz and Gary Swane. We also had Deacons Ronald Gilette and Montfort Naylor. They went to serve in other parishes where there were no permanent deacons and the need was greater. The deacon's spouses are very encouraging and helpful to their husbands; sacrificing family time, enabling them to minister to the needs of the people. At the council, as the Holy Father, with all the bishops and experts from around the world prayed and shared together, they could see clearly where the Holy Spirit was leading them. They came to understand from all of what the faithful believed and practiced, where the correct emphasis should be. All that was good and right in the church, already there, was more clearly perceived and put into right and clear order to be accepted and put into practice.

In the life of the church in my early years, and at the time I attended parish missions, the greatest emphasis was on "saving your soul." At every mission the four last things were preached, death, judgment, hell or heaven. That was what lay ahead for everyone without exception.

Over the entrance to the Seminary here on Long Island, carved in stone, we read, "salus animarum suprema lex"—the salvation of souls is the supreme law. In order to bring this about we must build the kingdom. Christ told us not to bury our talents but to use them to build his kingdom. "He who does not gather with me, scatters." It is Christ who saves.

To save my soul as most important is accomplished by using my gifts and talents to build the community of faith with others, helping one another to be the church, the budding forth of the kingdom of God on earth and be worthy to enter the fullness of the kingdom of God in heaven, where we will continue to sing together "all glory and honor is yours, almighty Father, for ever and ever." We have large numbers of laity committed to ministry in liturgy, religious education and outreach. Each of these areas of ministry has several subdivisions.

In the early days of the parish a course was offered in the seminary called Parish Renewal. It was conducted by a very talented Jesuit, Father Chuck Gallagher. There was a group of pastors taking the course and we enjoyed it very much. We were taught to do this in our parishes as weekends of renewal. It involved training some parishioners to work with the pastor. I came back to the parish feeling very enthusiastic about the program.

I trained a group of parishioners. Then we ran weekends where the people were encouraged to share their visions of the church and discuss what gifts they had which they would be willing to use in building up the community. We ran weekends during the Lenten season for several years. These weekends had a transforming affect on parishioners. A typical case was a man who came for a weekend and found it to be quite different from what he expected. At the sharing he told us he went to church to save his soul and he had come to the weekend for the same reason. Then he said, "What I am experiencing here is changing my mind and this is not easy." He discovered he had many talents: he found himself thinking of building community and not just of saving his own soul. He entered ministries and is using his gifts and talents in the service of the parish. He is now a much happier person, and others are much happier because of him. He said he used to think of just saving his soul: now he thinks of building the kingdom of God.

I kept reminding myself I must live up to what I said when I first became a pastor: a great pastor is not one who just does great things for the people, but one who also enables the people to do great things and become a great parish. We emphasized that all people by their baptism are called to ministry suitable to lay people. They were being called not just because there was a growing shortage of priests; shortage or not they were called by their baptism to be involved in building community. Now that the shortage has gotten much worse, making the church face a crisis, the trained lay people are essential to the life of the church. We have come a long way from what my former pastor, Monsignor Mike, told me when I was assigned as pastor to a new parish. There were far more priests in those days and he said the lay people should just "pray, pay and obey." I am grateful to all the good people who became involved in ministry, giving of themselves so generously, building up the parish and together with those whom they serve, growing in the faith.

Before the council only men and altar boys were permitted in the sanctuary, inside the altar rails, around the altar. Now women read scripture from the pulpit, come around the altar for communion, distribute communion to the faithful and take the Eucharist to those not able to come to church: they visit hospitals and nursing homes, bringing great comfort and consolation to so many who need this ministry. They can be authorized to run communion services, reading the scriptures and distributing pre-consecrated hosts. We have wonderful small Christian communities in districts of the parish, meeting regularly, sharing and growing in the faith. We have girls as well as boys serving at the altar. From the time in which I grew up things have changed. Gradually, the lay people are finding their rightful place in the life of the church.

Two cousins, Christy Fox and Michael Lynn are also priests. Father Christy was ordained five years after me and Father Michael was ordained with my brother Mike, ten years after me. They are both very good and talented priests, greatly respected and loved by the people they serve and by all in our families.

Christy is a missionary with the Mill Hill Fathers. He spent many fruitful years in Africa, starting communities in very remote areas, bringing the example of a living faith and helping the native people rise up from poverty and illiteracy as he shared himself, with all that he could give. On one of his visits to our parish in Sound Beach, we took up a collection to help him build a church in a remote village where they had only a shack. He was very impressed by the generosity of our people and later when the new church was built, he sent us a picture showing the old and the new.

Michael, after ordination, went with the Columban missionaries to Peru. He worked hard there serving the poor people in an area in Lima. He built up a parish with a church also catering to the needs of the many poor people there. After ten years Michael came back to his home diocese of Meath. He worked hard and served the people faithfully for many years as a curate in the parish of Tullamore where he was loved by all the people. From there he was sent as pastor to Duleek in Co. Meath. He is still there and the people hold him in very high esteem.

Christy and Michael join in all the family reunions when I come home every year, and we have a wonderful time with all the members of the extended family.

Father Christy Fox, Father Michael Lynn and I made our life decisions as teenagers, and we are still serving God's people, as are the vast majority of priests who made the big life decision in their teenage years. We are all helping the church through this time of turmoil.

There are many of our priest friends and large numbers we don't know, who left the active priesthood to get married. These are some of their thoughts. Christ said in Mtt: 19:10, "Some do not marry for the sake of the kingdom. Let him take who can." This is a gift from God. When God gives the gift of priesthood must he always give the gift of celibacy? If we expect God to give the gift of celibacy to everyone who confects the Eucharist for the faithful, and think God demands acceptance, and put this into church law, are we regulating God?

In this time of crisis in the church, are people going to be deprived of the Eucharist because of the requirement of celibacy? They claim these questions have not been fully answered.

And remember: Love is not love 'til it's given away.

CHAPTER 29

Semi-Retirement

At the time of retirement from administration, but not from ministry, I said to the people, among other things, open up your minds and behold the kingdom of God which you are. You are not called to just save your own souls: you are called to use your gifts and work together to build the kingdom of God on earth so that salvation can be shared by all. Let your light shine for one another.

You listened well and responded to every need. What you have become is due to your living faith, witnessing to the presence of the spirit within you, and ministering lovingly to one another and sacrificing willingly for the good of all. You never cease to impress me with your generous response in entering all the ministries responding to the many needs of our growing family of faith.

We listened well to one another. I was happy to hear you express yourselves, listen to your concerns and encourage your initiatives. You were happy with the concept of the church as the people of God and I as one of you, ordained to lead and serve. So you are the church, the kingdom of God on earth, always budding forth into the kingdom of God in heaven. Part of my role is to call all of you to serve the needs of one another in our parish and the larger community in which we live. We are also called to be aware of and support the greater church of the diocese and the world by prayer and sacrifice.

Father Joe Lynch, a priest psychologist, came to parishes on request and spent a day leading and teaching the staff in the skill of collaborating in all the parish ministries. As mentioned before, we invited him to our parish many times. He always commended us highly. At one meeting he asked each member of the staff to write a vision statement for our parish. He said he had done this in the many parishes he had helped in the dioceses of Brooklyn and Rockville

Center. Then he said he was giving us a challenge: he would like us to write a poetic vision for his next meeting with us. He asked us to try. I thought all would try, but at the next meeting, I was the only one with an attempted poetic vision of the parish. Father Joe was delighted someone tried, saying he was tired reading prose vision statements in many parishes and there was a great sameness to them. He read the poetic vision aloud for all to hear and commented very favorably.

The following was my poetic vision of the parish:

>We are human—we are God like.
>We are Sinners—we are Saints.
>We glorify God and his glory shines through us.
>We pursue wisdom and we share it.
>
>We are the voice of truth for a doubting world.
>We bring good tidings to the poor.
>We bear one another's burdens.
>We heal the broken-hearted.
>
>We are beautiful though scarred.
>We are joyful though suffering.
>We reconcile to God and one another.
>We open our hearts to all comers.
>
>We lend our shoulders to our children.
>To look for new horizons.
>When we hold them high enough,
>They can see into eternity.
>
>We are united: we listen: we learn.
>We let our light shine for all to see.
>We follow the lead of the Holy Spirit,
>In building up the kingdom of God on earth.

Visitors to our masses repeatedly spoke of the strong feelings of loving acceptance and welcome they experienced and enjoyed in sharing with our friendly family of faith. We belong to one another in this "holy family" and we must stay together, work and worship together. The family that prays together, stays together.

I am happy and privileged to be one of you and hope to remain for as long as God wills it.

The parish needs each one of you and you need the parish. Be faithful to your parish. In time of trial, stay together. Let nothing divide you. Grow from strength to strength. You built this parish for your children and for your children's children. Priests may come and go but you, as the strength of the parish, endure.

I was retiring from administration but not from ministry, being keenly aware that God had called me to ministry, to serve his people all my life.

The bishop came to the parish and thanked me and the parishioners for all the good work we did. He announced, speaking to me, that I was now free, meaning I would not have the burden of going to the office daily and running the parish; no more worrying about lights and locks and lawns and ledgers, raising funds and managing finances.

Greeting the people in the vestibule afterwards, the reaction of the families was that they did not want me to give over the reins, even though I assured them I would continue to serve them in ministry. People were hugging me and thanking me.

One lovely little girl of about ten embraced me and said, "I heard the bishop say you are now free, so you should get married." The family laughed. She went on, "You should have ten kids." The family laughed more. She continued, "I really mean it because you would be a great father." As I looked into her face, the thought came to me, this could be my own granddaughter.

I have thirty-five nieces and nephews, grandnieces and grand nephews, but no children of my own.

Thinking back on when I felt the call and made the decision, I remember the exact place by the river when I was able to say yes to God and felt confident his grace would support me. At that time I was keenly aware of the sacrifices that lay ahead. Having lived with these sacrifices for many years, they still continue. Total dedication to God and his people does not stifle the natural longing for deep human relationships and seeing the faces of children and grandchildren. This dedication is a continual sacrifice.

God continues to call me into close relationship with him and loving service of his people, in total commitment. I thank God every day for the gift of priesthood.

> The call continues,
> The sacrifice continues,
> And I continue to answer with the grace of God.

EPILOGUE

Dear God, you had no beginning.
You existed from eternity,
And will go on for all eternity,
I try to imagine eternity, but I cannot.
Eternity is infinite and my mind is finite.
Eternity goes both ways, back to no beginning
And forward to no ending.
So I am in the middle of eternity.
But it cannot be measured.
So where am I in this endless eternity?
Future eternity is easy to conceive,
just time never coming to an end.
Past eternity, having had no beginning,
is quite challenging to my mind.
I can have a concept of this,
but it is hard to fathom.

In reference to God it means,
He always was,
He had no beginning,
He existed from all eternity.
Can it be time was created for us,
that all time is present to God?
God revealed himself in the bible as I AM.

In John's gospel Jesus said at the last supper, "so that
You may believe that I AM." Also, in Chapter 17,
"Now glorify me, Father with you, with the glory that
I had with you before the world began."

You are infinite, filling infinite space in all directions.
Where do the directions start? From me?
Am I in the middle? But infinite cannot be measured.
So, where am I in the infinite space?
I get the concept of infinite space, but cannot imagine it.
When I think I've got it, there is more; my mind is finite.

You fill the infinite space with your eternal life.
How can you fill it when it's infinite?
No matter how much you fill it, there is more.
Full is a full measure, but infinite cannot be measured.

You created the universe—all the heavenly bodies.
Are they infinite in number?
Numbering is an instrument of the finite mind.
So, can we have an infinite number?

You created all life.
We only know life on this planet earth.
You may have created life on other planets.
You are the almighty and do what you will.

You created mankind: how long ago?
You brought mankind through stages.
You enabled man to multiply and fill the earth.
You looked on all men, women and children
As your family and what did you see?
You saw wealth and poverty, health and sickness.
The clever and the ignorant, myths and many gods.
Each group with a god of its own making.
Invoking the gods to win their battles,
You saw progress, reason and talents.
You saw regression, ignorance and depression,
You saw fighting for their gods.

You saw fighting for their lands.
You saw fighting for the seas.
You saw how many gods, all of man's making.
You saw pantheism, atheism and agnosticism.

You revealed yourself as the one, true God.
Fist to Abraham, then to many prophets.
We now have one God and one family of man.
This gift of revelation should unite all mankind.
They are one family with one creator, God.
Many stuck with their old gods out of fear and jealousy.

The Jews were first to know the one, true God,
Told to be a blessing to the nations.
Now they themselves are divided.
Each branch claiming to be right.
Christianity accepted Christ as the Messiah.
He was to unite all people.
Christianity is divided.
Each branch claiming to be the right one,
Even killing in wars to prove it.
Islam claims revelation came to Mohammad and
They have the one, true God.
Islam is divided.
Each division claims to be the right one.
They fight among themselves.

Dear God, what do you say?
Your children are fighting over you.
They are trying to divide you.
Each claims you are on their side.
The Jewish head Rabbi in the '56 war
Thanked you for being on their side.
The head Cleric of Islam in the same war,
Thanked you for being on their side.
One calls you Yahweh
The other calls you Allah.
Are you fighting on both sides?
Christians call you Our Father.

> Are you the same God with many names?
> Christians and Islam fought over your Holy City.
> Each claimed to be fighting for you.
>
> We can say one thing for certain.
> Mankind is prone to division. Revealing yourself as the one true God has not united them.
> Mankind is claiming you are divided also, fighting on two opposite sides in wars.
> How long will this go on?
> Will mankind continue to divide?
> Will mankind continue to fight over you?
>
> Is mankind grateful that you revealed yourself?
> Or is mankind going back to many gods?
> Each nation and each person having a god of their own making.
> You do want to unite us in love and peace.
> Our hope is in our children, but many are trapped.
> Trapped into continuing what their fathers do.

If I am looking in on the world from the outside, with no religion, an alien, I see believers, and unbelievers, then, religious leaders controlling people to appease their deities, and telling them it is for their own good. Leaders of Jews, Christians, Muslims, Buddhists, Hindu and others use control tactics. They use the fear of damnation and the reward of heaven. They coerce and ostracize, exorcise and excommunicate and in history have persecuted and even killed, all done in the name of God. What puzzles me most is how sure these leaders say they are, how they claim to know what God wants at every turn, and how so many people follow them like sheep, live in fear, give up their freedom, and control over their own lives. I see great differences from country to country and from one religion to another. There are countries where people can follow their own choice of religion or no religion. Their rights to freedom and choice are respected by governments. But even there, religious leaders can exercise control claiming divine knowledge, and using fear of damnation and hope of heavenly rewards. There are countries where people are not given a choice but must follow the religion of the leaders or suffer. I see religious leaders contradicting one another; yet all claiming to have knowledge from God, each one sure he is the only one right and all the others wrong. Surely, if there is a God, what does he think of this? All claim to have the truth, but the truth of the matter as it appears to me, is that man was made to find his fulfillment in relationships and until he recognizes that, he will sacrifice the truth to appear better than those he thinks are his enemies and give himself permission to hate and even to kill. Some have a kindly god, some a harsh god; some have a merciful god, some a condemning god, each one putting his own human stamp on his god.

I see the children who are the only future the world has, the human race has. In most areas of the world, they are educated and prepared to live out their lives on this earth, but I also see some abused in many ways, even sexually by the people committed to protecting them. I see a child sex slave trade. I see children coming into the world with clean hearts and pure minds and infinite potential for love and good works, only to be marred and scarred, made cruel and selfish, hating some instead of loving all, brought about by the example and words of their elders and leaders, sometimes even parents, even taught to kill others in God's name. I believe good will triumph over evil, but it seems to me that a great wave of children, good and pure with great loving potential must triumph over the ignorance and scandal of those elders who are agents of evil, trying to triumph over good.

Barriers of bias, hatred and mistrust have to be broken down and in their place, bridges of love and freedom built, so that future generations of children can grow up in the world where good has triumphed over evil.

To the children of the world, I say:

> We love you and cherish you most dearly.
> You are our greatest treasure.
> You are our only hope for the future.
> You are God's greatest gift to us.
> You brighten up our lives each day.
> You make our hearts rejoice along life's way.
> Your faces are our sunshine every morning.
> Your eyes reflect the truth there ever dawning.
> Your smiles make our lives worth living.
> Your laughter gives us a foretaste of heaven.
> Your crying tells us you belong to us.
> Your sleeping tells us you trust us all the time.
> We say, let no one abuse you or lead you astray.
> We say, let no one indoctrinate you in the wrong way.
> Your walking moves the world toward better days.

Your running says we have delayed too long.
You have to race to reach the goal of love and unity.
We cannot stop your growing up.
But we can change your life for better or worse.
We hear you say, take us on your shoulders that we may see new horizons.
That you have not been able to see.
But they will be seen by us if you hold us high enough.
Great will be our destiny, if you don't thwart us on our way.
-and drag us down into the clay.
We can bring the light of purest sanity.
To be enjoyed by all humanity.
Then freed from false indoctrination.
We will be a blessing in every nation.
We'll put an end to war and hate.
The ultimate insanity of our human race.

ADDENDUM: MY SISTERS AND BROTHERS

There were eight of us who grew up in the old home, Mary Jo, Marcella, Brian, Shane, Frank, Vera, Celene and Mike. Then there was baby, Tony Lynn, given to us as an infant, because his mother Teresa died after the birth. I want to give due recognition to all of them.

My sister Mary Joe, the oldest is still living. She married Ned Martin, a farmer, and they had four children, Seamus, Bernard, Edward and Celine. Seamus and his wife Marie have five children, Kenneth, Karl, Therese, Emer and David. Bernard, whom we call Ber, and his wife Mary, have four children Edel, Elaine, Louise and Edward. Edward or Eddie and his wife Margaret have two children, Stephen and Sinead. Celine married Jim O'Meara. They have three children, Ann Marie, John and Gemma.

My sister Marcella was second. She joined the Sisters of the Cross and Passion, and spent her life working in that order in England. She is now deceased and we all have wonderful memories of her.

Brian, deceased, was the third. He remained a farmer all his life. He and his wife Eileen had five children Bernard, John, Michael, Gerry and Aileen. John, who was an engineer, was killed in an accident by heavy machinery, a great tragedy. The family mourns him deeply. Bernard is a farmer. The others are in professions. None of them married yet.

Shane was the fourth. That's me. I became a priest, serving in Ireland, England Scotland, Rome and the United States. I am still active in ministry.

Frank was the fifth. He remained on the home farm with Brian for several years. Eventually, he bought another farm, moved there and married Mary Nally who lived on the farm next door with her mother, Mary Nally. Together they had six children, Evelyn, Celene, Joseph, Kathleen, Deirdre and Lela.

Grandma Mary was a very positive influence on all the grandchildren. Four of them are married and Evelyn, the oldest, has a daughter, Sophia. We all feel bad that Frank, who died a few years ago, did not live to see his first granddaughter.

Vera, living, was number six. She married Pat Timbs, a farmer. They had three children, Paraic, Marie and Michael. Paraic married Ann. They live in London and have three children, Catherine, Clare, and Patrick. Marie married Colin Flanagan. They live in Tipperary and have two children, William and Elinore.

Celine, deceased, was number seven. She married Jack Halligan, a farmer in County Longford. They had a son, Sean who remained on the farm. He married Deirdre and they have two children, Gerard and Noimh.

Mike, deceased, was number eight, the last. He became a priest and left after about ten years in the ministry. He married Alana. They had two daughters, Siobhan and Fiona, both of whom are still single.

Tony Lynn's mother, Teresa, who was my mother's sister, died after his birth. The father, Patrick Lynn, brought him to our house as an infant and gave him to my mother to be raised. We all accepted him as the ninth child in our family. He is still single and living in Dublin where he has worked most of his life.

Nephews and nieces, grandnephews and grandnieces now number over thirty. I love them all and enjoy their company when I come home on vacation.

Then there are all the cousins. We come together every year for a family reunion, over a hundred of us. This enables us to share our experiences to keep the family spirit alive and to respect our precious, common heritage.

I still relive the days of pain with the bone disease, the doctor lancing and the master slapping. Recently I visited the old schoolhouse, still standing there, all locked up. Looking through a window I see into the room where eight classes were taught, the old fireplace still there, all emptiness and silence now where so much activity once took place. I recently crossed the wall and went down into the bowl shaped hollow where I fought the bully. It still amazes me how I came through it all, and went on to complete the studies and become a priest. The life of ministry is a great fulfillment, meeting people in their needs and serving them well. The parish is my family. In this parish I feel I am a member of every family and happy to serve all.

The old home place is still in the family, empty now. When I go there it is a lonely place. There is no fire in the fireplace. The hearth is bare. I think of the happy days and nights sitting around that hearth, talking, laughing, telling stories and kneeling to pray. Something inside me is saying, stay awhile, as my childhood and young life come alive in my memory and overflows into my feelings. The hollow sound of the door closing behind me is saying it is all gone, it is all gone, but it is not dead. It all lives on in my memory. If those walls could speak, they would have lots to say. The kind words, the good deeds and the prayers are written in heaven by the recording angel.

I would like to acknowledge Terry and the children Colleen, Joanne, Peggy and Danny who shared my life, always willing to help, and making me part of their family.

I am commited to loving and serving everyone without exception. I endeavor to follow the summary of a priests life by Pere Lacordaire, O.P. which follows:

"To live in the midst of the world without wishing its pleasures; to be a member of each family, yet belonging to none; to share all sufferings; to penetrate all secrets; to heal all wounds; to go from men to God and offer Him their prayers to return from God to men and to bring pardon and hope; to have a heart of fire for charity and a heart of bronze for chastity; to teach and to pardon, console and bless always. My God, what a life! And it is yours, O Priest of Jesus Christ!"

> I am not my temptations.
> I am my decisions.
>
> And remember: Love is not love 'til it's given away.